C. W. Leadbeater

Collection Vol: 1

(4 Books)

Invisible Helpers,

The life After Death,

The Christian Creed,

An Outline of Theosophy.

CONTENTS

BOOK ONE

INVISIBLE HELPERS

CHARLES LEADBEATER

The author is considered a forward thinker and was way ahead of its time. However, please remember that this book is a product of its time and do not reflect the same views on race, gender, sexuality, ethnicity, and interpersonal relations as it would if it was written today.

Most references to "Man" must be read understanding "Man" as *human being, both male and female*, as the author intended from the beginning (as a writer of the New Thought Movement, he believed in and fought for the equality of women).

Although the wisdom in this book is ageless, parents might wish to discuss with their children how some things have changed since this book was written.

CHAPTER 1

THE UNIVERSAL BELIEF IN THEM

It is one of the most beautiful characteristics of Theosophy that it gives back to people in a more rational form everything which was really useful and helpful to them in the religions which they have outgrown. Many who have broken through the chrysalis of blind faith, and mounted on the wings of reason and intuition to the freer, nobler mental life of more exalted levels, nevertheless feel that in the process of this glorious gain a something has been lost - that in giving up the beliefs of their childhood they have also cast aside much of the beauty and the poetry of life.

If, however, their lives in the past have been sufficiently good to earn for them the opportunity of coming under the benign influence of Theosophy, they very soon discover that even in this particular there has been no loss at all, but an exceeding great gain - that the glory and the beauty and the poetry are there in fuller measure than they had ever hoped before, and no longer as a mere pleasant dream from which the cold light of common-sense may at any time rudely awaken them, but as truths of nature which will bear investigation - which become only brighter, fuller and more perfect as they are more accurately understood.

A marked instance of this beneficent action of Theosophy is the way in which the invisible world (which, before the great wave of materialism engulfed us, used to be regarded as the source of all living help) has been restored by it to modern life. All the charming folk-lore of the elf, the brownie and the gnome, of the spirits of air and water, of the forest, the mountain and the mine, is shown by it to be no more meaningless superstition, but to have a basis of actual and scientific fact behind it. Its answer to the great fundamental question "If a man die, shall he live again?" is equally definite and scientific, and its teaching on the nature and conditions of the life after death throws a flood of light upon much that, for the Western world at least, was previously wrapped in impenetrable darkness.

It cannot be too often repeated that in this teaching as to the immortality of the soul and the life after death, Theosophy stands in a position totally different from that of ordinary religion. It does not put forward these great truths merely on the authority of some sacred book of long ago; in speaking of these subjects it is not dealing with pious opinions , or metaphysical speculations, but with solid, definite facts, as real and as close to us as the air we breathe or the houses we live in - facts of which many among us have constant experience - facts among which lies the daily work of some of our students, as will presently be seen.

Among the beautiful conceptions which Theosophy has restored to us stands pre-eminent that of the great helpful agencies of nature. The belief in these has been world-wide from the earliest dawn of history, and is universal even now outside the narrow domains of Protestantism, which has emptied and darkened the world for its votaries by its attempt to do away with the natural and perfectly true idea of intermediate agents, and reduce everything to two factors of man and deity - a device whereby the conception of deity has been infinitely degraded, and man has remained unhelped.

A moment's thought will show that the ordinary view of providence - the conception of an erratic interference by the central power of the universe with the result of his own decrees - would imply the introduction of partiality into the scheme, and therefore of the whole train of evils which must necessarily follow upon its heels. The Theosophical teaching, that a man can be thus specially helped only when his past actions have been such as to deserve this assistance, and that even then the help will be given through those who are comparatively near his own level, is free from this serious objection; and it furthermore brings back to us the older and far grander conception of an unbroken ladder of living beings extending down from the Logos Himself to the very dust beneath our feet.

In the East the existence of the invisible helpers has always been recognized, though the names given and the characteristics attributed to them naturally vary in different countries; and even in Europe we have had the old Greek stories of the constant interference of the gods in human affairs, and the Roman legend that Castor and Pollux led the legions of the infant republic in the battle of Lake Regillus. Nor did such a conception die out when the classical period ended, for these stories have their legitimate successors in medieval tales of saints who appeared at critical moments and turned the fortune of war in favour of the Christian hosts, or of guardian angels who sometimes stepped in and saved a pious traveler from what would otherwise have been certain destruction.

CHAPTER II

SOME MODERN INSTANCES

EVEN in this incredulous age, and amidst the full whirl of our nineteenth-century civilization, in spite of the dogmatism of our science and the deadly dullness of our Protestantism, instances of intervention inexplicable from the materialistic standpoint may still be found by anyone who will take the trouble to look for them; and in order to demonstrate this to the reader I will briefly epitomize a few of the examples given in one or other of the recent collections of such stories, adding thereto one or two that have come within my own notice.

One very remarkable feature of these more recent examples is that the intervention seems nearly always to have been directed towards the helping or saving of children.

An interesting case which occurred in London only a few years ago was connected with the preservation of a child's life in the midst of a terrible fire, which broke out in a street near Holborn, and entirely destroyed two of the houses there. The flames had obtained such hold before they were discovered that the firemen were unable to save the houses, but they succeeded in rescuing all the inmates except two - an old woman who was suffocated by the smoke before they could reach her, and a child about five years old, whose presence in the house had been forgotten in the hurry and excitement of the moment.

The mother of the child, it seems, was a friend or relative of the landlady of the house, and had left the little creature in her charge for the night, because she was herself obliged to go down to Colchester on business. It was not until everyone else had been rescued, and the whole house was wrapped in flame, that the landlady remembered with a terrible pang the trust that had been confided to her. It seemed hopeless then to attempt to get at the garret where the child had been put to bed, but one of the firemen heroically resolved to make the desperate effort, and, after receiving minute directions as to the exact situation of the room, plunged in among the smoke and flame.

He found the child, and brought him forth entirely unharmed; but when he rejoined his comrades he had a very singular story to tell. He declared that when he reached the room he found it in flames, and most of the floor already fallen; but the fire had curved round the room towards the window in an unnatural and unaccountable manner, the like of which in all his experience he had never seen before, so that the corner in which the child lay was wholly untouched, although the very rafters of the fragment of floor on which his little crib stood were half burnt away. The child was naturally very much terrified, but the fireman distinctly and repeatedly declared that as at great risk he made his way towards him he saw a form like an angel - here his exact words are given - something "all gloriously white and silvery, bending over the bed and smoothing down the counterpane." He could not possibly have been mistaken about it, he said, for it was visible in a glare of light for some moments, and in fact disappeared only when he was within a few feet of it.

Another curious feature of this story is that the child's mother found herself unable to sleep that night down in Colchester, but was constantly harassed by a strong feeling that something was wrong with her child, insomuch that at last she was compelled to rise and spend some time in earnest prayer that the little one might be protected from the danger which she instinctively felt to be hanging over him. The intervention was thus evidently what a Christian would call an answer to a prayer; a Theosophist, putting the same idea in more scientific phraseology, would say that her intense outpouring of love constituted a force which one of our visible helpers was able to use for the rescue of her child from a terrible death.

A remarkable case in which children were abnormally protected occurred on the banks of the Thames near Maidenhead a few years earlier than our last example. This time the danger from which they were saved arose not from fire but from water. Three little ones, who lived, if I recollect rightly, in or near the village of Shottesbrook, were taken out for a walk along the towing-path by their nurse. They rushed suddenly round a corner upon a horse which was drawing a barge, and in the confusion two of them got on the wrong side of the tow-rope and were thrown into the water.

The boatman, who saw the accident, sprang forward to try to save them, and he noticed that they were floating high in the water "in quite an unnatural way, like," as he said, and moving quietly towards the bank. This was all that he and the nurse saw, but the children each declared that "a beautiful person, all white and shining," stood beside them in the water, held them up and guided them to the shore. Nor was their story without corroboration, for the bargeman's little daughter, who ran up from the cabin when she heard the screams of the nurse, also affirmed that she saw a lovely lady in the water dragging the two children to the bank.

Without fuller particulars than the story gives us, it is impossible to say with certainty from what class of helpers this "angel" was drawn; but the probabilities are in favour of its having been a developed human being functioning in the astral body, as will be seen when later on we deal with this subject from the other side, as it were - from the point of view of the helpers rather than the helped.

A case in which the agency is somewhat more definitely distinguishable is related by the well-known clergyman, Dr John Mason Neale. He states that a

5

man who had recently lost his wife was on a visit with his little children at the country house of a friend. It was an old, rambling mansion, and in the lower part of it there were long, dark passages, in which the children played about with great delight. But presently they came upstairs very gravely, and two of them related that as they were running down one of these passages they were met by their mother, who told them to go back again, and then disappeared. Investigation revealed the fact that if the children had run but a few steps farther they would have fallen down a deep uncovered well which yawned full in their path, so that the apparition of their mother had saved them from almost certain death.

In this instance there seems no reason to doubt that the mother herself was still keeping a loving watch over her children from the astral plane, and that (as has happened in some other cases) her intense desire to warn them of the danger into which they were so heedlessly rushing gave her the power to make herself visible and audible to them for the moment - or perhaps merely to impress their minds with the idea that they saw and heard her. It is possible, of course, that the helper may have been someone else, who took the familiar form of the mother in order not to alarm the children; but the simplest hypothesis is to attribute the intervention to the action of the ever-wakeful mother-love itself, undimmed by the passage through the gates of death.

This mother-love, being one of the holiest and most unselfish of human feelings, is also one of the most persistent on higher planes. Not only does the mother who finds herself upon the lower levels of the astral plane, and consequently still within touch of the earth, maintain her interest in and her care for her children as long as she is able to see them; even after her entry into the heaven-world these little ones are still the most prominent objects in her thought, and the wealth of love that she lavishes upon the images which she there makes of them is a great outpouring of spiritual force which flows down upon her offspring who are still struggling in this lower world, and surrounds them with living centres of beneficent energy which may not inaptly be described as veritable guardian angels. An illustration of this will be found in the sixth of our Theosophical manuals, page 38.

Not long ago the little daughter of one of our English bishops was out walking with her mother in the town where they lived, and in running heedlessly across a street the child was knocked down by the horses of a carriage which came quickly upon her round a corner. Seeing her among the horses' feet, the mother rushed forward, expecting to find her very badly injured, but she sprang up quite merrily, saying, "Oh, mamma, I am not at all hurt, for something all in white kept the horses from treading upon me, and told me not to be afraid."

A case which occurred in Buckinghamshire, somewhere in the neighborhood of Burnham Beeches, is remarkable on account of the length of time through which the physical manifestation of the succouring agency seems to have maintained itself. It will have been seen that in the instances hitherto given the intervention was a matter of but a few moments, whereas in this a phenomenon was produced which appears to have persisted for more than half an hour.

Two of the little children of a small farmer were left to amuse themselves while their parents and their entire household were engaged in the work of harvesting. The little ones started for a walk in the woods, wandered far from home, and then managed to lose their way. When the weary parents returned at dusk it was discovered that the children were missing, and after enquiring at some of the neighbours' houses the father sent servants and labourers in various directions to seek for them.

Their efforts were, however, unsuccessful, and their shouts unanswered; and they had reassembled at the farm in a somewhat despondent frame of mind, when they all saw a curious light some distance away moving slowly across some fields towards the road. It was described as a large globular mass of rich golden glow, quite unlike ordinary lamplight; and as it drew nearer it was seen that the two missing children were walking steadily along in the midst of it. The father and some others immediately set off running towards it; the appearance persisted until they were close to it, but just as they grasped the children it vanished, leaving them in the darkness.

The children's story was that after night came on they had wandered about crying in the woods for some time, and had at last lain down under a tree to sleep. They had been roused, they said, by a beautiful lady with a lamp, who took them by the hand and led them home; when they questioned her she smiled at them, but never spoke a word. To this strange tale they both steadily adhered, nor was it possible in any way to shake their faith in what they had seen. It is noteworthy, however, that though all present saw the light, and noticed that it lit up the trees and hedges which came within its sphere precisely as an ordinary light would, yet the form of the lady was visible to none but the children.

CHAPTER III

A PERSONAL EXPERIENCE

ALL the above stories are comparatively well known, and may be found in some of the books which contain collections of such accounts - most of them in Dr Lee's *More Glimpses of the World Unseen*; but the two instances which I am now about to give have never been in print before, and both occurred within the last ten years - one to myself, and the other to a very dear friend of mine, a prominent member of the Theosophical Society, whose accuracy of observation is beyond all shadow of doubt.

My own story is a simple one enough, though not unimportant to me, since the interposition undoubtedly saved my life. I was walking one exceedingly wet and stormy night down a quiet back street near Westbourne Grove, struggling with scant success to hold up an umbrella against the savage gusts of wind that threatened every moment to tear it from my grasp, and trying as I laboured along to think out the details of some work upon which I was just then engaged.

With startling suddenness a voice which I know well - the voice of an Indian teacher - cried in my ear "Spring back!" and in mechanical obedience I started violently backwards almost before I had time to think. As I did so my umbrella, which had swung forward with the sudden movement, was struck from my hand and a huge metal chimney pot crashed upon the pavement less than a yard in front of my face. The great weight of this article, and the tremendous force with which it fell, make it absolutely certain that but for the warning voice I should have been killed on the spot; yet the street was empty, and the voice was that of one whom I knew to be seven thousand miles away from me, as far as the physical body was concerned.

Nor was this the only occasion upon which I received assistance of this supernormal kind, for in early life, long before the foundation of the Theosophical Society, the apparition of a dear one who had recently died prevented me from committing what I now see would have been a serious crime, although by the light of such knowledge as I then had it appeared not only a justifiable but even a laudable act of retaliation. Again, at a later date, though still before the foundation of this Society, a warning conveyed to me from a higher plane amid most impressive surroundings enabled me to prevent another man from entering upon a course which I now know would have ended disastrously, though I had no reason to suppose so at the time. So it will be seen that I have a certain amount of personal experience to strengthen my belief in the doctrine of invisible helpers, even apart from my knowledge of the help that is constantly being given at the present time.

The other case is a very much more striking one. One of our members, who gives me permission to publish her story, but does not wish her name mentioned, once found herself in very serious physical peril. Owing to circumstances which need not be detailed here, she was in the very centre of a dangerous street fracas, and seeing several men struck down and evidently badly hurt close to her, was in momentary expectation of a similar fate, since escape from the crush seemed quite impossible.

Suddenly she experienced a curious sensation of being whirled out of the crowd, and found herself standing quite uninjured and entirely alone in a small bye-street parallel with the one in which the disturbance had taken place. She still heard the noise of the struggle, and while she stood wondering what on earth had happened to her, two or three men who had escaped from the crowd came running round the corner of the street, and on seeing her expressed great astonishment and pleasure, saying that when the brave lady so suddenly disappeared from the midst of the fight they had felt certain that she had been struck down.

At the time no sort of explanation was forthcoming, and she returned home in a very mystified condition; but when at a later period she mentioned this strange occurrence to Madame Blavatsky she was informed that, her karma being such as to enable her to be saved from her exceedingly dangerous position, one of the Masters had specially sent some one to protect her in view of the fact that her life was needed for the work.

Nevertheless the case remains a very extraordinary one, both with regard to the great amount of power exercised and the unusually public nature of its manifestation. It is not difficult to imagine the *modus operandi*; she must have been lifted bodily over the intervening block of houses, and simply set down in the next street; but since her physical body was not visible floating in the air, it is also evident that a veil of some sort (probably of etheric matter) must have been thrown round her while in transit.

If it be objected that whatever can hide physical matter must itself be physical, and therefore visible, it may be replied that by a process familiar to all occult students it is possible to bend rays of light (which, under all conditions at present known to science, travel only in straight lines unless refracted) so that after passing round an object they may resume exactly their former course; and it will at once be seen that if this were done such an object would to all physical eyes be absolutely invisible until the rays were allowed to resume their normal course. I am fully aware that this one statement alone is sufficient to brand any remarks as nonsense in the eyes of the scientist of the present day, but I cannot help that; I am merely stating a possibility in nature which the science of the future will no doubt one day discover, and for those who are not students of occultism the remark must wait until then for its justification.

The process, as I say, is comprehensible enough to anyone who understands a little about the more occult forces of nature; but the phenomenon still remains an exceedingly dramatic one, while the name of the heroine of the story, were I permitted to give it, would be a guarantee of its accuracy to all my readers.

Another recent instance of interposition, less striking, perhaps, but entirely successful, has been reported to me since the publication of the first edition of this book. A lady, being obliged

to undertake a long railway journey alone, had taken the precaution to secure an empty compartment; but just as the train was leaving the station, a man of forbidding and villainous appearance sprang in and seated himself at the other end of the carriage. The lady was much alarmed, thus to be left alone with so doubtful a character, but it was too late to call for help, so she sat still and commended herself earnestly to the care of her patron saint.

Soon her fears were redoubled, for the man arose and turned toward her with an evil grin, but he had hardly taken one step when he started back with a look of the most intense astonishment and terror. Following the direction of his glance, she was startled to see a gentleman seated directly opposite to her, gazing quietly but firmly at the baffled robber - a gentleman who certainly could not have entered the carriage by any ordinary means. Too much awed to speak, she watched him as though fascinated for a full half-hour; he uttered no word, and did not even look at her, but kept his eyes steadily upon the villain, who cowered trembling in the furthest corner of the compartment. The moment that the train reached the next station, and even before it came to a standstill, the would-be thief tore open the door and sprang hurriedly out. The lady, deeply thankful to be rid of him, turned to express her gratitude to the gentleman, but found only an empty seat, though it would have been impossible for any physical body to have left the carriage in the time.

The materialization was in this case maintained for a longer period than usual, but on the other hand it expended no force in action of any kind - nor indeed was it necessary that it should do so, as its mere appearance was sufficient to effect its purpose.

But these stories, all referring as they do to what would commonly be called angelic intervention, illustrate only one small part of the activities of our invisible helpers. Before, however, we can profitably consider the other departments of their work it will be well that we should have clearly in our minds the various classes of entities to which it is possible that these helpers may belong. Let that, then, be the portion of our subject to be next treated.

CHAPTER IV

THE HELPERS

HELP, then, may be given by several of the many classes of inhabitants of the astral plane. It may come from devas, from nature-spirits, or from those whom we call dead, as well as from those who function consciously upon the astral plane during life - chiefly the adepts and their pupils. But if we examine the matter a little more closely we shall see that though all the classes mentioned may, and sometimes do, take a part in this work, yet their shares in it are so unequal that it is practically left almost entirely to one class.

The very fact that so much of this work of helping has to be done either upon or from the astral plane goes far in itself towards explaining this. To anyone who has even a faint idea of what the powers at the command of an adept really are, it will be at once obvious that for him to work upon the astral plane would be a far greater waste of energy than for our leading physicians or scientists to spend their time in breaking stones upon the road.

The work of the adept lies in higher regions - chiefly upon the arûpa levels of the devachanic plane or heaven-world, where he may direct his energies to the influencing of the true individuality of man, and not the mere personality which is all that can be reached in the astral or physical world. The strength which he puts forth in that more exalted realm produces results greater, more far-reaching and more lasting than any which can be attained by the expenditure of even ten times the force down here; and the work up there is such as he alone can fully accomplish, while that on lower planes may be at any rate to some extent achieved by whose feet are yet upon the earlier steps of the great stairway which will one day lead them to the position where he stands.

The same remarks apply also in the case of the devas. Belonging as they do to a higher kingdom of nature than ours, their work seems for the most part entirely unconnected with humanity; and even those of their orders - and there are some such - which do sometimes respond to our higher yearnings or appeals, do so on the mental plane rather than on the physical or astral, and more frequently in the periods between our incarnations than during our earthly lives.

It may be remembered that some instances of such help were observed in the course of investigations into the subdivisions of the devachanic plane which were undertaken when the Theosophical manual on the subject was in preparation. In one case a deva was found teaching the most wonderful celestial music to a chorister; and in another one of a different class was giving instruction and guidance to an astronomer who was seeking to comprehend the form and structure of the universe.

These two were but examples of many instances in which the great deva kingdom was found to he helping onward the evolution and responding to the higher aspirations of man after death; and there are methods by which, even during earth-life, these great ones may be approached, and an infinity of knowledge acquired from them, though even then such intercourse is gained rather by rising to their plane than by invoking them to descend to ours.

In the ordinary events of our physical life the deva very rarely interferes - indeed, he is so fully occupied with the far grander work of his own plane that he is probably scarcely conscious of this; and though it may occasionally happen that he becomes aware of some human sorrow or difficulty which excites his pity and moves him to endeavour to help in some way, his wider vision undoubtedly recognizes that at the present stage of evolution such interpositions would in the vast majority of cases be productive of infinitely more harm than good.

There was indubitably a period in the past - in the infancy of the human race - when it was much more largely assisted from outside than is at present the case. At the time when all its Buddhas and Manus, and even its more ordinary leaders and teachers, were drawn either from the ranks of the deva evolution or from the perfected humanity of a more advanced planet, any such assistance as we are considering in this treatise must also have been given by these exalted beings. But as man progresses he becomes himself qualified to act as a helper, first on the physical plane and then on higher levels; and we have now reached a stage at which humanity ought to be able to provide, and to some slight extent does provide, invisible helpers for itself, thus setting free for still more useful and elevated work those beings who are capable of it.

It becomes obvious then that such assistance as that to which we are here referring may most fitly be given by men and women at a particular stage of their evolution; not by the adepts, since they are capable of doing far grander and more widely useful work, and not by the ordinary person of no special spiritual development, for he would be unable to be of any use. Just as these considerations would lead us to expect, we find that this work of helping on the astral and lower mental planes is chiefly in the hands of the pupils of the Masters - men who, though yet far from the attainment of adeptship, have evolved themselves to the extent of being able to function consciously upon the planes in question.

Some of these have taken the further step of completing the links between the physical consciousness and that of the higher levels, and they therefore have the undoubted advantage of recollecting in waking life what they have done and what they have learnt in those other worlds; but there are my others who, though as yet unable to carry their consciousness through unbroken, are nevertheless by no means wasting the hours when they think they are asleep, but spending them in noble and unselfish labour for their fellow-men.

What this labour is we will proceed to consider, but before we enter upon that part of the subject we will refer to an objection which is very frequently brought forward with regard to such work, and we will also dispose of the comparatively rare cases in which the agents are either nature-spirits or men who have cast off the physical body.

People whose grasp of Theosophical ideas is as yet imperfect are often in doubt as to whether it is allowable for them to try to help some one whom they find in sorrow or difficulty, lest they should interfere with the fate which has been decreed for him by the absolute justice of the eternal law of karma. "The man is in his present position," they say in effect, "because he has deserved it; he is now working out the perfectly natural result of some evil which he has committed in the past; what right have I to interfere with the action of the great cosmic law by trying to ameliorate his condition, either on the astral plane or the physical.

Now the good people who make such suggestions are really, however unconsciously to themselves, exhibiting the most colossal conceit, for their position implies two astounding assumptions; first, that they know exactly what another man's karma has been, and how long it has decreed that his sufferings shall last; and secondly, that they - the insects of a day - could absolutely override the cosmic law and prevent the due working-out of karma by any action of theirs. We may be well assured that the great kârmic deities are perfectly well able to manage their business without our assistance, and we need have no fear that any steps we may take can by any possibility cause them the slightest difficulty or uneasiness.

If a man's karma is such that he cannot be helped, then all our well-meant efforts in that direction will fail, though we shall nevertheless have gained good karma for ourselves by making them. What the man's karma has been is no business of ours; our duty is to give help to the utmost of our power, and our right is only to the act; the result is in other and higher hands. How can we tell how a man's account stands? For all we know he may just have exhausted his evil karma, and be at this moment at the very point where a helping hand is needed to give relief and raise him out of his trouble or depression; why should not we have the pleasure and privilege of doing that good deed as well as another? If we *can* help him, then that fact of itself shows that he has deserved to be helped; but we can never know unless we try. In any case the law of karma will take care of itself, and we need not trouble ourselves about it.

The cases in which assistance is given to mankind by nature-spirits are few. The majority of such creatures shun the haunts of man, and retire before him, disliking his emanations and the perpetual bustle and unrest which he creates all around him. Also, except some of their higher orders, they are generally inconsequent and thoughtless - more like happy children at play under exceedingly favourable physical conditions than like grave and responsible entities. Still it sometimes happens that one of them will become attached to a human being, and do him many a good turn; but at the present stage of its evolution this department of nature cannot be relied upon for anything like steady co-operation in the work of invisible helpers. For a fuller account of the nature-spirits the reader is referred to the fifth of our Theosophical manuals.

Again, help is sometimes given by those recently departed - those who are still lingering on the astral plane, and still in close touch with earthly affairs, as (probably) in the above-mentioned case of the mother who saved her children from falling down a well. But it will readily be seen that the amount of such help available must naturally be exceedingly limited. The more unselfish and helpful a person is, the less likely is he to be found after death lingering in full consciousness on the lower levels of the astral plane, from which the earth is most readily accessible. In any case, unless he were an exceptionally bad man, his stay within the realm whence alone any interference would be possible would be comparatively short; and although from the heaven-world he may still shed benign influence upon those whom he has loved on earth, it will usually be rather of the nature of a general benediction than a force capable of bringing about definite results in a specific case, such as those which we have been considering.

Again, many of the departed who wish to help those whom they left behind, find themselves quite unable to influence them in any way, since to work from one plane upon an entity on another requires either very great sensitiveness on the part of that entity, or a certain amount of knowledge and skill on the part of the operator. Therefore, although instances of apparitions shortly after death are by no means uncommon, it is rare to find one in which the departed person has really done anything useful, or succeeded in impressing what he wished upon the friend or relation whom he visited. There are such cases, of course - a good many of them when we come to put them all together; but they are not numerous compared to the great number of ghosts who have succeeded in showing themselves. So that but little help is usually given by the dead - indeed, as will presently be explained, it is far more common for them to be themselves in need of assistance than to be able to accord it to others.

At present, therefore, the main bulk of the work which has to be done along these lines falls to the share of those living persons who are able to function consciously on the astral plane

CHAPTER V

THE REALITY OF SUPERPHYSICAL LIFE

IT seems difficult for those who are accustomed only to the ordinary and somewhat materialistic lines of thought of the nineteenth century, to believe in and realize fully a condition of perfect consciousness apart from the physical body. Every Christian, at any rate, is bound by the very foundations of his creed to believe that he possesses a soul; but if you suggest to him the possibility that that soul may be a sufficiently real thing to become visible under certain conditions apart from the body either during life or after death, the chances are ten to one that he will scornfully tell you that he does not believe in ghosts, and that such an idea is nothing but an anachronistic survival of an exploded medieval superstition.

If, therefore, we are at all to comprehend the work of the band of invisible helpers, and perchance ourselves to learn to assist in it, we must shake ourselves free from the trammels of contemporary thought on these subjects, and endeavour to grasp the great truth (now a demonstrated fact to many among us) that the physical body is in simple truth nothing but a vehicle or vesture of the real man. It is put off permanently at death, but it is also put off temporarily every night when we go to sleep - indeed the process of falling asleep consists in this very action of the real man in his astral vehicle slipping out of the physical body.

Again I repeat, this is no mere hypothesis or ingenious supposition. There are many among us who are able to perform (and *do* perform every day of their lives) this elementary act of magic in full consciousness - who pass from one plane to the other at will; and if that is clearly realized, it will become apparent how grotesquely absurd to them must appear the ordinary unreasoning assertion that such a thing is utterly impossible. It is like telling a man that it is impossible for him to fall asleep, and that if he thinks he has ever done so he is under a hallucination.

Now the man who has not yet developed the link between the astral and physical consciousness is unable to leave his denser body at will, or to recollect most of what happens to him while away from it; but the fact nevertheless remains that he leaves it every time he sleeps, and may be seen by any trained clairvoyant either hovering over it or wandering about at a greater or less distance from it, as the case may be.

The entirely undeveloped person usually floats close above his physical body, scarcely less asleep than it is, and comparatively shapeless and inchoate, and it is found that he cannot be drawn away from the immediate neighbourhood of that physical body without causing serious discomfort which would in fact awaken it. As the man evolves, however, his astral body grows more definite and more conscious, and so becomes a fitter vehicle for him. In the case of the majority of intelligent and cultured people the degree of consciousness is already very considerable, and a man who is at all spiritually developed is as fully himself in that vehicle as in this denser body.

But though he may be fully conscious on the astral plane during sleep, and able to move about on it freely if he wishes to do so, it does not yet follow that he is ready to join the band of helpers. Most people at this stage are so wrapped up in their own train of thought - usually a continuation of some line taken up in waking hours - that they are like a man in a brown study, so much absorbed as to be practically entirely heedless of all that is going on about them. And in many ways it is well that this is so, for there is much upon the astral plane which might be unnerving and terrifying to one who had not the courage born of full knowledge as to the real nature of all that he would see.

Sometimes a man gradually rouses himself out of this condition - wakes up to the astral world around him, as it were; but more often he remains in that state until someone who is already active there takes him in hand and wakens him. This is, however, not a responsibility to be lightly undertaken, for while it is comparatively easy thus to wake a man up on the astral plane, it is practically impossible, except by a most undesirable exercise of mesmeric influence, to put him to sleep again. So that before a member of the band of workers will thus awaken a dreamer, he must fully satisfy himself that the man's disposition is such that he will make good use of the additional powers that will then be put into his hands, and also that his knowledge and his courage are sufficient to make it reasonably certain that no harm will come to him as a result of the action.

Such awakening so performed will put a man in a position to join if he will the band of those who help mankind. But it must be clearly understood that this does not necessarily or even usually bring with it the power of remembering in the waking consciousness anything which has been done. That capacity has to be attained by the man for himself, and in most cases it does not come for years afterwards - perhaps not even in the same life. But happily this lack of memory in the body in no way impedes the work out of the body; so that, except for the satisfaction to a man of knowing during his waking hours upon what work he has been engaged during his sleep, it is not a matter of importance. What really matters is that the work should be done - not that we should remember who did it.

CHAPTER VI

A TIMELY INTERVENTION

VARIED as is this work on the astral plane, it is all directed to one great end - the furtherance, in however humble a degree, of the processes of evolution. Occasionally it is connected with the development of the lower kingdoms, which it is possible slightly to accelerate under certain conditions. A duty towards these lower kingdoms, elemental as well as animal and vegetable, is distinctly recognized by our adept leaders, since it is in some cases only through connection with or use by man that their progress takes place.

But naturally by far the largest and most important part of the work is connected with humanity in some way or other. The services rendered are of many and various kinds, but chiefly concerned with man's spiritual development, such physical interventions as are recounted in the earlier part of this book being exceedingly rare. They do, however, occasionally take place, and though it is my wish to emphasize rather the possibility of extending mental and moral help to our fellow-men, it will perhaps be well to give two or three instances in which friends personally known to me have rendered physical assistance to those in sore need of it, in order that it may be seen how these examples from the experience of the helpers gear in with the accounts given by those who have received the supernormal aid - such stories, I mean, as those which are to be found in the literature of so-called "supernatural occurrences."

In the course of the recent rebellion in Matabeleland one of our members was sent upon an errand of mercy which may serve as an illustration of the way in which help upon this lower plane has occasionally been given. It seems that one night a certain farmer and his family in that country were sleeping tranquilly in fancied security, quite unaware that only a few miles away relentless hordes of savage foes were lying in ambush maturing fiendish plots of murder and rapine. Our member's business was in some way or other to arouse the sleeping family to a sense of the terrible danger which so unexpectedly menaced them, and she found this by no means an easy matter.

An attempt to impress the idea of imminent peril upon the brain of the farmer failed utterly, and as the urgency of the case seemed to demand strong measures, our friend decided to materialize herself sufficiently to shake the housewife by the shoulder and adjure her to get up and look about her. The moment she saw that she had been successful in attracting attention she vanished, and the farmer's wife has never from that day to this been able to find out *which* of her neighbours it was who roused her so opportunely, and thus saved the lives of the entire family, who but for this mysterious intervention would undoubtedly have been massacred in their beds half an hour later; nor can she even now understand how this friend in need contrived to make her way in, when all the windows and doors were found so securely barred.

Being this abruptly awakened, the housewife was half inclined to consider the warning a mere dream; however, she arose and looked around just to see that all was right, and fortunate it was that she did so, for though she found nothing amiss indoors she had no sooner thrown open a shutter than she saw the sky red with a distant conflagration. She at once roused her husband and the rest of the family, and owing to this timely notice they were able to escape to a place of concealment near at hand just before the arrival of the horde of savages, who destroyed the house and ravaged the fields indeed, but were disappointed of the human prey which they had expected. The feelings of the rescuer may be imagined when she read in the newspaper some time afterwards an account of the providential deliverance of this family.

CHAPTER VII

THE "ANGEL STORY."

ANOTHER instance of intervention on the physical plane which occurred a short time ago makes a very beautiful little story, though this time only one life was saved. It needs, however, a few words of preliminary explanation. Among our band of helpers here in Europe are two who were brothers long ago in ancient Egypt, and are still warmly attached to one another. In this present incarnation there is a wide difference in age between them, one being advanced in middle life, while the other was at that time a mere child in the physical body, though an ego of considerable advancement and promise. Naturally it falls to the lot of the elder to train and guide the younger in the occult work to which they are so heartily devoted, and as both are fully conscious and active on the astral plane they spend most of the time during which their grosser bodies are asleep in labouring together under the direction of their common Master, and giving to both living and dead such help as is within their power.

I will quote the story of the particular incident which I wish to relate from a letter written by the elder of the two helpers immediately after it occurrence, as the description there given is more vivid and picturesque than any account in the third person could possibly be.

"We were going about quite other business, when Cyril suddenly cried, 'What's that?' for we heard a terrible scream of pain or fright. In a moment we were on the spot, and found that a boy of about eleven or twelve had fallen over a cliff on to some rocks below, and was very badly hurt. He had broken a leg and an arm, poor fellow, but what was still worse was a dreadful cut in the thigh, from which blood was pouring in a torrent. Cyril cried, 'Let us help him quick, or he'll die!'

"In emergencies of this kind one has to think quickly. There were clearly two things to be done; that bleeding must be stopped, and physical help must be procured. I was obliged to materialize either Cyril or myself, for we wanted physical hands at once to tie a bandage, and besides it seemed better that the poor boy should *see* someone standing by him in his trouble. I felt that while undoubtedly he would be more at home with Cyril than with me, I should probably be more readily able to procure help than Cyril would, so the division of labour was obvious.

"The plan worked capitally. I materialized Cyril instantly (he does not know yet how to do it for himself), and told him to take the boy's neckerchief and tie it round the thigh, and twist a stick through it. 'Won't it hurt him terribly? said Cyril; but he *did* it, and the blood stopped flowing. The injured boy seemed half unconscious, and could scarcely speak, but he looked up at the shining little form bending so anxiously over him, and asked, 'Be you an angel, master?' Cyril smiled so prettily, and replied, 'No, I'm only a boy, but I've come to help you;' and then I left him to comfort the sufferer while I rushed off to the boy's mother, who lived about a mile away.

"The trouble I had to force into that woman's head the conviction that something was wrong, and that she must go and see about it, you would never believe; but at last she threw down the pan she was cleaning, and said aloud, 'Well, I don't know what's come over me, but I must go and find the boy.' When she once started I was able to guide her without much difficulty, though at the time I was holding Cyril together by will-power, lest the poor child's angel should suddenly vanish from before his eyes.

"You see, when you materialize a form you are changing matter from its natural state into another - temporarily opposing the cosmic will, as it were; and if you take your mind off it for one half-second, back it flies into its original condition like a flash of lightning. So I could not give more than half my attention to that woman, but still I got her along somehow, and as soon as she came round the corner of the cliff I let Cyril disappear; but she had seen him, and now that village has one of the best-attested stories of angelic intervention on record!

"The accident happened in the early morning, and the same evening I looked in (astrally) upon the family to see how matters were going on. The poor boy's leg and arm had been set, and the great cut bandaged, and he lay in bed looking very pale and weak, but evidently going to recover in time. The mother had a couple of neighbours in, and was telling them the story; and a curious tale it sounded to one who knew the real facts.

"She explained, in very many words, how she couldn't tell what it was, but something came over her all in a minute like, making her feel something had happened to the boy, and she *must* go out and see after him; how at first she thought it was nonsense, and tried to throw off the feeling, 'but it warn't no use - she just had to go.' She told how she didn't know what made her go round by that cliff more than any other way, but it just happened so, and as she turned round the corner there she saw him lying propped up against a rock, and kneeling beside him was the 'beautifullest child ever she saw, dressed all in white and shining, with rosy cheeks and lovely brown eyes;' and how he smiled at her 'so heavenly like,' and then all in a moment he was not there, and at first she was so startled she didn't know what to think; and then all at once she felt what it was, and fell on her knees and thanked God for sending one of his angels to help her poor boy.

"Then she told how when she lifted him to carry him home she wanted to take off the handkerchief that was cutting into his poor leg so, but he would not let her, because he said the angel had tied it and said he was not to touch it; and how when she told the doctor this afterwards he explained to her that if she *had* unfastened it the boy would certainly have died.

"Then she repeated the boy's part of the tale - how the moment after he fell this lovely little angel came to him (he knew it *was* an angel because he knew there had been nobody in sight for half a mile round when he was at the top of the cliff just before - only he could not understand why it hadn't any wings, and why it said it was only a boy) - how it lifted him against the rock and tied up his leg, and then began to talk to him and tell him he need not be frightened, because somebody was gone to fetch mother, and she would be there directly; how it kissed him and tried to make him comfortable, and how its soft, warm, little hand held his all the time, while it told him strange, beautiful stories which he could not clearly remember, but he knew they were very good, because he had almost forgotten he was hurt until he saw his mother coming; and how then it assured him he would soon be well again, and smiled and squeezed his hand, and then somehow it was gone.

"Since then there has been quite a religious revival in that village! Their minister has told them that so signal an interposition of divine providence must have been meant as a sign to them, to rebuke scoffers and to prove the truth of holy scripture and of the Christian religion - and nobody seems to see the colossal conceit involved in such an astonishing proposition.

"But the effect on the boy had been undoubtedly good, morally as well as physically; by all accounts he was a careless enough young scamp before, but now he feels 'his angel' may be near him at any time, and he will never do or say anything rough or coarse or angry, lest it should see or hear. The one great desire of his life is that some day he may see it again, and he knows that when he dies its lovely face will be the first to greet him on the other side."

A beautiful and pathetic little story, truly. The moral dawn from the occurrence by the village and its minister is perhaps somewhat of a *non sequitur*; yet the testimony to the existence of at least something beyond this material plane must surely do the people more good than harm, and after all the mother's conclusion from what she saw was a perfectly correct one, though more accurate knowledge would probably have led her to express it a little differently.

An interesting fact afterwards discovered by the investigations of the writer of the letter throws a curious side-light upon the reasons underlying such incidents. It was found that the two boys had met before, and that some thousands of years ago the one who fell from the cliff had been the slave of the other, and had once saved his young master's life at the risk of his own, and had been liberated in consequence; and now, long afterwards, the master not only repays the debt in kind, but also gives his former slave a high ideal and an inducement to morality of life which will probably change the whole course of his future evolution. So true is it that no good deed ever goes unrewarded by karma, however tardy it may seem in its action - that

Though the mills of God grind slowly

Yet they grind exceeding small;

Though with patience stands
He waiting

With exactness grinds He all.

CHAPTER VIII

THE STORY OF A FIRE

ANOTHER piece of work done by the same boy Cyril furnishes an almost exact parallel to some of the stories from the books which I have given in earlier pages. He and his older friend, it seems, were passing along in the prosecution of their usual work one night, when they noticed the fierce glare of a big fire below them, and promptly dived down to see if they could be of any use.

It was a great hotel which was in flames, a huge caravanserai on the edge of a great lake. The house, many stories in height, formed three sides of a square round a sort of garden, planted with trees and flowers, while the lake formed the fourth side. The two wings ran right down to the lake, the big bay windows which terminated them almost projecting over the water, so as to leave only quite a narrow passage-way under them at the two sides.

The front and wings were built round inside wells, which contained also the lattice-work shafts of the lifts, so that when once the fire broke out, it spread with almost incredible rapidity, and before our friends saw it on their astral journey all the middle floors in each of the three great blocks were in flames. Fortunately the inmates - except one little boy - had already been rescued, though some of them had sustained very serious burns and other injuries.

This little fellow had been forgotten in one of the upper rooms of the left wing, for his parents were out at a ball, and knew nothing of the fire, while naturally enough no one else thought of the lad till it was far too late. The fire had gained such a hold on the middle floors of that wing that nothing could have been done, even if anyone had remembered him, as his room faced on to the inner garden which has been mentioned, so that he was completely cut off from all outside help. Besides, he was not even aware of his danger, for the dense, suffocating smoke had so gradually filled the room that his sleep had grown deeper and deeper, till he was all but stupefied.

In this state he was discovered by Cyril, who seems to be specially attracted towards children in need or danger. He first tried to make some of the people remember the boy, but in vain; and in any case it seemed scarcely possible that they could have helped him, so that it was soon evident that this was merely a waste of time. The older helper then materialized, Cyril, as before, in the room, and set him to work to awaken and rouse up the more than half-stupefied child. After a good deal of difficulty this was accomplished to some extent, but the boy remained in a half-dazed, semi-conscious condition through all that followed, so that he needed to be pushed and pulled about, guided and helped at every turn.

The two boys first crept out of the room into the central passage which ran through the wing, and then, finding that the smoke and the flames beginning to come through the floor made it impassable for a physical body, Cyril got the other boy back into the room again and out of the window on to a stone ledge, about a foot wide, which ran right along the block just below the windows. Along this he managed to guide his companion, half balancing himself on the extreme edge of the ledge, and half floating on air, but always placing himself outside of the other, so as to keep him from dizziness and prevent him from feeling afraid of a fall.

Towards the end of the block nearest the lake, in which direction the fire seemed less developed, they climbed in through an open window and again reached the passage, hoping to find the staircase at that end still passable. But it, too, was full of flame and smoke; so they crawled back along the passage, Cyril advising his companion to keep his mouth close to the ground, till they reached the latticed cage of the lift running down the long well in the centre of the block.

The lift of course was at the bottom, but they managed to clamber down the lattice work inside the cage till they stood on the roof of the elevator itself. Here they found themselves blocked, but luckily Cyril discovered a doorway opening from the cage of the lift on to a sort of *entresol* just above the ground floor. Through this they reached a passage, which they crossed, the little boy being half-stifled by the smoke; then they made their way through one of the rooms opposite, and finally, clambering out of the window, found themselves on the top of the veranda which ran along in front of the ground floor, between it and the garden.

There it was easy enough to swarm down one of the pillars and reach the garden itself; but even there the heat was intense, and the danger, when the walls should fall, very considerable. So Cyril tried to conduct his charge round the end first of one, then of the other wing; but in both cases the flames had burst through, and the narrow, overhung passages were quite impassable. Finally they took refuge in one of the pleasure boats which were moored to the steps of the quay at the side of the garden next the lake, and, casting loose, rowed out on to the water.

Cyril intended to row round past the burning wing and land the boy whom he had saved; but when they got some little way out, they fell in with a passing lake steamer, and were seen - for the whole scene was lit up by the glare of the burning hotel, till everything was as plain as in broad daylight. The steamer came alongside the boat to take them off; but instead of the two boys they had seen, the crew found only one - for his older friend had promptly allowed Cyril to slip back into his astral form, dissipating the denser matter which had made for the time a material body, and he was therefore now invisible.

A careful search was made, of course, but no trace of the second boy could be found, and so it was concluded that he must have fallen overboard and been drowned just as they came alongside. The child who had been rescued fell into a dead faint as soon as he was safe on board, so they could get no information from him, and when he did recover, all he could say was that he had seen the other boy the moment before they came alongside, and then knew nothing more.

The steamer was bound down the lake to a place some two days' sail distant, and it was a week or so before the rescued boy could be restored to his parents, who of course thought that he had perished in the flames, for though an effort was made to impress on their minds the fact that their son had been saved, it was found impossible to convey the idea to them, so it may be imagined how great was the joy of the meeting.

The boy is still well and happy, and is never weary of relating his wonderful adventure. Many a time he has regretted that the kind friend who saved him should have perished so mysteriously at the very moment when all the danger seemed over at last. Indeed, he has even ventured to suggest that perhaps he *didn't* perish after all - that perhaps he was a fairy prince; but of course this idea elicits nothing but tolerant smiles of superiority from his elders. The kârmic link between him and his preserver has not yet been traced, but no doubt there must be one somewhere.

CHAPTER IX

MATERIALIZATION AND REPERCUSSION

ON meeting with a story such as this, students often enquire whether the invisible helper is perfectly safe amidst these scenes of deadly peril - whether, for example, this boy who was materialized in order to save another from a burning house was not himself in some danger - whether his physical body would not have suffered in any way by repercussion if his materialized form had passed through the flames, or fallen from the high ledge on the edge of which he walked so unconcernedly. In fact, since we know that in many cases the connection between a materialized form and a physical body is sufficiently close to produce repercussion, might it not have occurred in this case?

Now this subject of repercussion is an exceedingly abstruse and difficult one, and we are by no means yet in a position fully to explain its very remarkable phenomena; in order to understand the matter perfectly, it would probably be necessary to comprehend the laws of sympathetic vibration on more planes than one. Still, we do know by observation some of the conditions which permit its action, and some which definitely exclude it, and I think we are warranted in saying that it was absolutely impossible here.

To see why this is so we must first remember that there are at least three well-defined varieties of materialization, as anyone who has at all an extended experience of spiritualism will be aware. I am not concerned at the moment to enter upon any explanation as to how these three varieties are respectively produced, but am merely stating the indubitable fact of their existence.

There is the materialization which, though tangible, is not visible to ordinary physical sight. Of this nature are the unseen hands which so often clasp one's arm or stroke one's face at a *séance,* which sometimes carry physical objects through the air or make raps upon the table - though of course both these latter phenomena may easily be produced without a materialized hand at all.

There is the materialization which though visible is not tangible - the spirit-form through which one's hand passed as through empty air. In some cases this variety is obviously misty and impalpable, but in others its appearance is so entirely normal that its solidity is never doubted until some one endeavours to grasp it.

There is the perfect materialization which is both visible and tangible - which not only bears the outward semblance of your departed friend but shakes you cordially by the hand with the very clasp that you know so well.

Now while there is a good deal of evidence to show that repercussion takes place under certain conditions in the case of this third kind of materialization., it is by no means so certain that it can occur with the first or second class. In the case of the boy-helper it is probable that the materialization would not be of the third type, since the greatest care is always taken not to expend more force than is absolutely necessary to produce whatever result may be required, and it is obvious that less energy would be used in the production of the more partial forms which we have called the first and second classes. The probability is that only the arm with which the boy held his little companion would be solid to the touch, and that the rest of his body, though looking perfectly natural, would have proved far less palpable if it had been tested.

But, apart from this probability, there is another point to be considered. When a full materialization takes place, whether the subject be living or dead, physical matter of some sort has to be gathered together for the purpose. At a spiritualistic *séance* this matter is obtained by drawing largely upon the etheric double of the medium - and sometimes even upon his physical body also, since cases are on record in which his weight has been very considerably decreased while manifestations of this character were taking place.

This method is employed by the directing entities of the *séance* simply because when an available medium is within reach it is very much the easiest way in which a materialization can be brought about; and the consequence is that the very closest connection is thus set up between that medium and the materialized body, so that the phenomenon which (although very imperfectly understanding it) we call repercussion, occurs in its clearest form. If, for example, the hands of the materialized body be rubbed with chalk, that chalk will afterwards be found on the hands of the medium, even though he may have been all the time carefully locked up in a cabinet under circumstances which absolutely preclude any suspicion of fraud. If any injury be inflicted upon the materialized form, that injury will be accurately reproduced upon the corresponding part of the medium's body: while sometimes food of which the spirit-form has partaken will be found to have passed into the body of the medium - at least that happened in one case at any rate within my own experience.

It would be far otherwise, however, in the case which we have been describing. Cyril was thousands of miles from his sleeping physical body, and it would therefore be quite impossible for his friend to draw etheric matter from it, while the regulations under which all pupils of the great Masters of Wisdom perform their work of helping man would assuredly prevent him, even for the noblest purpose, from putting such a strain upon any one else's body. Besides, it would be quite unnecessary, for the far less dangerous method invariably employed by the helpers when materialization seems desirable would be ready to his hand - the condensation from the circumambient ether, or even from the physical air, of such an amount of matter as may be requisite. This feat, though no doubt beyond the power of the average entity manifesting at a *séance*, presents no difficulty to a student of occult chemistry.

But mark the difference in the result obtained. In the case of the medium we have a materialized form in the closest possible connection with the physical body, made out of its very substance, and therefore capable of producing all the phenomena of repercussion. In the case of the helper we have indeed an exact reproduction of the physical body, but it is created by a mental effort out of matter entirely foreign to that body, and is no more capable of acting upon it by repercussion than an ordinary marble statue of the man would be.

Thus it is that a passage through the flames or a fall from a high window-ledge would have had no terrors for the boy-helper, and that on another occasion a member of the band, though materialized, was able without any inconvenience to the physical body to go down in a sinking vessel (see page 77).

In both the incidents of his work that have been described above, it will have been noticed that the boy Cyril was unable to materialize himself, and that the operation had to be performed for him by an older friend. One more of his experiences is worth relating, for it gives us a case in which by intensity of pity and determination of will he *was* able to show himself - a case somewhat parallel to that previously related of the mother whose love enabled her somehow to manifest herself in order to save her children's lives.

Inexplicable as it may seem, there is no doubt whatever of the existence in nature of this stupendous power of will over matter of all planes, so that if only the power be great enough, practically *any* result may be produced by its direct action, without any knowledge or even thought on the part of the man exercising that will as to *how* it is to do its work. We have had plenty of evidence that this power holds good in the case of materialization, although ordinarily it is an art which must be learnt just like any other. Assuredly an average man on the astral plane could no more materialize himself without having previously learnt how to do it than the average man on this plane could play the violin without having previously learnt it; but there are exceptional cases, as will be seen from the following narrative.

CHAPTER X

THE TWO BROTHERS

This story has been told by a pen of far greater dramatic capability than mine, and with a wealth of detail for which I have here no space, in *The Theosophical Review* of November, 1897, page 229. To that account I would refer the reader, since my own description of the case will be a mere outline, as brief as is consistent with clearness. The names given are of course fictitious, but the incidents are related with scrupulous accuracy.

Our *dramatis personae* are two brothers, the sons of a country gentleman - Lancelot, aged fourteen, and Walter, aged eleven - very good boys of the ordinary healthy, manly type, like hundreds of others in this fair realm, with no obvious psychic qualifications of any sort, except the possession of a good deal of Celtic blood. Perhaps the most remarkable feature about them was the intensity of the affection that existed between them, for they were simply inseparable - neither would go anywhere without the other, and the younger idolized the elder as only a younger boy can.

One unlucky day Lancelot was thrown from his pony and killed, and for Walter the world became empty. The child's grief was so real and terrible that he could neither eat not sleep, and his mother and nurse were at their wits' end as to what to do for him. He seemed deaf alike to persuasion and blame; when they told him that grief was wicked, and that his brother was in heaven, he simply answered that he could not be certain of that, and that even if it were true, he knew that Lancelot could no more be happy in heaven without him than he could on earth without Lancelot.

Incredible as it may sound, the poor child was actually dying of grief, and what made the case even more pathetic was the fact that, all unknown to him, his brother stood at his side all the time, fully conscious of his misery, and himself half-distracted at the failure of his repeated attempts to touch him or speak to him.

Affairs were still in this most pitiable condition on the third evening after the accident, when Cyril's attention was drawn to the two brothers - he cannot tell how. "He just happened to be passing," he says; yet surely the will of the Lords of Compassion guided him to the scene. Poor Walter lay exhausted yet sleepless - alone in his desolation, so far as he knew, though all the time his sorrowing brother stood beside him. Lancelot, free from the chains of the flesh, could see and hear Cyril, so obviously the first thing to do was to soothe his pain with a promise of friendship and help in communicating with his brother.

As soon as the dead boy's mind was thus cheered with hope, Cyril turned to the living one, and tried with all his strength to impress upon his brain the knowledge that his brother stood beside him, not dead, but living and loving as of yore. But all his efforts were in vain; the dull apathy of grief so filled poor Walter's mind that no suggestion from without could enter, and Cyril knew not what to do. Yet so deeply was he moved by the sad sight, so intense was his sympathy and so firm his determination to help in some way or other at any cost of strength to himself, that somehow (even to this day he cannot tell how) he found himself able to touch and speak to the heart-broken child.

Putting aside Walter's questions as to who he was and how he came there, he went straight to the point, telling him that his brother stood beside him, trying hard to make him hear his constantly repeated assurances that he was not dead, but living and yearning to help and comfort him. Little Walter longed to believe, yet hardly dared to hope; but Cyril's eager insistence vanquished his doubts at last, and he said, "Oh! I do believe you, because you're so kind; but if I could only see him, then I should *know*, then I should be quite sure; and if I could only hear his voice telling me he was happy, I shouldn't mind a bit his going away again afterwards."

Young though he was at the work, Cyril knew enough to be aware that Walter's wish was one not ordinarily granted, and was beginning regretfully to tell him so, when suddenly he felt a Presence that all the helpers know, and though no word was spoken it was borne in upon his mind that instead of what he had meant to say, he was to promise Walter the boon his heart desired. "Wait till I come back," he said, "and you shall see him then." And then - he vanished.

That one touch from the Master had shown him what to do and how to do it, and he rushed to fetch the older friend who had so often helped him before. This older man had not yet retired for the night, but on hearing Cyril's hurried summons, he lost no time in accompanying him, and in a few minutes they were back at Walter's bedside. The poor child was just beginning to believe it all a lovely dream, and his delight and relief when Cyril reappeared were beautiful to see. Yet how much more beautiful was the scene a moment later, when, in obedience to a word from the Master, the elder man materialized the eager Lancelot, and the living and the dead stood hand in hand once more!

Now in very truth for both the brothers had sorrow been turned into joy unspeakable, and again and again they both declared that now they should never feel sad any more, because they knew that death had no power to part them. Nor was their gladness damped even when Cyril explained carefully to them, at his older friend's suggestion, that this strange physical reunion would not be repeated, but that all day long Lancelot would be near Walter, even though the latter could not see him, and every night Walter would slip out of his body and be consciously with his brother once more.

Hearing this, poor weary Walter sank to sleep at once and proved its truth, and was amazed to find with what hitherto unknown rapidity he and his brother could fly together from one to another of their old familiar haunts. Cyril thoughtfully warned him that he would probably forget most of his freer life when he awoke next day; but by rare good fortune he did *not* forget, as so many of us do. Perhaps the shock of the great joy had somewhat aroused the latent psychic faculty which belongs to the Celtic blood; at any rate he forgot no single detail of all that had happened, and next morning he burst upon the house of mourning with a wondrous tale which suited it but ill.

His parents thought that grief had turned his brain, and, since he is now the heir, they have been watching long and anxiously for further symptoms of insanity, which happily they have not found. They still think him a monomaniac on this point, though they fully recognize that his "delusion" has saved his life; but his old nurse (who is a Catholic) is firm in her belief that all he says is true - that the Lord Jesus, who was once a child himself, took pity on that other child as he lay dying of grief, and sent one of His angels to bring his brother back to him from the dead as a reward for a love which was stronger than death. Sometimes popular superstition gets a good deal nearer to the heart of things than does educated skepticism!

Nor does the story end here, for the good work begun that night is still progressing, and none can say how far the influence of that one act may ramify. Walter's astral consciousness, once having been thus thoroughly awakened, remains in activity; every morning he brings back into his physical brain the memory of his night's adventures with his brother; every night they meet their dear friend Cyril, from whom they have learned so much about the wonderful new world that has opened before them, and the other worlds to come that lie higher yet. Under Cyril's guidance they also - the living and the dead alike - have become eager and earnest members of the band of helpers; and probably for years to come - until Lancelot's vigorous young astral body disintegrates - many a dying child will have cause to be grateful to these three who are trying to pass on to others something of the joy that they have themselves received.

Nor is it to the dead alone that these new converts have been of use, for they have sought and found some other living children who show consciousness on the astral plane during sleep; and one at least of those whom they have thus brought to Cyril has already proved a valuable little recruit to the children's band, as well as a very kind little friend down here on the physical plane.

Those to whom all these ideas are new sometimes find it very difficult to understand how children can be of any use in the astral world. Seeing, they would say, that the astral body of a child must be undeveloped, and the ego thus limited by childhood on the astral as well as the physical plane, in what way could such an ego be of use, or be able to help towards the spiritual, mental and moral evolution of humanity, which we are told is the chief concern of the helpers?

When first such a question was asked, shortly after the publication of one of these stories in our magazine, I sent it to Cyril himself, to see what he would say to it, and his answer was this:

"It is quite true, as the writer says, that I am only a boy, and know very little yet, and that I shall be much more useful when I have learnt more. But I am able to do a little even now, because there are so many people who have learnt nothing about Theosophy yet, though they may know very much more than I do about everything else. And you see when you want to get to a certain place, a little boy who knows the way can do more for you than a hundred wise men who don't know it."

It may be added that when a child had been awakened upon the astral plane the development of the astral body would proceed so rapidly that he would very soon be in a position upon that plane but little inferior to that of the awakened adult, and would of course be much in advance, so far as usefulness is concerned, of the wisest man who was as yet unawakened. But unless the ego expressing himself through the child-body possessed the necessary qualification of a determined yet loving disposition, and had clearly manifested it in his previous lives, no occultist would take the very serious responsibility of awakening him upon the astral plane. When, however their karma is such that it is possible for them to be thus aroused, children very often prove most efficient helpers, and throw themselves into their work with a whole-souled devotion which is very beautiful to see. And so is fulfilled once more the ancient prophecy "a little child shall lead them."

Another question that suggests itself to one's mind in reading this last story of the two brothers is this: Since Cyril was somehow able to materialize himself by sheer force of love and pity and strength of will, is it not strange that Lancelot, who had been trying so much longer to communicate, had not succeeded in doing the same thing.

Well, there is of course no difficulty in seeing why poor Lancelot was unable to communicate with his brother, for that inability is simply the normal condition of affairs, the wonder is that Cyril *was* able to materialize himself, not that Lancelot was *not*. Not only, however, was the feeling probably stronger in Cyril's case, but he also knew exactly what he wanted to do - knew that such a thing as materialization was a possibility, and had some general idea as to how it was done - while Lancelot naturally knew nothing of all this then, though he does now.

CHAPTER XI

WRECKS AND CATASTROPHES

SOMETIMES it is possible for members of the band of helpers to avert impending catastrophes of a somewhat larger order. In more than one case when the captain of a vessel has been carried unsuspecting far out of his course by some unknown current or through some mistaken reckoning, and has thereby run into serious danger, it has been possible to prevent shipwreck by repeatedly impressing upon his mind a feeling that something was wrong; and although this generally comes through into the captain's brain merely as a vaguely warning intuition, yet if it occurs again and again he is almost certain to give it some attention and take such precautions as suggest themselves to him.

In one case, for example, in which the master of a barque was much nearer in to the land than he supposed, he was again and again pressed to heave the lead, and though he resisted this suggestion for some time as being unnecessary and absurd, he at last gave the order in a somewhat hesitating way. The result astounded him, and he at once put his vessel about and stood off from the coast, though it was not until morning came that he realized how very close he had been to an appalling disaster.

Often, however, a catastrophe is kârmic in its nature, and consequently cannot be averted; but it must not therefore be supposed that in such cases no help can be given. It may be that the people concerned are destined to die, and therefore cannot be saved from death; but in many cases they may still be to some extent prepared for it, and may certainly be helped upon the other side after it is over. Indeed, it may be definitely stated that wherever a great catastrophe of any kind takes place, there is also a special sending of help.

Two recent cases in which such help was given were the sinking of the *Drummond Castle* off Cape Ushant, and the terrible cyclone which devastated the city of St Louis in America. On both these occasions a few minutes' notice was given, and the helpers did their best to calm and raise men's minds, so that when the shock came upon them it would be less disturbing than it might otherwise have been. Naturally, however, the greater part of the work done with the victims in both these calamities was done upon the astral plane after they had left their physical bodies; but of this we shall speak later.

It is sad to relate how often when some catastrophe is impending the helpers are hindered in their kindly offices by wild panic among those whom the danger threatens - or sometimes, worse still, by a mad outburst of drunkenness among those whom they are trying to assist. Many a ship has gone to her doom with almost every soul on board mad with drink, and therefore utterly incapable of profiting by any assistance offered either before death or for a very long time afterwards.

If it should ever happen to any of us to find ourselves in a position of imminent danger which we can do nothing to avert, we should try to remember that help is certainly near us, and that it rests entirely with ourselves to make the helper's work easy or difficult. If we face the danger calmly and bravely, recognizing that the true ego can in no way be affected by it, our minds will then be open to receive the guidance which the helpers are trying to give, and this cannot but be best for us, whether its object be to save us from death or, when that is impossible, to conduct us safely through it.

Assistance of this latter kind has not infrequently been given in cases of accidents to individuals, as well as of more general catastrophes. It will be sufficient to mention one example as an illustration of what is meant. In one of the great storms which did so much damage around our coasts a few years ago, it happened that a fishing boat was capsized far out at sea. The only people on board were an old fisherman and a boy, and the former contrived to cling for a few minutes to the overturned boat. There was no physical help at hand, and even if there had been in such a raging storm it would have been impossible for anything to be done, so that the fisherman knew well enough that there was no hope of escape, and that death could only be a question of a few moments. He felt a great terror at the prospect, being especially impressed by the awful loneliness of that vast waste of waters, and he was also much troubled with thoughts of his wife and family, and the difficulties in which they would be left by his sudden decease.

A passing helper seeing all this endeavoured to comfort him, but finding his mind too much disturbed to be impressionable, she thought it advisable to show herself to him in order to assist him the better. In relating the story afterwards she said that the change which came over the fisherman's face at sight of her was wonderful and beautiful to see; with the shining form standing upon the boat above him he could not think that an angel had been sent to comfort him in his trouble, and therefore he felt that not only would he himself be carried safely through the gates of death, but his family would assuredly be looked after also. So, when death came to him a few moments later, he was in a frame of mind very different from the terror and perplexity which had previously overcome him; and naturally when he recovered consciousness upon the astral plane and found the "angel" still beside him he felt himself at home with her, and was prepared to accept her advice as regards the new life upon which he had entered.

Some time later the same helper was engaged in another piece of work of very similar character, the story of which she has since told as fellows: "You remember that steamer that went down in the cyclone at the end of last November; I betook myself to the cabin where about a dozen women had been shut in, and found them wailing in the most pitiful manner, sobbing and moaning with fear. The ship had to founder - no aid was possible - and to go out of the world in this state of frantic terror is the worst possible way to enter the next. So in order to calm them I materialized myself, and of course they thought I was an angel, poor souls; they all fell on their knees and prayed me to save them, and one poor mother pushed her baby into my arms imploring me to save that at least. They soon grew quiet and composed as we talked, and the wee baby went to sleep smiling, and presently they all fell asleep peacefully, and I filled their minds with thoughts of the heaven-world, so that they did not wake up when the ship made her final plunge downwards. I went down with them to ensure their sleeping through the last moments, and they never stirred as their sleep became death."

Evidently in this case, too, those who were thus helped had not only the enormous advantage of being enabled to meet death calmly and reasonably, but also the still greater one of being received on its farther shore by one whom they were already disposed to love and trust - one who thoroughly understood the new world in which they found themselves, and could not only reassure them as to their safety, but advise them how to order their lives under these much altered circumstances. And this brings us to the consideration of one of the largest and most important departments of the work of invisible helpers - the guidance and assistance which they are able to give to the dead.

CHAPTER XII

WORK AMONG THE DEAD

IT is one of the many evils resulting from the absurdly erroneous teaching as to conditions after death which is unfortunately current in our western world, that those who have recently shaken off this mortal coil are usually much puzzled and often very seriously frightened at finding everything so different from what their religion had led them to expect. The mental attitude of a large number of such people was pithily voiced the other day by an English general, who three days after his death met one of the band of helpers whom he had known in physical life. After expressing his great relief that he had at last found someone with whom he was able to communicate, his first remark was: "But if I am dead, where am I? For if this is heaven I don't think much of it; and if it is hell, it is better than I expected."

But unfortunately a far greater number take things less philosophically. They have been taught that all men are destined to eternal flames except a favoured few who are superhumanly good; and since a very small amount of self-examination convinces them that they do not belong to *that* category, they are but too often in a condition of panic terror, dreading every moment that the new world in which they find themselves may dissolve and drop them into the clutches of the devil, in whom they have been sedulously taught to believe. In many cases they spend long periods of acute mental suffering before they can free themselves from the fatal influence of this blasphemous doctrine of everlasting punishment - before they can realize that the world is governed, not according to the caprice of a hideous demon who gloats over human anguish, but according to a benevolent and wonderfully patient law of evolution, which is absolutely just indeed, but yet again and again offers to man opportunities of progress, if he will but take them, at every stage of his career.

It ought in fairness to be mentioned that it is only among what are called protestant communities that this terrible evil assumes its most aggravated form. The great Roman Catholic Church, with its doctrine of purgatory, approaches much more nearly to a conception of the astral plane, and it devout members at any rate realize that the state in which they find themselves shortly after death is merely a temporary one, and that it is their business to endeavour to raise themselves out of it as soon as may be by intense spiritual aspiration, while they accept any suffering which may come to them as necessary for the wearing away of the imperfections in their character before they can pass to higher and brighter regions.

It will thus be seen that there is plenty of work for the helpers to do among the newly dead, for in the vast majority of cases they need to be calmed and reassured, to be comforted and instructed. In the astral, just as in the physical world, there are many who are but little disposed to take advice from those who know better than they; yet the very strangeness of the conditions surrounding them renders many of the dead willing to accept the guidance of those to whom these conditions are obviously familiar; and many a man's stay on that plane has been considerably shortened by the earnest efforts of this band of energetic workers.

Not, be it understood, that the karma of the dead man can in any way be interfered with; he has built for himself during life an astral body of a certain degree of density, and until that body is sufficiently dissolved he cannot pass on into the heaven-world beyond; but he need not lengthen the period necessary for that process by adopting an improper attitude.

All students ought clearly to grasp the truth that the length of a man's astral life after he has put off his physical body depends mainly upon two factors - the nature of his past physical life, and his attitude of mind after what we call death. During his earth life he is constantly influencing the building of matter into his astral body. He affects it directly by the passions, emotions and desires which he allows to hold sway over him; he affects it indirectly by the action upon it of his thoughts from above, and of the details of his physical life - his continence or his debauchery, his cleanliness or his uncleanliness, his food and his drink - from below.

If by persistence in perversity along any of these lines he is so stupid as to build for himself a coarse and gross astral vehicle, habituated to responding only to the lower vibrations of the plane, he will find himself after death bound to that plane during and long and slow process of that body's disintegration. On the other hand if by decent and careful living he gives himself a vehicle mainly composed of finer material, he will have very much less *post-mortem* trouble and discomfort, and his evolution will proceed much more rapidly and easily.

This much is generally understood, but the second great factor - his attitude of mind after death - seems often to be forgotten. The desirable thing is for him to realize his position on this particular little arc of his evolution - to learn that he is at this stage withdrawing steadily inward towards the plane of the true ego, and that consequently it is his business to disengage his thoughts as far as may be from things physical, and to fix his attention more and more upon those spiritual matters which will occupy him during his life in the heaven-world. By doing this he will greatly facilitate the natural astral disintegration, and will avoid the sadly common mistake of unnecessarily delaying himself upon the lower levels of what should be so temporary a residence.

But many of the dead very considerably retard the process of dissolution by clinging passionately to the earth which they have left; they simply will not turn their thoughts and desires upward, but spend their time in struggling with all their might to keep in full touch with the physical plane, thus causing great trouble to any one who may be trying to help them. Earthly matters are the only ones in which they have had any living interest, and they cling to them with desperate tenacity even after death. Naturally as time passes on they find it increasingly difficult to keep hold of things down here, but instead of welcoming and encouraging this process of gradual refinement and spiritualization they resist it vigorously by every means in their power.

Of course the mighty force of evolution is eventually too strong for them, and they are swept on in its beneficent current, yet they fight every step of the way, thereby not only causing themselves a vast amount of entirely unnecessary pain and sorrow, but also very seriously delaying their upward progress and prolonging their stay in astral regions to an almost indefinite extent. In convincing them that this ignorant and disastrous opposition to the cosmic will is contrary to the laws of nature, and persuading them to adopt an attitude of mind which is the exact reversal of it, lies a great part of the work of those who are trying to help.

It happens occasionally that the dead are earthbound by anxiety - anxiety sometimes about duties unperformed or debts undischarged, but more often on account of wife or children left unprovided for. In such cases as this it has more than once been necessary, before the dead man was satisfied to pursue his upward path in peace, that the helper should to some extent act as his representative upon the physical plane, and attend on his behalf to the settlement of the business which was troubling him. An illustration taken from our recent experience will perhaps make this clearer.

One of the band of pupils was trying to assist a poor man who had died in one of our western cities, but found it impossible to withdraw his mind from earthly things because of his anxiety about two young children whom his death had left without means of support. He had been a working man of some sort, and had been unable to lay by any money for them; his wife had died some two years previously and his landlady, though exceedingly kindhearted and very willing to do anything in her power for them, was herself far too poor to be able to adopt them, and very reluctantly came to the conclusion that she would be obliged to hand them over to the parish authorities. This was a great grief to the dead father, though he could not blame the landlady, and was himself unable to suggest any other course.

Our friend asked him whether he had no relative to whom he could entrust them, but the father knew of none. He had a younger brother, he said, who would certainly have done something for him in this extremity, but he had lost sight of him for fifteen years, and did not even know whether he was living or dead. When last heard of he had been apprenticed to a carpenter in the north, and he was then described as a steady young fellow who, if he lived, would surely get on.

The clues at hand were certainly very slight, but since there seemed no other prospect of help for the children, our friend thought it worth while to make a special effort to follow them up. Taking the dead man with him he commenced a patient search after the brother in the town indicated; and after a great deal of trouble they were actually successful in finding him. He was now a master carpenter in a fairly flourishing way of business - married, but without children though earnestly desiring them, and therefore apparently just the man for the emergency.

The question now was how the information could be conveyed to this brother. Fortunately he was found to be so far impressionable that the circumstances of his brother's death and the destitution of his children could be put vividly before him in a dream, and this was repeated three times, the place and even the name of the landlady being clearly indicated to him. He was immensely impressed by this recurring vision, and discussed it earnestly with his wife, who advised him to write to the address given. This he did not like to do, but was strongly inclined to travel down into the west country, find out whether there was such a house as that which he had seen, and if so make some excuse to call there. He was a busy man, however, and he finally decided that he could not afford to lose a day's work for what after all might well prove to be nothing but the baseless fabric of a dream.

The attempt along these lines having apparently failed, it was determined to try another method, so one of the helpers wrote a letter to the man detailing the circumstances of his brother's death and the position of the children, exactly as he had seen them in his dream. On receipt of this confirmation he no longer hesitated, but set off the very next day for the town indicated, and was received with open arms by the kind-hearted landlady. It had been easy enough for the helpers to persuade her, good soul that she was, to keep the children with her for a few days on the chance that something or other would turn up for them, and she has ever since congratulated herself that she did so. The carpenter of course took the children back with him and provided them with a happy home, and the dead father, now no longer anxious, passed rejoicing on his upward journey.

Since some Theosophical writers have felt it their duty to insist in vigorous terms upon the evils so frequently attendant upon the holding of spiritual séances, it is only fair to admit that on several occasions good work similar to that of the helper in the case just described has been done through the agency of a medium or of some one present at a circle. Thus, though spiritualism has too often detained souls who but for it would have attained speedier liberation, it must be set to the credit of its account that it has also furnished the means of escape to others, and thus opened up the path of advancement for them. There have been instances in which the defunct has been able to appear unassisted to his relatives or friends and explain his wishes to them; but these are naturally rare, and most souls who are earth-bound by anxieties of the kind indicated can satisfy themselves only by means of the services of the medium or the conscious helper.

Another case very frequently encountered on the astral plane is that of the man who cannot believe that he is dead at all. Indeed, most people consider the very fact that they are still conscious to be an absolute proof that they have not passed through the portals of death; somewhat of a satire this, if one thinks of it, on the practical value of our much vaunted belief in the immortality of the soul! However they may have labeled themselves during life, the great majority of those who die, in this country at any rate, show themselves by their subsequent attitude to have been to all intents and purposes materialists at heart; and those who on earth have honestly called themselves so are often no more difficult to deal with than others who would have been shocked at the very name.

A very recent instance was that of a scientific man who, finding himself fully conscious, and yet under conditions differing radically from any that he had ever experienced before, had persuaded himself that he was still alive, and merely the victim of a prolonged and unpleasant dream. Fortunately for him there happened to be among the band of those able to function upon the astral plane a son of an old friend of his, a young man whose father had commissioned him to search for the departed scientist and endeavour to render him some assistance. When after some trouble the youth found and accosted him, he frankly admitted that he was in a condition of great bewilderment and discomfort, but still clung desperately to his dream hypothesis as on the whole the most probable explanation of what he saw, and even went so far as to suggest that his visitor was nothing but a dream-figure himself!

At last, however, he so far gave way as to propose a kind of test, and said to the young man, "If you are, as you assert, a living person, and the son of my old friend, bring me from him some message that shall prove to me your objective reality." Now although under all ordinary conditions of the physical plane the giving of any kind of phenomenal proof is strictly forbidden to the pupils of the Masters, it seemed as though a case of this kind hardly came under the rules; and therefore, when it had been ascertained that there was no objection on the part of higher authorities, an application was made to the father, who at once sent a message referring to a series of events which had occurred before the son's birth. This convinced the dead man of the real existence of his young friend, and therefore of the plane upon which they were both functioning; and as soon as he felt this established, his scientific training at once reasserted itself, and he became exceeding eager to acquire all possible information about this new region.

Of course the message which he so readily accepted as evidence was in reality no proof at all, since the facts to which it referred might have been read from his own mind or from the records of the past by any creature possessed of astral senses! But his ignorance of these possibilities enabled this definite impression to be made upon him, and the Theosophical instruction which his young friend is now nightly giving to him will undoubtedly have a stupendous effect upon his future, for it cannot but greatly modify not only the heaven-state which lies immediately before him, but also his next incarnation upon earth.

The main work, then, done for the newly dead by our helpers is that of soothing and comforting them - of delivering them when possible from the terrible though unreasoning fear which but too often seizes them, and not only causes them much unnecessary suffering, but retards their progress to higher spheres - and of enabling them as far as may be to comprehend the future that lies before them.

Others who have been longer on the astral plane may also receive much help, if they will but accept it, from explanations and advice as to their course through its different stages. They may, for example, be warned of the danger and delay caused by attempting to communicate with the living through a medium, and sometimes (though rarely) an entity already drawn into a spiritualistic circle may be guided into higher and healthier life. Teaching thus given to persons on this plane is by no means lost for though the memory of it cannot of course be directly carried over to the next incarnation, there always remains the real inner knowledge, and therefore the strong predisposition to accept it immediately when heard again in the new life.

A rather remarkable instance of service rendered to the dead was the first achievement of a very recent recruit to the band of helpers - one who is hardly as yet a fully-fledged member. This young aspirant had not long before lost an aged relation for whom he had felt an especially warm affection; and his earliest request was to be taken by a more experienced friend to visit her in the hope that he might be of some service to her. This was done and the effect of the meeting of the living and the dead was very beautiful and touching. The older person's astral life was already approaching its end, but a condition of apathy, dullness and uncertainty prevented her from making any immediate progress.

But when the boy, who had been so much to her in earth-life, stood once more before her and dissolved by the sunlight of his love the grey mist of depression which had gathered around her, she was aroused from her stupor; and soon she understood that he had come in order to explain to her her situation, and to tell her of the glories of the higher life toward which her thoughts and aspirations ought now to be directed. But when this was fully realized, there was such an awakening of dormant feeling in her and such an outrush of devoted affection towards her earnest young helper, that the last fetters which bound her to the astral life were broken, and that one great outburst of love and gratitude swept her forthwith into the higher consciousness of the heaven-world. Truly there is no greater and more beneficent power in the universe than that of pure, unselfish love.

CHAPTER XIII

OTHER BRANCHES OF THE WORK

BUT turning back again now from the all-important work among the dead to the consideration of the work among the living, we must briefly indicate a great branch of it, without a notice of which our account of the labours of our invisible helpers would indeed be incomplete, and that is the immense amount which is done by suggestion - by simply putting good thoughts into the minds of those who are ready to receive them.

Let there be no mistake as to what is meant here. It would be perfectly easy - easy to a degree which would be quite incredible to those who do not understand the subject practically - for a helper to dominate the mind of any average man, and make him think just as he pleased, and that without arousing the faintest suspicion of any outside influence in the mind of the subject. But, however admirable the result might be, such a proceeding would be entirely inadmissible. All that may be done is to throw the good thought into the person's mind as one among the hundreds that are constantly sweeping through it; whether the man takes it up, makes it his own, and acts upon it, depends upon himself entirely. Were it otherwise, it is obvious that all the good karma of the action would accrue to the helper only, for the subject would have been a mere tool, and not an actor - which is not what is desired.

The assistance given in this way is exceedingly varied in character. The consolation of those who are suffering or in sorrow at once suggests itself, as does also the endeavour to guide toward the truth those who are earnestly seeking it. When a person is spending much anxious thought upon some spiritual or metaphysical problem, it is often possible to put the solution into his mind without his being at all aware that it comes from external agency.

A pupil too may often be employed as an agent in what can hardly be described otherwise than as the answering of prayer; for though it is true that any earnest spiritual desire, such as might be supposed to find its expression in prayer, is itself a force which automatically brings about certain results, it is also a fact that such a spiritual effort offers an opportunity of influence to the Powers of Good, of which they are not slow to take advantage; and it is sometimes the privilege of a willing helper to be made the channel through which their energy is poured forth. What is said of prayers is true to an even greater extent of meditation, for those to whom this higher exercise is a possibility.

Besides these more general methods of help there are also special lines open only to the few. Again and again such pupils as are fitted for the work have been employed to suggest true and beautiful thoughts to authors, poets, artists and musicians; but obviously it is not every helper who is capable of being used in this way.

Sometimes, though more rarely, it is possible to warn persons of the danger to their moral development of some course which they are pursuing, to clear away evil influences from about some person or place, or to counteract the machinations of black magicians. It is not often that direct instruction in the great truths of nature can be given to people outside the circle of occult students, but occasionally it is possible to do something in that way by putting before the minds of preachers and teachers a wider range of thought or a more liberal view of some question than they would otherwise have taken.

Naturally as an occult student progresses on the Path he attains a wider sphere of usefulness. Instead of assisting individuals only, he learns how classes, nations and races are dealt with, and he is entrusted with a gradually increasing share of the higher and more important work done by the adepts themselves. As he acquires the requisite power and knowledge he begins to wield the greater forces of the mental and the astral planes and is shown how to make the utmost possible use of each favourable cyclic influence. He is brought into relation with those great Nirmânakâyas who are sometimes symbolized as the Stones of the Guardian Wall, and he becomes - at first of course in the very humblest capacity - one of the and of their almoners, and learns how those forces are dispersed which are the fruit of their sublime self-sacrifice. Thus he rises gradually higher and higher until, blossoming at length into adeptship, he is able to take his full share of the responsibility which lies upon the Masters of Wisdom, and to help others along the road which he has trodden.

On the mental plane the work differs somewhat, since teaching can be both given and received in a much more direct, rapid and perfect manner, while the influences set in motion are infinitely more powerful, because acting on so much higher a level. But (though it is useless to speak of it in detail at present, since so few of us are yet able to function consciously upon this plane during life) here also - and even higher still - there is always plenty of work to be done, as soon as ever we can make ourselves capable of doing it; and there is certainly no fear that for countless æons we shall ever find ourselves without a career of unselfish usefulness open before us.

CHAPTER XIV

THE QUALIFICATIONS REQUIRED

HOW, it may be asked, are we to make ourselves capable of sharing in this great work? Well, there is no mystery as to the qualifications which are needed by one who aspires to be a helper; the difficulty is not in learning what they are, but in developing them in oneself. To some extent they have been already incidentally described, but it is nevertheless as well that they should be set out fully and categorically.

Single-mindedness. The first requisite is that we shall have recognized the great work which the Masters would have us do, and that it shall be for us the one great interest in our lives. We must learn to distinguish not only between useful and useless work, but between the different kinds of useful work, so that we may each devote ourselves to the very highest of which we are capable, and not fritter away our time in labouring at something which, however good it may be for the man who cannot yet do anything better, is unworthy of the knowledge and capacity which should be ours as Theosophists. A man who wishes to be considered eligible for employment on higher planes must begin by doing the utmost that lies in his power in the way of definite work for Theosophy down here.

Of course I do not for a moment mean that we are to neglect the ordinary duties of life. We should certainly do well to undertake no new worldly duties of any sort, but those which we have already bound upon our shoulders have become a kârmic obligation which we have no right to neglect. Unless we have done to the full the duties which karma has laid upon us we are not free for the higher work. But this higher work must nevertheless be to us the one thing really worth living for - the constant background of a life which is consecrated to the service of the Masters of Compassion.

Perfect self-control. Before we can be safely trusted with the wider powers of the astral life, we must have ourselves perfectly in hand. Our temper, for example, must be thoroughly under control, so that nothing that we may see or hear can cause real irritation in us, for the consequences of such irritation would be far more serious on that plane than on this. The force of thought is always an enormous power, but down here it is reduced and deadened by the heavy physical brain-particles which it has to set in motion. In the astral world it is far freer and more potent, and for a man with fully awakened faculty to feel anger against a person there would be to do him serious and perhaps even fatal injury.

Not only do we need control of temper, but control of nerve, so that none of the fantastic or terrible sights that we may encounter may be able to shake our dauntless courage. It must be remembered that the pupil who awakens a man upon the astral plane incurs thereby a certain amount of responsibility for his actions and for his safety, so that unless his neophyte had courage to stand alone the whole of the older worker's time would be wasted in hovering round to protect him, which it would be manifestly unreasonable to expect.

It is to make sure of this control of nerve, and to fit them for the work that has to be done, that candidates are always made, now as in days of old, to pass what are called the tests of earth, water, air and fire.

In other words, they have to learn with that absolute certainty that comes not by theory, but by practical experience, that in their astral bodies none of these elements can by any possibility be hurtful to them - that none can oppose any obstacle in the way the work which they have to do.

In this physical body we are fully convinced that fire will burn us, that water will drown us, that the solid rock forms an impassable barrier to our progress, that we cannot with safety launch ourselves unsupported into the ambient air. So deeply is this conviction ingrained in us that it costs most men a good deal of effort to overcome the instinctive action which follows from it, and to realize that in the astral body the densest rock offers no impediment to their freedom of motion, that they may leap with impunity from the highest cliff, and plunge with the most absolute confidence into the heart of the raging volcano or the deepest abysses of the fathomless ocean.

Yet until a man *knows* this - knows it sufficiently to act upon his knowledge instinctively and confidently - he is comparatively useless for astral work, since in emergencies that are constantly arising he would be perpetually paralyzed by imaginary disabilities. So he has to go through his tests, and through many another strange experience - to meet face to face with calm courage the most terrifying apparitions amid the most loathsome surroundings - to show in fact that his nerve may be thoroughly trusted under any and all of the varied groups of circumstances in which he may at any moment find himself.

Further, we need control of mind and of desire; of mind, because without the power of concentration it would be impossible to do good work amid all the distracting currents of the astral plane; of desire, because in that strange world to desire is very often to have, and unless this part of our nature were well controlled we might perchance find ourselves face to face with creations of our own of which we should be heartily ashamed.

Calmness. This is another most important point - the absence of all worry and depression. Much of the work consists in soothing those who are disturbed, and cheering those who are in sorrow; and how can a helper do that work if his own aura is vibrating with constant fuss and worry, or grey with the deadly gloom that comes from perpetual depression? Nothing is more hopelessly fatal to occult progress or usefulness than our nineteenth century habit of ceaselessly worrying over trifles - of eternally making mountains out of molehills. Many of us simply spend our lives in magnifying the most absurd trivialities - in solemnly and elaborately going to work to make ourselves miserable about nothing.

Surely we who are Theosophists ought, at any rate, to have got beyond this stage of irrational worry and causeless depression; surely we, who are trying to acquire some definite knowledge of the cosmic order, ought by this time to have realized that the optimistic view of everything is always nearest to the divine view, and therefore to the truth, because only that in any person which is good and beautiful can by any possibility be permanent, while the evil must by its very nature be temporary. In fact, as Browning said, "the evil is null, is naught, is silence implying sound," while above and beyond it all "the soul of things is sweet, the Heart of Being is celestial rest." So They who know maintain unruffled calm, and with Their perfect sympathy combine the joyous serenity which comes from the certainty that all will at last be well; and those who wish to help must learn to follow Their example.

Knowledge. To be of use the man must at least have some knowledge of the nature of the plane on which he has to work, and the more knowledge he has in any and every direction the more useful he will be. He must fit himself for this task by carefully studying Theosophical literature; for he cannot expect those whose time is already so fully occupied to waste some of it in explaining to him what he might have learnt down here by taking the trouble to read the books. No one who is not already as earnest a student as his capacities and opportunities permit, need begin to think of himself as a candidate for astral work.

Unselfishness. It would seem scarcely needful to assist upon this as a qualification, for surely everyone who has made the least study of Theosophy must know that while the slightest taint of selfishness remains in a man, he is not yet fit to be entrusted with higher powers, not yet fit to enter upon a work of whose very essence it is that the worker should forget himself but to remember the good of others. He who is still capable of selfish thought, whose personality is still so strong in him that he can allow himself to be turned aside from his work by feelings of petty pride or suggestions of wounded dignity - that man is not yet ready to show the selfless devotion of the helper.

Love. This, the last and greatest of the qualifications, is also the most misunderstood. Most emphatically it is *not* the cheap, namby-pamby backboneless sentimentalism which is always overflowing into vague platitudes and gushing generalities, yet fears to stand firm for the right lest it should be branded by the ignorant as "unbrotherly." What is wanted is the love which is strong enough *not* to boast itself, but to act without talking about it - the intense desire for service which is ever on the watch for an opportunity to render it, even though it prefers to do so anonymously - the feeling which springs up in the heart of him who has realized the great work of the Logos, and having once seen it, knows that for him there can be in the three worlds no other course but to identify himself with it to the utmost limit of his power - to become, in however humble a way, and at however great a distance, a tiny channel of that wondrous love of God which, like the peace of God, passeth man's understanding.

These are the qualities toward the possession of which the helper must ceaselessly strive, and of which some considerable measure at least must be his before he can hope that the Great Ones who stand behind will deem him fit for full awakening. The ideal is in truth a high one, yet none need therefore turn away disheartened, nor think that while he is still but struggling toward it he must necessarily remain entirely useless on the astral plane, for short of the responsibilities and dangers of that full awakening there is much that may safely and usefully be done.

There is hardly one among us who would not be capable of performing at least one definite act of mercy and good will each night while we are away from our bodies. Our condition when asleep is usually one of absorption in thought, be it remembered - a carrying on of the thoughts that have principally occupied us during the day, and especially of the last thought in the mind when sinking into sleep. Now if we make that last thought a strong intention to go and give help to some one whom we know to be in need of it, the soul when freed from the body will undoubtedly carry out that intention, and the help will be given. There are several cases on record in which, when this attempt has been made, the person thought of has been fully conscious of the effort of the would-be helper, and has even seen his astral body in the act of carrying out the instructions impressed upon it.

Indeed, no one need sadden himself with the thought that he can have no part nor lot in this glorious work. Such a feeling would be entirely untrue, for every one who can think can help. Nor need such useful action be confined to our hours of sleep. If you know (and who does not?) of some one who is in sorrow or suffering, though you may not be able consciously to stand in astral form by their bedside, you can nevertheless send them loving thoughts and earnest good wishes; and be well assured that such thoughts and wishes are real and living and strong - that when you so send them they do actually go and work your will in proportion to the strength which you have put into them. Thoughts are things, intensely real things, visible enough to those whose eyes have been opened to see, and by their means the poorest man may bear his part in the good work of the world as fully as the richest. In this way at least, whether we can yet function consciously upon the astral plane or not, we all can join, and we all ought to join, the army of invisible helpers.

But the aspirant, who definitely desires to become one of the band of astral helpers who are working under the direction of the great Masters of Wisdom, will make his preparation part of a far wider scheme of development. Instead of merely endeavouring to fit himself for this particular branch of their service, he will undertake with high resolution the far greater task of training himself to follow in their footsteps, of bending all the energies of his soul to attain even as they have attained, so that his power of helping the world may not be confined to the astral plane, but may extend to those higher levels which are the true home of the divine self of man.

For him the path has been marked out long ago by the wisdom of those who have trodden it in days of old - a path of self-development which sooner or later all must follow, whether they choose to adopt it of their own free will, or to wait until, after many lives and an infinity of suffering, the slow, resistless force of evolution drives them along it among the laggards of the human family. But the wise man is he who eagerly enters upon it immediately, setting his face resolutely toward the goal of adeptship, in order that, being safe for ever from all doubt and fear and sorrow himself, he may help others into safety and happiness also. What are the steps of this Path of Holiness, as the Buddhists call it, and in what order they are arranged, let us see in our next chapter.

CHAPTER XV

THE PROBATIONARY PATH

EASTERN books tell us that there are four means by which a man may be brought to the beginning of the path of spiritual advancement: 1. By the companionship of those who have already entered upon it. 2. By the hearing or reading of definite teaching on occult philosophy. 3. By enlightened reflection; that is to say, that by sheer force of hard thinking and close reasoning he may arrive at the truth, or some portion of it, for himself. 4. By the practice of virtue, which means that a long series of virtuous lives, though it does not necessarily involve any increase of intellectuality, does eventually develop in man sufficient intuition to enable him to grasp the necessity of entering upon the path, and show him in what direction it lies.

When, by one or another of these means, he has arrived at this point, the way to the highest adeptship lies straight before him, if he chooses to take it. In writing for students of occultism it is hardly necessary to say that at our present stage of development we cannot expect to learn all, or nearly all, about any but the lowest steps of this path; whilst of the highest we know little but the names, though we may get occasional glimpses of the indescribable glory which surrounds them.

According to the esoteric teachings these steps are grouped in three great divisions:

The probationary period, before any definite pledges are taken, or initiations (in the full sense of the word) are given. This carries a man to the level necessary to pass successfully through what in Theosophical books is usually called the critical period of the fifth round.

The period of pledged discipleship, or the path proper, whose four stages are often spoken of in Oriental books as the four paths of holiness. At the end of this the pupil obtains adeptship - the level which humanity should reach at the close of the seventh round.

What we may venture to call the official period, in which the adept takes a definite part (under the great Cosmic Law) in the government of the world, and holds a special office connected therewith, Of course every adept - every pupil even, when once definitely accepted, as we have seen in the earlier chapters - takes a part in the great work of helping forward the evolution of man; but those standing on the higher levels take charge of special departments, and correspond in the cosmic scheme to the ministers of the crown in a well-ordered earthly state. It is not proposed to make any attempt in this book to treat of this official period; no information about it has ever been made public, and the whole subject is too far above our comprehension to be profitably dealt with in print. We will confine ourselves therefore to the two earlier divisions.

Before going into details of the probationary period it is well to mention that in most of the Eastern sacred books this stage is regarded as merely preliminary, and scarcely as part of the path at all, for they consider that the latter is really entered upon only when definite pledges have been given. Considerable confusion has been created by the fact that the numbering of the stages occasionally commences at this point, though more often at the beginning of the second great division; sometimes the stages themselves are counted, and sometimes the initiations leading into or out of them, so that in studying the books one has to be perpetually on one's guard to avoid misunderstanding.

This probationary period, however, differs considerably in character from the others; the divisions between its stages are less decidedly marked than are those of the higher groups, and the requirements are not so definite or so exacting. But it will be easier to explain this last point after giving a list of the five stages of this period, with their respective qualifications. The first four were very ably described by Mr Mohini Mohun Chatterji in the first Transaction of the London Lodge, to which readers may be referred for fuller definitions of them than can be given here. Much exceedingly valuable information about them is also given by Mrs. Besant in her books *The Path of Discipleship* and *In the Outer Court.*

The names given to the stages will differ somewhat, for in those books the Hindu Sanskrit terminology was employed, whereas the Pâli nomenclature used here is that of the Buddhist system; but although the subject is thus approached from a different side as it were, the qualifications exacted will be found to be precisely the same in effect even when the outward form varies. In the case of each word the mere dictionary meaning will first be given in parentheses, and the explanation of it which is usually given by the teacher will follow. The first stage, then is called among Buddhists.

Manodvâravajjana (the opening of the doors of the mind, or perhaps escaping by the door of the mind) - and in it the candidate acquires a firm intellectual conviction of the impermanence and worthlessness of mere earthly aims. This is often described as learning the difference between the real and the unreal; and to learn it often takes a long time and many hard lessons. Yet it is obvious that it must be the first step toward anything like real progress, for no man can enter whole-heartedly upon the path until he has definitely decided to "set his affection upon things above, not on things on the earth," and that decision comes from the certainty that nothing on earth has any value as compared with the higher life. This step is called by the Hindus the acquirement of Viveka or discrimination, and Mr. Sinnett speaks of it as the giving allegiance to the higher self.

Parikamma (preparation for action) - the stage in which the candidate learns to do the right merely because it is right, without considering his own gain or loss either in this world or the future, and acquires, as the Eastern books put it, perfect indifference to the enjoyment of the fruit of his own actions. This indifference is the natural result of the previous step; for when the neophyte has once grasped the unreal and impermanent character of all earthly rewards, he ceases to crave for them; when once the radiance of the real has shone upon the soul, nothing below that can any longer be an object of desire. This higher indifference is called by the Hindus Vairâgya.

Upachâro (attention or conduct) - the stage in which what are called "the six qualifications" (the Shatsampatti of the Hindus) must be acquired. These are called in Pâli:

a. Samo (quietude) - that purity and calmness of thought which comes from perfect control of the mind - a qualification exceedingly difficult of attainment, and yet most necessary, for unless the mind moves only in obedience to the guidance of the will it cannot be a perfect instrument for the Master's work in the future. This qualification is a very comprehensive one, and includes within itself both the self-control and the calmness which were described in chapter xiv. as necessary for astral work.

b. Damo (subjugation) - a similar mastery over, and therefore purity in, one's actions and words - a quality which again follows necessarily from its predecessor.

c. Uparti (cessation) - explained as cessation from bigotry or from belief in the necessity of any act or ceremony prescribed by a particular religion - so leading the aspirant to independence of thought and to a wide and generous tolerance.

d. Titikkhâ (endurance or forbearance) - by which is meant the readiness to bear with cheerfulness whatever one's karma may bring upon one, and to part with anything and everything worldly whenever it may be necessary. It also includes the idea of complete absence of resentment for wrong, the man knowing that those who do him wrong are but the instruments of his own karma.

e. Samâdhâna (intentness) - one-pointedness involving the incapability of being turned aside from one's path by temptation. This corresponds very closely with the single-mindness spoken of in the previous chapter.

f.Saddhâ (faith) - confidence in one's Master and oneself: confidence, that is, that the Master is a competent teacher, and that, however diffident the pupil may feel as to his own powers, he has yet within him that divine spark which when fanned into a flame will one day enable him to achieve even as his Master has done.

Anuloma (direct order or succession, signifying that its attainment follows as a natural consequence from the other three) - the stage in which is acquired that intense desire for liberation from earthly life, and for union with the highest, which is called by the Hindus Mumukshatva.

Gotrabhû (the condition of fitness for initiation); in this stage the candidate gathers up, as it were, his previous acquisitions, and strengthens them to the degree necessary for the next great step, which will set his feet upon the path proper as an accepted pupil. The attainment of this level is followed very rapidly by initiation into the next grade. In answer to the question, "Who is the Gotrabhû?" Buddha says, "The man who is in possession of those conditions upon which the commencement of sanctification immediately ensues - he is the Gotrabhû

The wisdom necessary for the reception of the path of holiness is called Gotrabhû-gñâna.

Now that we have hastily glanced at the steps of the probationary period, we must emphasize the point to which reference was made at the commencement - that the *perfect* attainment of these accomplishments and qualifications is not expected at this early stage. As Mr. Mohini says, "If all these are equally strong, adeptship is attained in the same incarnation." But such a result is of course extremely rare. It is in the direction of these acquirements that the candidate must ceaselessly strive, but it would be an error to suppose that no one has been admitted to the next step without possessing all of them in the fullest possible degree. Nor do they necessarily follow one another in the same definite order as the later steps; in fact, in many cases a man would be developing the various qualifications all at the same time - rather side by side than in regular succession.

It is obvious that a man might easily be working along a great part of this path even though he was quite unaware of its very existence, and no doubt many a good Christian, many an earnest freethinker is already far on the road that will eventually lead him to initiation, though he may never have heard the word occultism in his life. I mention these two classes especially, because in every other religion occult development is recognized as a possibility, and would certainly therefore be intentionally sought by those who felt yearnings for something more satisfactory than the exoteric faiths.

We must also note that the steps of this probationary period are not separated by initiations in the full sense of the word, though they will certainly be studded with tests and trials of all sorts and on all planes, and may be relieved by encouraging experiences, and by hints and help whenever these may safely be given. We are apt sometimes to use the word initiation somewhat loosely, as for example when it is applied to such tests as have just been mentioned; properly speaking it refers only to the solemn ceremony at which a pupil is formally admitted to a higher grade by an appointed official, who in the name of the One Initiator receives his plighted vow, and puts into his hands the new key of knowledge which he is to use on the level to which he has now attained. Such an initiation is taken at the entrance to the division which we shall next consider, and also at each passage from any one of its steps to the next.

CHAPTER XVI

THE PATH PROPER

IT is in the four stages of this division of the path that the ten Samyojana, or fetters which bind man to the circle of rebirth and hold him back from Nirvâna, must be cast off. And here comes the difference between this period of pledged discipleship and the previous probation. No partial success in getting rid of these fetters is sufficient now; before a candidate can pass on from one of the steps to the next he must be *entirely* free from certain of these clogs; and when they are enumerated it will be seen how far-reaching this requirement is, and there will be little cause to wonder at the statement made in the sacred books that seven incarnations are sometimes required to pass through this division of the path.

Each of these four steps or stages is again divided into four: for each has (1) its Maggo, or way, during which the student is striving to cast off the fetters; (2) its Phala (result or fruit) when he finds the results of his action in so doing showing themselves more and more; (3) its Bhavagga or consummation, the period when, the result having culminated, he is able to fulfil satisfactorily the work belonging to the step on which he now firmly stands; and (4) its Gotrabhû, meaning, as before, the time when he arrives at a fit state to receive the next initiation. The first stage is:

Sotâpatti or Sohan. The pupil who has attained this level is spoken of as the Sowani or Sotâpanna - "he who has entered the stream, - "because from this period, though he may linger, though he may succumb to more refined temptations and turn aside from his course for a time, he can no longer fall back altogether from spirituality and become a mere worldling. He has entered upon the stream of definite higher human evolution, upon which all humanity must enter by the middle of the next round, unless they are to be left behind as temporary failures by the great life-wave, to wait for further progress until the next chain of worlds.

The pupil who is able to take this initiation has therefore already outstripped the majority of humanity to the extent of an entire round of all our seven planets, and in doing so has definitely secured himself against the possibility of falling out of the stream in the fifth round. He is consequently sometimes spoken of as "the saved" or "the safe one." It is from a misunderstanding of this idea that there arises the curious theory of salvation promulgated by a certain section of the Christian community. The "æonian salvation" of which some of its documents speak is not, as has been blasphemously supposed by the ignorant, from eternal torture, but simply from wasting the rest of this æon or dispensation by falling out of its line of progress. This also is the meaning, naturally, of the celebrated clause in the Athanasian Creed, "Whosoever will be saved, before all things it is necessary that he hold the catholic faith" (See *The Christian Creed*, p.91). The fetters which he must cast off before he can pass into the next stage are:

Sakkâyaditthi - the delusion of self.

Vichikichchhâ - doubt or uncertainty.

Sîlabbataparâmâsa - superstition.

The first of these is the "I am I" consciousness, which as connected with the *personality* is nothing but an illusion, and must be got rid of at the very first step of the real upward path. But to cast off this fetter completely means even more than this, for it involves the realization of the fact that the individuality also is in very truth one with the All, that it can therefore never have any interests opposed to those of its brethren, and that it is most truly progressing when it most assists the progress of others.

For the very sign and seal of the attainment of the Sotâpatti level is the first entrance of the pupil into the plane next above the mental - that which we usually call the buddhic. It may be - nay, it will be - the merest touch of the lowest sub-plane of that stupendously exalted condition that the pupil can as yet experience, even with his Master's help; but even that touch is something that can never be forgotten - something that opens a new world before him, and entirely revolutionizes his feelings and conceptions. Then for the first time, by means of the extended consciousness of that plane, he truly realizes the underlying unity of all, not as an intellectual conception merely, but as a definite fact that is patent to his opened eyes; then first he really knows something of the world in which he lives - then first he gets some slight glimpse of what the love and compassion of the great Masters must be.

As to the second fetter, a word of caution is necessary. We who have been trained in European habits of thought are unhappily so familiar with the idea that a blind unreasoning adhesion to certain dogmas may be claimed from a disciple, that or hearing that occultism considers *doubt* as an obstacle to progress, we are likely to suppose that it also requires the same unquestioning faith from its followers as modern superstitions do. No idea could be more certainly false.

It is true that doubt (or rather uncertainty) on certain questions is a bar to spiritual progress, but the antidote to that doubt is not blind faith (which is itself considered as a fetter, as will presently be seen) but the certainty of conviction founded on individual experiment or mathematical reasoning. While a child doubted the accuracy of the multiplication table he would hardly acquire proficiency in the higher mathematics; but his doubts could be satisfactorily cleared up only by his attaining a comprehension, founded on reasoning or experiment, that the statements contained in the table are true. He believes that twice two are four, not merely because he has been told so, but because it has become to him a self-evident fact. And this is exactly the method, and the only method, of resolving doubt known to occultism.

Vichikichchhâ has been defined as doubt of the doctrines of karma and reincarnation, and of the efficacy of the method of attaining the highest good by this path of holiness; and the casting off of this Samyojana is the arriving at absolute certainty, based either upon personal first-hand knowledge or upon reason, that the occult teaching upon these points is true.

The third fetter to be got rid of comprehends all kinds of unreasoning or mistaken belief, all dependence on the efficacy of outward rites and ceremonies to purify the heart. He who would cast it off must learn to depend upon himself alone, not upon others, nor upon the outer husk of any religion.

The first three fetters are in a coherent series. The difference between individuality and personality being fully realized, it is then possible to some extent to appreciate the actual course of reincarnation, and so as to dispel all doubt on that head. This done, the knowledge of the spiritual permanence of the true ego gives rise to reliance on one's own spiritual strength, and so dispels superstition.

II. Sakadâgâmî. The pupil who has entered upon this second stage is spoken of as a Sakridâgâmin - "the man who returns but once" - signifying that a man who has reached this level should need but one more incarnation before attaining arahatship. At this step no additional fetters are cast off, but the pupil is occupied in reducing to a minimum those which still enchain him. It is, however, usually a period of considerable psychic and intellectual advancement.

If what are commonly called psychic faculties have not been previously acquired, they must be developed at this stage, as without them it would be impossible to assimilate the knowledge which must now be given, or to do the higher work for humanity in which the pupil is now privileged to assist. He must have the astral consciousness at his command during his physical waking life, and during sleep the heaven-world will be open before him - for the consciousness of a man when away from his physical body is always one stage higher than it is while he is still burdened with the house of flesh.

III. Anâgâmi. The Anâgâmin (he who does not return) is so called because, having reached this stage, he ought to be able to attain the next one in the life he is then living. He enjoys, while moving through the round of his daily work, all the splendid possibilities of progress given by the full possession of the priceless faculties of the heaven-world, and when he leaves his physical vehicle at night he enters once more into the wonderfully-widened consciousness that belongs to the buddhi. In this step he finally gets rid of any lingering remains of the two fetters of

Kâmarâga - attachment to the enjoyment of sensation, typified by earthly love, and

Patigha - all possibility of anger or hatred.

The student who has cast off these fetters can no longer be swayed by the influence of his senses either in the direction of love or hatred, and is free from either attachment to or impatience of physical plane conditions.

Here again we must guard against a possible misconception - one with which we frequently meet. The purest and noblest human love *never* dies away - is *never* in any way diminished by occult training; on the contrary, it is increased and widened until it embraces all with the same fervour which at first was lavished on one or two. But the student does in time rise above all considerations connected with the mere*personality* of those around him, and so is free from all the injustice and partiality which ordinary love so often brings in its train.

Nor should it for a moment be supposed that in gaining this wide affection for all he loses the especial love for his closer friends. The unusually perfect link between Ânanda and the Buddha, as between S. John and Jesus, is on record to prove that on the contrary this is enormously intensified; and the tie between a Master and his pupils is stronger far than any earthly bond. For the affection which flourishes upon the path of holiness is an affection between egos, and not merely between personalities; therefore it is strong and permanent, without fear of diminution or fluctuation, for it is that "perfect love which casteth out fear."

IV. Arahat (the venerable, the perfect). On attaining this level the aspirant constantly enjoys the consciousness of the buddhic plane, and is able to use its powers and faculties while still in the physical body; and when he leaves that body in sleep or trance he passes at once into the unutterable glory of the nirvânic plane. In this stage the occultist must cast off the last remains of the five remaining fetters, which are:

Rûparâga - desire for beauty of form or for physical existence in a form, even including that in the heaven-world.

Arûparâga - desire for formless life

Mâno - pride.

Uddhachcha - agitation or irritability.

10.Avijjâ - ignorance.

On this we may remark that the casting off of Rûparâga involves not only getting rid of desire for earthly life, however grand or noble that life may be, and astral or devachanic life, however glorious, but also of all liability to be unduly influenced or repelled by the external beauty or ugliness of any person or thing.

Arûparâga - desire for life either in the highest and formless planes of the heaven-world or in the still more exalted buddhic plane -would be merely a higher and less sensual form of selfishness, and must be cast off just as much as the lower. Uddhachcha really means "liability to be disturbed in mind," and a man who had finally cast off this fetter would be absolutely unruffled by anything whatever that might happen to him - perfectly impervious to any kind of attack upon his dignified serenity.

The getting rid of ignorance of course implies the acquisition of perfect knowledge - practical omniscience as regards our planetary chain. When all the fetters are finally cast off the advancing ego reaches the fifth stage - the stage of full adeptship - and becomes.

V. Asekha, "the one who has no more to learn," again as regards our planetary chain. It is quite impossible for us to realize at our present level what this attainment means. All the splendor of the nirvânic plane lies open before the waking eyes of the adept, while when he chooses to leave his body he has the power to enter upon something higher still - a plane which to us is the merest name. As Professor Rhys Davids explains, "He is now free from all sin; he sees and values all things in this life and their true value; all evil being rooted from his mind he experiences only righteous desires for himself and tender pity and regard and exalted love for others."

To show how little he has lost the sentiment of love, we read in the Metta Sutta of the state of mind of one who stands at this level: "As a mother loves, who even at the risk of her own life protects her only son, such love let there be toward all beings. Let goodwill without measure prevail in the whole world, above, below, around, unstinted, unmixed with any feeling of differing or opposing interests. When a man remains steadfastly in this state of mind all the while, whether he be standing or walking, sitting or lying down, then is come to pass the saying which is written, 'Even in this life has holiness been found.' "

CHAPTER XVII

WHAT LIES BEYOND

BEYOND this period it is obvious that we can know nothing of the new qualifications required for the still higher levels which yet lie before the perfect man. It is abundantly clear, however, that when man has become Asekha he has exhausted all the possibilities of moral development, so that further advancement for him can only mean still wider knowledge and still more wonderful spiritual powers. We are told that when man has thus attained his spiritual majority, whether in the slow course of evolution or by the shorter path of self-development he assumes the fullest control of his own destinies and makes choice of his future line of evolution among seven possible paths which he sees opening before him.

Naturally at our present level we cannot expect to understand much about these, and the faint outline of some of them which is all that can be sketched in for us conveys very little to the mind, except that most of them take the adept altogether away from our earth-chain, which no longer affords sufficient scope for his evolution.

One path is that of those who, as the technical phrase goes, "accept Nirvâna." Through what incalculable æons they remain in that sublime condition, for what work they are preparing themselves, what will be their future line of evolution, are questions upon which we know nothing; and indeed if information upon such points could be given it is more than likely that it would prove quite incomprehensible to us at our present stage.

But this much at least we may grasp - that the blessed state of Nirvâna is not, as some have ignorantly supposed, a condition of blank nothingness, but on the contrary of far more intense and beneficent activity; and that ever as man rises higher in the scale of nature his possibilities become greater, his work for others ever grander and more far-reaching, and that infinite wisdom and infinite power mean for him only infinite capacity for service, because they are directed by infinite love.

Another class chooses a spiritual evolution not quite so far removed from humanity, for though not directly connected with the next chain of our system it extends through two long periods corresponding to its first and second rounds, at the end of which time they also appear to "accept Nirvâna," but at a higher stage than those previously mentioned.

Others join the deva evolution, whose progress lies along a grand chain consisting of seven chains like ours, each of which to them is as one world. This line of evolution is spoken of as the most gradual and therefore the least arduous of the seven courses; but though it is sometimes referred to in the books as "yielding to the temptation to become a god." it is only in comparison with the sublime height of renunciation of the Nirmânakâya that it can be spoken of in this half-disparaging manner, for the adept who chooses this course has indeed a glorious career before him, and though the path which he selects is not the shortest, it is nevertheless a very noble one.

Yet another group are the Nirmânakâyas - those who, declining all these easier methods, choose the shortest but steepest path to the heights which still lie before them. They form what is poetically termed the "guardian wall," and, as *The Voice of the Silence* tells us, "protect the world from further and far greater misery and sorrow," not indeed by warding off from it external evil influences, but by devoting all their strength to the work of pouring down upon it a flood of spiritual force and assistance without which it would assuredly be in far more hopeless case than now.

Yet again there are those who remain even more directly in association with humanity, and continue to incarnate among it, choosing the path which leads through the four stages of what we have called above the official period; and among these are the Masters of Wisdom - those from whom we who study Theosophy have learnt such fragments as we know of the mighty harmony of evolving Nature. But it would seem that only a certain comparatively small number adopt this course - probably only so many as are necessary for the carrying on of this physical side of the work.

In hearing of these different possibilities, people sometimes exclaim rashly that there could of course be no thought in a Master's mind of choosing any but that course which most helps humanity - a remark which greater knowledge would have prevented them from making. We should never forget that there are other evolutions in the solar system besides our own, and no doubt it is necessary for the carrying out of the vast plan of the Logos that there should be adepts working on all the seven lines to which we have referred. Surely the choice of the Master would be to go wherever his work was most needed - to place his services with absolute selflessness at the disposal of the Powers in charge of this part of the great scheme of evolution.

This then is the path which lies before us, the path which each one of us should be beginning to tread. Stupendous though its heights appear we should remember that they are attained but gradually and step by step, and that those who now stand near the summit once toiled in the mire of the valleys, even as we are doing. Although this path may at first seem hard and toilsome, yet ever as we rise our footing becomes firmer and our outlook wider, and thus we find ourselves better able to help those who are climbing beside us.

Because it is at first thus hard and toilsome to the lower self, it has sometimes been called by the very misleading title of "the path of woe;" but, as Mrs. Besant has beautifully written, "through all such suffering there is a deep and abiding joy, for the suffering is of the lower nature, and the joy of the higher." When the last shred of the personality is gone all that can thus suffer has passed away, and in the perfected Adept there is unruffled peace and everlasting joy. He sees the end toward which all is working, and rejoices in that end, knowing that earth's sorrow is but a passing phase in human evolution.

"That of which little has been said is the profound content which comes from being on the path, from realizing the goal and the way to it, from knowing that the power to be useful is increasing, and that the lower nature is being gradually extirpated. And little has been said of the rays of joy which fall upon the path from loftier levels, the dazzling glimpses of the glory to be revealed, the serenity which the storms of earth cannot ruffle. To any one who has entered on the path all other ways have lost their charm, and its sorrows have a keeper bliss than the best joys of the lower world." (Vâhan, vol. v., No. 12.)

Let no man therefore despair because he thinks the task too great for him; what man has done man can do, and just in proportion as we extend our aid to those whom we can help, so will those who have already attained be able in their turn to help us. So from the lowest to the highest we who are treading the steps of the path are bound together by one long chain of mutual service, and none need feel neglected or alone, for though sometimes the lower flights of the great staircase may be wreathed in mist, we know that it leads up to happier regions and purer air, where the light is always shining.

The End

BOOK TWO

THE CHRISTIAN CREED

CHAPTER I
THE EARLIER CREEDS

THERE are many students of Theosophy who have been, and indeed still are, earnest Christians; and though their faith has gradually broadened out into unorthodoxy, they have retained a strong affection for the forms and ceremonials of the religion into which they were born. It is a pleasure to them to hear the recitation of the ancient prayers and creeds, the time-honoured psalms and canticles, though they try to read into them a higher and wider meaning than the ordinary orthodox interpretation.

I have thought that it might be of interest to such students to have some slight account of the real meaning and origin of those very remarkable basic formulae of the Church which are called the Creeds, so that when they hear them or join in their recital the ideas brought into their minds thereby may be the grander and nobler ones originally connected with them, rather than the misleading materialism of modern misapprehension.

I have spoken of the ideas originally connected with them; I ought perhaps rather to say the ideas connected with the ancient formula upon which all the most valuable portion of them is based. For I do not mean to say for a moment that any large number of the members, or even of the leaders, of the Church which now recites these Creeds have for many a century known their true meaning. I do not even claim that the ecclesiastical councils which edited and authorized them ever realized the full and glorious signification of the rolling phrases which they used; for much of the true meaning had already been lost, much of the materializing corruption had been introduced, long before those unfortunate assemblies were convoked.

But this at least does seem certain - that narrowed, degraded and materialized as the Christian faith has been, corrupt almost beyond recognition as its scriptures have become, an attempt has at least been made by some of the higher powers to guide those who have compiled for it these great symbols called the Creeds, so that, whatever they may themselves have known, their language still clearly conveys the grand truths of the ancient wisdom to all who have ears to hear; and much that in these formulae seems false and incomprehensible when the endeavour is made to read them in accordance with modern misconceptions, becomes at once luminous and full of meaning when understood in that inner sense which exalts it from a fragment of unreliable biography into a declaration of eternal truth.

It is with the elucidation of this inner sense of the Creeds that I am concerned; and although in writing of this it will be necessary for me to make some reference to their real history, I need hardly say that I am not in any way attempting to approach the subject from the ordinary scholarly standpoint. Such information as I have to give about the Creeds is obtained neither from the comparison of ancient manuscripts nor from the study of the voluminous works of theological writers, but is simply the result of an investigation into the records of Nature made by a few students of occultism. Their notice was incidentally attracted to the question while following up quite another line of research, and it was then seen that the matter was of sufficient interest to repay further and more detailed examination.

It will perhaps be a new idea to some of my readers that there is such a thing as a record of Nature - that there are methods by which it is possible to recover with absolute certainty the true story of the past. The fact that this can be done is well known to those who have studied the subject, and much ancient history of most vivid interest has already been examined in this way. To explain the process would be outside the scope of this treatise, and I would refer those who desire further information upon this matter to my little book on *Clairvoyance*.

The Christian Church at present uses three formulations of belief, called respectively the Apostles' Creed, the Nicene Creed, and the Athanasian Creed. The first and second of these have many points in common, and may easily be examined together; the third is so much longer and so different in character, that it will be more convenient to devote a separate chapter to its consideration later. As at present found in the Prayer-book of the Church of England, these Creeds are as follows:

THE APOSTLES' CREED.

I believe in God the Father Almighty, Maker of heaven and earth; and in Jesus Christ his only Son our Lord, who was conceived by the Holy Ghost, born of the Virgin Mary, suffered under Pontius Pilate, was crucified, dead and buried; he descended into hell; the third day he rose again from the dead; he ascended into heaven, and sitteth on the right hand of God the Father Almighty; from thence he shall come to judge the quick and the dead.

I believe in the Holy Ghost, the holy catholic Church, the communion of saints, the forgiveness of sins, the resurrection of the body, and the life everlasting.

THE NICENE CREED.

I believe in one God, the Father Almighty, maker of heaven and earth, and of all things visible and invisible; and in one Lord Jesus Christ, the only-begotten Son of God, begotten of his Father before all worlds, God of God, Light of Light, very God of very God, begotten, not made, being of one substance with the Father, by whom all things were made; who for us men and for our salvation came down from heaven, and was incarnate by the Holy Ghost of the Virgin Mary, and was made man, and was crucified also for us under Pontius Pilate; he suffered and was buried, and the third day he rose again according to the scriptures, and ascended into heaven, and sitteth on the right hand of the Father; and he shall come again with glory to judge both the quick and the dead, whose kingdom shall have no end.

And I believe in the Holy Ghost, the Lord and giver of life, who proceedeth from the Father and the Son, who with the Father and the Son together is worshipped and glorified, who spake by the prophets; and I believe one catholic and apostolic Church; I acknowledge one baptism for the remission of sins, and I look for the resurrection of the dead and the life of the world to come.

Since for the comprehension of the Nicene Creed so much depends upon accurate translation from the Greek original, I append here the received text for comparison.

THEIR DATE AND HISTORY.

Before describing the true origin of these Creeds, let me very briefly epitomize the current ideas of orthodox theologians as to their date and history. At one time the ecclesiastical theory was that the Nicene and the Athanasian formulae were merely amplifications of the Apostles' Creed, but it is now universally recognized that the Nicene Creed is historically the oldest of the three. Let us take them one by one, and glance at what is commonly known of them.

Some sort of brief and simple Creed seems to have been in use from a very early period, not only as a symbol of faith, but as a pass-word in military style. But the wording of this formula appears to have varied considerably in different countries, and it was not until centuries later that anything like uniformity was attained. An example of the earlier form is the Creed given by Irenaeus in his work *Against Heresies*: "I believe in One God almighty, of whom are all things ... and in the Son of God, by whom are all things."

The earliest mention of a Creed bearing the name of the Apostles occurs in the fourth century in the writings of Rufinus, who states that it is so called because it consists of twelve articles, one of which was contributed by each of the twelve Apostles assembled in solemn conclave for the purpose. But Rufinus is not regarded as any great historical authority, and even in the Roman Catholic encyclopaedia of Wetzer and Welte his story is considered as a mere pious legend.

The Apostles' Creed is not found in anything like its present form till fully four centuries after the composition of the Nicene symbol, and the most authoritative writers on the subject suppose it to be a mere conglomerate slowly formed by the gradual collation of earlier and simpler expressions of belief. Occult investigation negatives this idea, as will be explained later, and, though quite admitting its composite character, assigns to part of it at any rate a far higher origin than even that claimed by Rufinus.

Much more definite and satisfactory, from the ordinary point of view, is the history of the longer formula called the Nicene Creed, which appears in the mass of the Roman Church and the communion service of the Church of England. Practically all writers seem agreed that with the exception of two notable omissions it was drawn up at the Council of Nicaea in the year 325. As most readers will be aware, that council was summoned in order to settle the controversies then raging among ecclesiastical authorities as to the exact nature of the Christ. The Athanasian or materialistic party declared him to be of the same substance as the Father, while the followers of Arius preferred not to commit themselves to anything stronger than the statement that he was of *like* substance, nor were they willing to admit that he also was without beginning.

The point seems a small one to have caused so much excitement and ill-feeling; but it appears to be one of the characteristics of theological controversy that the smaller the difference of opinion the more acrimonious is the hatred between the disputants. Suggestions have been made that Constantine himself exercised a somewhat undue influence over the deliberations of the council; however that may have been, its decision was in favour of the Athanasian party, and the Nicene Creed was accepted as the expression of the faith of the majority. As then drawn up, it ended (if we omit the awful anathema, which shows very clearly the real spirit of the council) with the words, "I believe in the Holy Ghost," and the clauses with which it now concludes were added at the Council of Constantinople in the year 381, with the exception of the words "and the Son," which were inserted by the Western Church at the Council of Toledo in the year 589.

CHAPTER II.
THEIR ORIGIN.

HAVING thus very briefly epitomized what is generally accepted by orthodox scholars with regard to the history of the Creeds, I will now proceed to recount what was discovered in relation to them in the course of the investigations to which I have already referred.

The first point to bear in mind is that all the Creeds as we have them now are essentially composite productions, and that the only one of them which in any way represents a single original document is the latest of all - the Athanasian. I am perfectly aware that even this opening statement flies directly in the face of the ideas ordinarily received upon this subject, but I cannot help that; I am simply stating the facts as the investigators found them.

These Creeds, then, embody statements which are derived from three quite separate sources, and we shall find it of great interest to endeavour to disentangle these three elements from one another, and to assign to each of them respectively those clauses of the Creed (as we have it now) which have flowed from them. These are:

(a) An ancient formula of cosmogenesis, resting on very high authority indeed.

(b) The rubric for the guidance of the hierophant in the Egyptian form of the Sohan or Sotapatti initiation.

(c) The materializing tendency which mistakenly sought to interpret these two documents (a) and (b) as relating the biography of an individual.

Let us consider each of these sources a little more in detail.

THE LIFE OF THE CHRIST.

It is not my intention here to enter at length into the extremely interesting information which clairvoyant investigation has given to us with regard to the true life-story of the great teacher Christ. That will be a work to be done hereafter, but it will assuredly not be undertaken unless and until it is possible for us to adduce in support of our statements evidence entirely apart from that of clairvoyance - evidence such as will appeal to the minds of the scholar and the antiquarian. It will, however, be necessary for a comprehension of the purpose of the ancient formula above mentioned that just a few words upon that subject should be introduced into this treatise.

When the Churchman ends his prayer with the words "through Jesus Christ our Lord," he is confusing together three entirely separate ideas - (a) the disciple Jesus; (b) the great Master whom men call the Christ, though he is known by another and far grander name among the Initiates; and (c) the Second Aspect or Person of the Logos. With regard to the first of these, Mrs. Besant writes in that wonderful book, Esoteric Christianity:

"The child whose Jewish name has been turned into that of Jesus was born in Palestine B.C. 105, during the consulate of Publius Rutilius Rufus and Gnaeus Mallius Maximus. His parents were well-born though poor, and he was educated in a knowledge of the Hebrew scriptures. His fervent devotion and a gravity beyond his years led his parents to dedicate him to the religious and ascetic life, and soon after a visit to Jerusalem, in which the extraordinary intelligence and eagerness for knowledge of the youth were shown in his seeking of the doctors in the temple, he was sent to be trained in an Essene community in the southern Judaean desert. When he had reached the age of nineteen he went on to the Essene monastery near Mount Serbal, a monastery which was much visited by learned men travelling from Persia and India to Egypt, and where a magnificent library of occult works - many of them Indian of the trans-Himalayan regions - had been established. From this seat of mystic learning he proceeded later to Egypt. He had been fully instructed in the secret teachings which were the real fount of life among the Essenes, and was initiated in Egypt as a disciple of that one sublime Lodge from which every great religion has its Founder. For Egypt has remained one of the world-centres of the true Mysteries, whereof all semi-public Mysteries are the fain and far-off reflections. The Mysteries spoken of in history as the Egyptian were the shadow of the true things 'in the Mount,' and there the young Hebrew received the solemn consecration which prepared him for the royal priesthood he was later to attain" (p. 129).

Indeed, this was a young man of such wondrous devotion and such surpassing purity that he was found worthy of the highest honour that can come to man - he was permitted to yield up his body for the use of a mighty Teacher sent out by the Great Brotherhood to found a new religion, to present in yet another form the wonderful truth, many-sided because divine, which now we are studying under the name of Theosophy. This Great One took possession of the body when it was twenty-nine years old, and used it for three years, two of which were occupied in instructing the heads of the Essene community in the Mysteries of the Kingdom of Heaven, and one in preaching to the general public among the hills and fields of Palestine. It is of this last year's work only that some traditions are preserved in the gospel story, though even those traditions are so corrupted and overlaid that it is all but impossible to sift the truth from the falsehood in them. Both the disciple Jesus and the great Master Christ are men of our own humanity, however far in advance of us they are along the path of evolution. It is therefore incorrect to speak of either of them as a direct manifestation or incarnation of the Second Person of the Trinity, though it is true that there is a certain mystical connection here which is fully understood only by the advanced student.

THE FORMULA WHICH HE TAUGHT.

For the purposes of our present inquiry, however, we need not consider that side of the question at all, but may simply think of the Christ as a teacher within the bosom of the Essene community, living amongst them and instructing them for some time before his public ministry commenced. The heads of this community were already in possession of fragments of more or less accurate information - possibly obtained from Buddhist sources - with regard to the origin of all things. These the Christ put together and rendered coherent, casting them for the purpose of ready memorization into the shape of a formula of belief which may be regarded as the first source of the Christian Creed.

The original of this formula may perhaps some day be exactly translated into English; but such an undertaking would need the co-operation of several persons, and very minute care as to the niceties of meaning and choice of words. The attempt will therefore not be made here; yet, since many have inquired what clauses were included in it, it may be well to give a rough idea of it in the words which follow - it being of course understood that this is a paraphrase of its meaning as enshrined in the hearts of those to whom it had been taught, rather than an attempt at an accurate rendering of it.

"We believe in God the Father, from whom comes the system - yea, our world and all things therein, whether seen or unseen;

"And in God the Son, most holy, alone-born from His Father before all the aeons, not made but emanated, being of the very substance of the Father, true God from the true God, true Light from the true Light, by whom all forms were made; who for us men came down from heaven and entered the dense sea, yet riseth thence again in ever greater glory to a kingdom without end;

"And in God the Holy Ghost, the Lifegiver, emanating also from the Father, equal with Him and with the Son in glory; who manifesteth through His Angels;

"We recognize one brotherhood of holy men as leading to the Greater Brotherhood above, one initiation for emancipation from the fetters of sin and for escape from the wheel of birth and death into eternal life."

The purpose for which this symbol was constructed was to condense into a form easily remembered the teaching as to the origin of the cosmos which the Christ had been giving to the heads of the Essene community. Each phrase of it would recall to their minds much more than the mere words in which it was expressed; in fact, it was a mnemonic such as the Buddha used when he gave to his hearers the Four Noble Truths, and no doubt each clause was taken as a text for explanation and expansion, much in the same way as Madame Blavatsky wrote the whole of The Secret Doctrine upon the basis of the Stanzas of Dzyan.

THE EGYPTIAN RUBRIC.

In considering the second source, which we have decided to mark as (b), we have to remember that the Egyptian religion expressed itself principally through a multiplicity of forms and ceremonies, and that even in its Mysteries the same tendency repeatedly showed itself. The highest step of these Mysteries placed a man definitely upon the Path, as we should now call it; that is to say, it corresponded with what in Buddhist terminology is called the Sotapatti initiation. An elaborate symbolical ritual was performed in connection with this step, and part of our Creed is a direct reproduction of the instructions laid down by that ritual for the officiating hierophant, the only difference being that what there stood as a series of directions has been recast into the form of a historical narrative describing that descent of the Logos into matter which the original ritual was intended to symbolize.

This rubric of initiation, in the new form which we have described, was inserted in the formula (a) by the leaders of the Essene community shortly after the Christ's departure from among them, in order that the details as to the descent of the Logos (which he had so often illustrated for them by reference to the ritual of this initiation) might be commemorated in the same symbol which gave the great outline of the doctrine.

Teaching similar in character and similarly illustrated by symbol was given by him with regard to the work of the Logos in His First and Third Aspects, though comparatively little of it has been preserved to us; but there seems no doubt that special importance was attached by the Christ to the accurate comprehension by his disciples of the descent into matter of the monadic essence which is outpoured by the Logos in His Second Aspect.

This is readily comprehensible if we reflect that it is this monadic essence which ensouls all the forms around us, and that it is only through its study that the great principle of evolution can be grasped, and the law of love which sways the universe at all understood. For though undoubtedly evolution is also taking place in the case of the life which ensouls atoms and molecules, its progress is entirely beyond our ken; and assuredly the same may be said, at any rate as regards the vast majority of men, with reference to that far higher evolution which we must suppose to be in operation in connection with that third great outpouring which comes from the First of the great Divine manifestations.

Thus it is evident that it is only through the study of the method of this second outpouring that a comprehension of the whole system may be approached, and this would account for the emphasis which the Christ seems to have laid upon this part of his teaching. Knowing as they did the necessity for this emphasis, it is not wonderful that those who felt themselves responsible for handing on the teaching should have incorporated this symbolical outline of it into the special formula which was intended to epitomize their faith. No doubt in doing so they were actuated by the highest and purest motives, and it was not possible for them to foresee that this very insertion would presently open the way for the degrading and destructive action of tendency (c), of which in their time there was as yet no sign.

It may perhaps be asked why the Christ should have chosen the somewhat complicated and material symbolism of this Egyptian rite to illustrate his teaching on such a subject. We are in no position to presume to criticize the methods adopted by one who knows; but perhaps we may venture to suggest that a possible reason may be found in the close connection of the Essenes with the Egyptian tradition, and in the fact that Jesus himself had in earlier life spent some considerable time in Egypt and passed through at least one initiation according to its methods.

MATERIALISM AND DEGRADATION.

(c) At a very early period in the history of the movement which afterwards became known as Christianity we find two rival schools or tendencies asserting themselves, which are in reality the outcome of two phases of the lifework of the Christ. As has been said, the greater portion of his time was devoted to giving definite instruction within the boundaries of the Essene community; but in addition to this, and in opposition to the views of the official leaders of that community, he also passed beyond these comparatively narrow limits, and devoted a short period at the close of his life to public preaching.

It was obviously impossible for him to put before the ignorant multitude those deeper teachings of the Ancient Wisdom which he had imparted to the few who by special education and a long life of ascetic training had fitted themselves, at least to some extent, for their reception. We find, therefore, that his public addresses may be divided into two classes, the first consisting of the λογια or proverbs, a series of short sentences each containing either an important truth or a rule of conduct, and the second being composed of the παρακλητηρια or "words of comfort" - those eloquent discourses which were called forth by the deep compassion he felt for the profound misery almost universal at that time among the lower classes, and the terrible atmosphere of despair, depression and degradation by which they were overwhelmed.

Some traditional fragments of the Logia have been incorporated here and there in what are now called the gospels; and what seems to be a genuine leaf from a collection of them was discovered some time ago in Egypt by Messrs. Grenfell and Hunt. Christ himself appears to have written nothing, or at any rate nothing that he wrote is now known to us; but during the first two centuries after his death (which, be it remembered, took place considerably before what we now call the Christian era) many of his disciples seem to have made and written down collections of the sayings which were ascribed to him by the current oral tradition. In such collections, however, no attempt was made to give a biography of the Christ; though sometimes a few words of introduction described the occasion upon which certain sayings were uttered, just as in the Buddhist books we constantly find a sermon of the Buddha's introduced by the statement, "On a certain occasion the Blessed One was dwelling in the bamboo garden at Rajagriha," etc.

WORDS OF COMFORT MISUNDERSTOOD.

Though some of his Logia have been distorted, and many sayings have been attributed to him which he certainly never uttered, yet he has been still more seriously misrepresented with reference to the "words of comfort " or Para-kleteria, and with even more disastrous consequences. The general tenour of these addresses was an endeavour to inspire fresh hope in the hearts of the despairing, by explaining to them that if they followed the teaching which he put before them they would assuredly find themselves in better case in the future than in the present, and that though now they were poor and suffering they might yet so live as to ensure for themselves an existence after death and conditions of life upon their next return to earth far more desirable than the fate of those who now so cruelly oppressed them.

It was perhaps not unnatural that many of the more ignorant of his hearers should apprehend his meaning but dimly, and should go away with a general impression that he was vaguely prophesying a future in which what they considered injustice should be righted according to their wishes - in which savage retribution should overtake the rich man, mainly for the crime of being rich, while they themselves should inherit all kinds of power and glory merely because they now were poor.

It will be readily understood that this was a doctrine which easily secured the adhesion of all the least desirable elements of the community, and among such classes in the ancient world it seems to have spread with marvellous rapidity. Nor is it wonderful that such men should have altogether eliminated from their doctrine the condition of good living, and simply banded themselves together, often in orgies of the most objectionable character, as believers in "a good time coming," when they should revenge themselves upon all their personal enemies, and without effort of their own enter forthwith into possession of the wealth and luxury which had been accumulated by the labours of others.

As this tendency developed, it naturally assumed a more and more political and revolutionary character, until it came to be true of the leaders of this faction as of David of old, that "every one that was in distress, and every one that was in debt, and every one that was discontented, gathered themselves unto them." It is little wonder, therefore, that the organization which gathered round such men, filled as it was with jealous hatred of any knowledge superior to its own, should eventually come to regard ignorance as practically a qualification for salvation, and to look with uncomprehending contempt upon the Gnosis possessed by those who still retained some tradition of the real teaching of the Christ.

THREE MAIN TENDENCIES.

It must not, however, be supposed that this turbulent and covetous majority comprised the whole of the early Christian movement. Apart from the various bodies of Gnostic philosophers who had inherited a more or less accurate tradition from authentic sources of the secret teaching given by the Christ to the Essenes, there was also a steadily increasing body of comparatively quiet and respectable people who, though without any knowledge of the Gnosis, took what they knew of the Logia of the Christ as their guide in life, and this body eventually became the predominant force in what was afterwards called the orthodox party.

Thus we see that in the course of the development of the Christian movement three main streams of tendency may be clearly recognised as resulting from the teaching of the Christ; first, the vast congeries of Gnostic sects which, generally speaking, represented something of

the inner teaching given to the Essenes, though in many cases tinged with ideas derived from various outside sources, such as Zoroastrianism, Sabaism, etc.; second, the moderate party who at first troubled themselves little about doctrine, but adopted the reputed sayings of the Christ as their rule of life; and third, the ignorant horde nicknamed "poor men," whose only real religion was a vague hope of revolution.

As Christianity gradually spread, its followers became sufficiently numerous to earn recognition as a political factor, and thus to gain a certain amount of social influence. By degrees the representatives of our second and third tendencies gradually drew together into a party which called itself orthodox. Being united in its distrust of the higher teachings of the Gnostics, it found itself compelled to develope some sort of doctrinal system to offer instead of theirs. By this time, however, the original Essene community had been broken up, and the formula (which among them had never been written, but was handed down from mouth to mouth) had in various more or less imperfect forms become practically public property among all the sects; and of course the orthodox party found itself obliged to produce an interpretation of it to set up against the true one as propounded by the Gnostics.

A DISASTROUS MISUNDERSTANDING.

Then it was that there dawned upon their mental horizon one of the most colossal mis-understandings ever invented by the crass stupidity of man. It occurred to somebody probably

it had long before occurred to the densely ignorant "poor men" - that the beautiful allegorical illustration of the descent into matter of the Second Person of the Trinity which is contained in the symbolic ritual of the Egyptian initiation was not an allegory at all, but the life-story of a physical human being whom they identified with Jesus the Nazarene. No idea could have been more degrading to the grandeur of the faith, or more misleading to the unfortunate people who accepted it, yet one can understand its welcome by the grossly ignorant, as being more nearly within the grasp of their very small mental calibre than the magnificent breadth of the true interpretation.

The slight additions necessary to engraft this unworthy theory upon the growing Creed were easily made, and not very long after this period fragmentary versions of it began to be committed to writing. So that the commonly accepted idea that the Creed is a conglomerate gradually gathered together is, though not quite in the sense usually supposed, partially true, but the tradition which assigns its authorship to the twelve apostles is entirely unworthy of credit. The true genesis of the greater part of it is indeed far higher than that, as we have seen, and the early fragments are imperfect recollections of an oral tradition, out of which eventually a very fair representation of the original was compiled, and this was formally adopted by the Council of Nicaea, though that council showed its absolute miscomprehension of the whole thing by concluding it with a curse entirely foreign to its spirit.

THE CREED OF THE COUNCIL.

In order that we may have before us the exact form of Creed which was the outcome of this exceedingly turbulent council, I subjoin here a careful translation of it, given by Mr. Mead in Lucifer, vol. ix. p. 204:

"We believe in one God, the Father Almighty, Maker of all things both visible and invisible; and in one Lord, Jesus Christ; the Son of God, begotten of the Father, only-begotten, that is to say, of the substance of the Father, God of God, Light of Light, very God of very God, begotten, not made, being of one substance with the Father, by whom all things were made, both things in heaven and things in earth - who for us men and for our salvation came down and was made flesh, and was made man, suffered and rose again on the third day, went up into the heavens, and is to come again to judge the quick and the dead; and in the Holy Ghost. But those who say, 'There was when he was not,' and 'before he was begotten he was not,' and that 'he came into existence from what was not,' or who profess that the Son of God is of a different person or substance, or that he is created, or changeable, or variable, are anathematized by the Catholic Church."

It will be perceived that though this form is broadly similar to that which now occurs in the communion service of the Church of England, there are yet several not unimportant points of difference. Much of the materialistic quasi historical corruption has not yet found entrance, though even already the fatal identification of the Christ with Jesus, and of both of them with the Second Logos, shows itself all too plainly. But since all accounts agree that the members of this celebrated council were in the main ignorant and turbulent fanatics, drawn together largely by the hope of promoting their personal interests, it is small wonder that the narrower rather than the wider idea commended itself to them. Still it will be noted that the confusion of the conception by the Holy Ghost and the birth from the Virgin does not appear; the symbol of the crucifixion is not degraded into a historical fact, nor has the clumsy attempt been made to give an air of verisimilitude to the story by importing into it an entirely inaccurate date in the shape of an unwarranted reference to that unfortunate and much-maligned man, Pontius Pilate.

All these missing clauses, however, appear in what is called "The Roman Confession," which is usually assigned to an earlier date; but we are in no way concerned in this discussion, since we recognize that most of these clauses are merely slight distortions of the Egyptian formula of initiation, which had certainly existed for many centuries.

THE MATERIALIZATION OF THE GOSPELS.

Whatever may have been the date (and it was undoubtedly an early one) at which the degradation of allegory into pseudo-biography first took place, we see its influence working upon other documents as well as upon the Creed. The gospels also have suffered under an exactly similar materializing mania, for the beautiful parable of the original has again and again been corrupted by the addition of popular legends and the interspersion of some of the traditional Logia, until in what are now called the gospels we have a confused compilation - hopelessly impossible, if regarded as history, and exceedingly difficult to sort out into its component parts.

The knowledge that the gospel is a parable shows itself occasionally among the earlier Christians. Origen, for example, speaks very plainly with regard to the difference between the ignorant faith of the undeveloped multitude, based only on the gospel history, and the higher and reasonable faith which was founded upon definite knowledge. He calls the former "the popular, irrational faith," and says of it "what better method could be devised to assist the masses?" In Inge's *Christian Mysticism*, p. 89, he is quoted as explaining that "the Gnostic or sage no longer needs the crucified Christ. The eternal or spiritual gospel which is his possession shows clearly all things concerning the Son of God himself, both the mysteries shown by his words and the things of which his acts were the symbols." We may not feel quite so sure as Mr. Inge does that "It is not that Origen denies or doubts truth of the gospel history"; but we can cordially agree when he says that "Origen feels that events which happened only once can be of no importance, and regards the life, death and resurrection of Christ as only one manifestation of a universal law, which was really enacted not in this fleeting world of shadows, but in the eternal counsels of the Most High. He considers that those who are thoroughly convinced of the universal truths revealed by the incarnation and the atonement need trouble themselves no more about their particular manifestations in time."

This subject of the true meaning of the original allegory in the gospels is one of great interest; we must not, however, allow ourselves to be led away into its fascinating bye-paths, but must confine ourselves to the consideration of the Creed.

CHAPTER III.
THE DESCENT INTO MATTER.

BEFORE, however, it will be possible for the reader to appreciate fully the real meaning of the various clauses of the Creed, it is necessary that he should understand as far as may be possible the outline of the system of cosmogenesis which it was originally intended to indicate. This is of course identical with that taught by the Wisdom-Religion, and the statement of it with which we are now concerned is in fact an outline of the respective functions of the Three Aspects of the Logos in human evolution.

It is of course understood from the beginning that this is a subject of which none of us can hope to attain perfect comprehension for many an aeon to come, for he who grasps it thoroughly must be consciously one with the Highest. Some indications may, however, be given which will perhaps help us in our thinking, though it is most emphatically necessary to bear in mind all the way through that, since we are looking at the problem from below instead of from above, from the standpoint of our extreme ignorance instead of from that of omniscience, any conception that we may form of it must be imperfect and therefore inaccurate.

We are told that what happens at the beginning of a solar system (such as our own) is, allowing for certain obvious differences in the surrounding conditions, identical with what happens at the re-awakening after one of the great periods of cosmic rest; and it will probably be more possible for us not entirely to misunderstand if we endeavour to direct our attention to the former rather than to the latter.

It should be realized, to begin with, that in the evolution of a solar system three of the highest principles of the Logos of that system correspond to and respectively fulfil the functions of the three Great Logoi in cosmic evolution; in point of fact, those three principles are identical with the three Great Logoi in a manner which to us down here is wholly incomprehensible, even though we may see that it must be so.

Yet we should be careful, while recognizing this identity in essence, on no account to confuse the respective functions of beings differing so widely in their sphere of action. It should be remembered that from the First Logos, which stands next to the Absolute, emanates the

Second or Dual Logos, from which in turn comes the Third. From that Third Logos come forth the Seven Great Logoi, called sometimes the Seven Spirits before the throne of God; and as the divine out-breathing pours itself ever further outward and downward, from each of these we have upon the next plane seven Logoi also, together making up on that plane forty-nine.

It will be observed that we have already passed through many stages on the great downward sweep towards matter; yet, omitting the detail of intermediate hierarchies, it is said that to each of these forty-nine belong millions of solar systems, each energized and controlled by its own solar Logos. Though, at levels so exalted as these, differences in glory and power can mean but little to us, we may yet to some extent realize how vast is the distance between the three Great Logoi and the Logos of a single system, and so avoid a mistake into which careless students are constantly falling.

Yet, though it is true that the distance between the Absolute and the Logos of our own solar system is greater than our minds can grasp, it is nevertheless also certain that all the greatest of the qualities which we have ever attributed to the Deity-His love, wisdom and power, His patience and compassion, His omniscience, omnipresence, and omnipotence - all these and many more are possessed to the fullest extent by the solar Logos, in whom in very truth we live and move and have our being. Let it never be forgotten that in Theosophy we do not offer this as an article of religious belief, or a pious opinion; to the clairvoyant investigator this Mighty existence is a definite certainty, for unmistakable evidence of His action and His purpose surrounds us on every side as we study the life of the higher planes. Unmistakable also is the evidence given by His work of His threefold nature - the Trinity in Unity of which the Creeds speak; but a fuller consideration of this will fall into place when we come to deal with the Athanasian Creed, which so especially devotes itself to this question.

THE PLANES OF NATURE.

It has often been stated that each of the planes of our system is divided into seven sub-planes, and that the matter of the highest sub-plane in each may be regarded as atomic qua its particular plane-that is to say, that its atoms cannot be further subdivided without passing from that plane to the one next above it. Now these seven atomic sub-planes, taken by themselves and entirely without reference to any of the other sub-planes which are afterwards called into existence by the various combinations of their atoms, compose the lowest of the great cosmic planes, and are themselves its seven subdivisions. (See Diagram I.)

So that before a solar system comes into existence we have on its future site, so to speak, nothing but the ordinary conditions of interstellar space - that is to say, we have probably matter of the seven subdivisions of the lowest cosmic plane, and from our point of view this is simply the atomic matter of each of our planes without the various combinations of which we are accustomed to think as linking them together and leading us gradually from one to the other.

Diagram I.

Now in the evolution of a system the action of the three higher principles or aspects of its Logos (generally called the three Logoi of the system) upon this antecedent condition of affairs takes place in what we may call a reversed order. In the course of the great work each of them pours out his influence, but the outpouring which comes first in time is from that principle of our Logos which corresponds to the mind in man, though of course on an infinitely higher plane. This is usually spoken of as the Third Logos, or Mahat, corresponding to the Holy Ghost in the Christian system - the "Spirit of God which broods over the face of the waters" of space, and so brings the worlds into existence.

An attempt is made in Diagram I. to indicate the scheme of the planes of Nature, as understood in the Theosophical teaching. A diagram of this kind, however, while it may be of the greatest assistance to our minds in one direction, is almost invariably a limitation in another; so in studying this one it is necessary to bear in mind certain qualifications. In speaking of the movement from finer matter into grosser it is customary to use the word "descent"; and for that reason it seems natural to represent these planes of matter in a diagram as though they lay one above the other, like the shelves of a book-case - nor, indeed, is there any other method by which their relations can so readily be diagrammatically expressed. Nevertheless, in reality the matter of all these planes occupies the same space; and this apparent impossibility is readily achieved by a system of interpenetration. Science teaches us that ether interpenetrates every physical substance, even the hardest and densest, and that even in the diamond itself no two physical atoms or molecules ever touch another, but each is floating in a sea of ether. Science has not yet taken the next step, which would bring it to recognize that ether itself is also atomic, and that its atoms in turn do not touch one another, but float in a sea of still finer matter to which we give the name of astral. Astral atoms in their turn float in mental matter, and so on as far as the most highly-developed senses of any investigator can reach. So that when we speak of the Divine life as "descending" into matter, it must be clearly understood that no motion in space is implied, but simply the vivification of degrees or stages of matter of steadily increasing density.

In Diagram II. we see again the seven planes of our system, arranged just as before, though in this case the names are not given. In Diagram I. the three Aspects or Persons of the Logos are represented as already descended into our system of planes and manifesting themselves upon the seventh, sixth and fifth respectively. In Diagram II., however, we are supposed to be dealing with an earlier condition of affairs, and so the symbols of the three Aspects are placed outside of time and space, and only the streams of influence from them descend into our system of planes. The symbols here employed to designate the three Persons are of extreme antiquity, and are copied from those employed by Madame Blavatsky to represent the corresponding Aspects of the Highest Logos of all. As it will be necessary in a later chapter to take up this symbolism in some detail, I will say no more of it now, premising merely that the three signs arranged one above the other represent in due order what are commonly called the three Persons of the Trinity.

It will be seen that from each of them an outpouring of life or force is projected into the planes below. The first of these in order is the straight line which descends from the third Aspect; the second is that part of the large oval which lies upon our left hand - the stream which descends from the second Aspect until it has touched the lowest point in matter, and then rises again up the side on our right hand until it reaches the lower mental level. It will be noted that in both of these outpourings the divine life becomes darker and more veiled as it descends into matter, until at the lowest point we might almost fail to recognize it as divine life at all; but as it rises again when it has passed its nadir it shows itself somewhat more clearly.

Diagram II.

The third outpouring which descends from the highest Aspect of the Logos differs from the others in that it is in no way clouded by the matter through which it passes, but retains its virgin purity and splendour untarnished. It will be noted that this outpouring descends only to the level of the buddhic plane, and that the link between the two is formed by a triangle in a circle, representing the individual soul of man - the reincarnating ego. Here the triangle is contributed by the third outpouring and the circle by the second; but of this we shall have more to say later. For the moment let us turn our attention to the first of these great streams, which descends from the third Aspect of the Logos.

The result of this first great outpouring is the quickening of that wonderful and glorious vitality which pervades all matter (inert though it may seem to our dim physical eyes), so that the atoms of the various planes develope, when electrified by it, all sorts of previously latent attractions and repulsions, and enter into combinations of all kinds, thus by degrees bringing into existence all the lower subdivisions of each level, until we have before us in full action the marvellous complexity of the forty-nine sub-planes as we see them to-day.

For this reason is it that in the Nicaean symbol the Holy Ghost is so beautifully described as "the Lord and Giver of Life"; and some clue as to the method of His working may be obtained by any one who will study carefully Sir William Crookes' paper on "The Genesis of the Elements," read before the Royal Institution of Great Britain on February 18th, 1887.

THE SECOND OUTPOURING.

When matter of all the sub-planes of the system is already in existence and the field has thus been prepared for its activity, the second great outpouring begins - the outflow of what we have sometimes called the monadic essence; and it comes this time from that higher principle corresponding in our system to the Second Logos, of whom the Christian writers speak as God the Son. Much that has been said of Him, though beautiful and true when rightly understood, has been grossly degraded and misinterpreted by those who could not grasp the grand simplicity of the truth; but to this we shall return later.

Slowly and steadily, but with resistless force, this great influence pours itself forth, each successive wave of it spending a whole aeon in each of the kingdoms of nature - the three elemental, the mineral, the vegetable, the animal and the human. It is thus obvious that at any given point in our evolution we have always present with us seven of these successive life-waves from the Second Aspect of the Logos, animating these seven kingdoms. On the downward arc of its mighty curve this monadic essence simply aggregates round itself the different kinds of matter on the various planes, so that all may be accustomed and adapted to act as its vehicles; but when it has reached the lowest point of its destined immeshing in matter, and turns to begin the grand upward sweep of evolution towards divinity, its object is to develope consciousness in each of these grades of matter in turn, beginning of course with the lowest.

Thus it is that man, although possessing in a more or less latent condition so many higher principles, is yet for a long time at first fully conscious in his physical body only, and afterwards very gradually becomes so in his astral vehicle, and later still in his mind-body.

Diagram III. expresses for us these stages of development in an ingenious fashion. Although in appearance this drawing differs wholly from Diagram II., it is nevertheless only another representation of part of the same facts as those given in the earlier illustration. The particoloured column on our left as we examine Diagram III. corresponds to the left side of the large oval in Diagram II., for they both depict the downward sweep or descent into matter of the second great outpouring.

In this case, however, the different kingdoms are indicated by the use of certain colours which have been appropriated to their respective planes by Madame Blavatsky in one of the tables which she gives us in *The Secret Doctrine*. It is well that we should clearly understand that these different colours are merely for the purpose of distinction, and that they do not in any way represent real characteristics of the planes. All the colours that we know, and some with which as yet we are not acquainted, exist upon every one of these higher planes, so that the use of a colour to distinguish one plane from another must not be supposed to indicate any preponderance of that colour in the plane which bears it. It would not be difficult to suggest fanciful reasons for their assignment - such as, for example, that the colour of sand or earth is very appropiate for the physical plane, and the rosy hue of affection or the lurid red of animal passion have a certain connection with the astral; but all this is mere speculation, and the only fact upon which it is necessary to insist is that the astral plane is not as a matter of fact pervaded by a roseate hue nor the lower mental by a vivid green.

The pointed columns or bands of colour which fill the rest of Diagram III. all correspond to various stages of the upward curve at the right hand in Diagram II., and the intention of them is to express for us in a form convenient of apprehension the extent to which consciousness is developed in each of the great kingdoms. The scheme is that where the consciousness is fully manifesting, the band of the column is of full width, but it narrows down as we reach the levels upon which that consciousness is only just beginning to function. In the case of the mineral kingdom it will be observed that full development exists only in that part of the band which represents the three lower subdivisions of the physical - the solid, the liquid, and the gaseous, and that as we pass through the etheric, the super-etheric, the sub-atomic and the atomic sub-planes, the power to exercise consciousness grows less and less; while on the astral plane we have only a tiny point - indicating that slight though decided manifestation of desire commonly called chemical affinity.

LIFE IN THE MINERAL.

Only a short time ago the fact that definite life manifested itself at all in the mineral kingdom would have been disputed by all except students of occultism; but recent discoveries are gradually altering the previously materialistic scientific position. Within the last few years three distinct lines of evidence have conspired to show the reality of life in the mineral. The researches of Professor Bose at Calcutta have shown that a mineral can be poisoned, and German chemists have devoted themselves to an exhaustive inquiry into an infectious disease which they have called the tin-pest, which attacks tin roofs, and may be communicated from one roof to another. They are even hoping to acquire from this study great practical advantage and additional safety; for they think that it may be possible to learn along these lines to prevent many of the accidents arising from what have hitherto been supposed to be unavoidable causes - such, for example, as the sudden and inexplicable breaking of a steel tyre. At present, all that can be done to safeguard us against an accident that may arise from such a possibility is to test the tyre frequently for hidden flaws; they suggest that in many cases sudden collapse may be due to weakness induced by disease, and that an additional test for health might usefully be applied to the metal.

But by far the fullest and most satisfactory demonstration of the existence of life in the mineral world has been given by the experimental researches of Professor Otto von Schrön of Naples. By the employment of exceedingly powerful micro-photographic instruments he has been enabled to watch in detail various processes, the very existence of which had never before been suspected. He has shown that crystals possess not only movement, but also the power of reproduction, and that they exhibit various processes of generation exactly analogous to those employed in the vegetable kingdom. He gives us clear examples of generation by division, generation by budding, and generation by endogenesis with emigration. In this latter case the new crystal forms itself and comes to the surface of the mother crystal, withdrawing itself by a double movement, propulsive and rotary, exactly as do the zoospores of algae. When last at Naples, I had myself, through the courtesy of Professor von Schrön, the opportunity of examining a very large number of his exceedingly beautiful photographs, and also of seeing something of the mechanism by which his very wonderful results have been obtained. An outline of these most interesting investigations will be found in *The Theosophical Review*, vol. xxxi. page 142.

As to the power of evolution possessed by the mineral kingdom, perhaps I can hardly do better than quote a remarkable passage from Ruskin's Ethics *of the Dust*, page 232.

THE CRYSTAL REST.

"A pure and holy state of anything is that in which all its parts are helpful and consistent. The highest and first law of the universe, and the other name of life, is therefore 'help.' The other name of death is 'separation.' Government and co-operation are in all things, and eternally, the laws of life. Anarchy and competition are, eternally, and in all things, the laws of death.

"Perhaps the best, though the most familiar, example we could take of this nature and power of consistence, will be that of the possible changes in the dust we tread on.

"Exclusive of animal decay, we can hardly arrive at a more absolute type of impurity than the mud or slime of a damp, over-trodden path, in the outskirts of a manufacturing town. I do not say mud of the road, because that is mixed with animal refuse; but take merely an ounce or two of the blackest slime of a beaten footpath, on a rainy day, near a manufacturing town. That slime we shall find in most cases composed of clay (or brick-dust, which is burnt clay), mixed with soot, a little sand, and water. All these elements are at helpless war with each other, and destroy reciprocally each other's nature and power: competing and fighting for place at every tread of your foot; sand squeezing out clay, and clay squeezing out water, and soot meddling everywhere, and defiling the whole. Let us suppose that this ounce of mud is left in perfect rest, and that its elements gather together, like to like, so that their atoms may get into the closest relations possible.

"Let the clay begin. Ridding itself of all foreign substance, it gradually becomes a white earth, already very beautiful, and fit, with help of congealing fire, to be made into finest porcelain, and to be painted on, and to be kept in Kings' palaces. But such artificial consistence is not its best. Leave it still quiet, to follow its own instinct of unity, and it becomes, not only white, but clear; not only clear, but hard; not only clear and hard, but so set that it can deal with light in a wonderful way, and gather out of it the loveliest blue rays only, refusing all the rest. We call it then a sapphire.

»Such being the consummation of the clay, we give similar condition of quiet to the sand. It also becomes, first, a white earth, then proceeds to grow clear and hard, and at last arranges itself in mysterious, infinitely fine parallel lines, which have the power of reflecting, not merely the blue rays, but blue, green, purple and red rays in the greatest beauty in which they can be seen through any hard material whatsoever. We call it then an opal.

"In next order the soot sets to work. It cannot make itself white at first, but, instead of being discouraged, tries harder and harder, and comes out clear at last, and the hardest thing in the world; and for the blackness that it had, obtains in exchange the power of reflecting all the rays of the sun at once, in the vividest blaze that any solid thing can shoot. We call it then a diamond.

"Last of all, the water purifies, or unites itself; contented enough if it only reaches the form of a dew-drop; but if we insist on its proceeding to a more perfect consistence, it crystallizes into the shape of a star. And for the ounce of slime which we had by political economy of competition, we have, by political economy of co-operation, a sapphire, an opal, and a diamond, set in the midst of a star of snow."

THE VEGETABLE KINGDOM.

All this helps us to understand how consciousness slowly but steadily presses upward. We have life and evolution in the mineral, and the first faint beginnings of desire as shown in chemical affinity; but in the vegetable kingdom we find desire much more prominent and decided, while the life-force is working actively for evolution in a far more definite way. Indeed, many plants exercise a great deal of ingenuity and sagacity in attaining their ends, limited though these ends may be.

We shall not be surprised, therefore, to find that the band in Diagram III, symbolizing consciousness in the vegetable kingdom, indicates a considerable degree of advancement. The full width of the band here extends through the higher as well as the lower subdivisions of the physical plane, while the point upon the astral plane has much increased in size. It is in fact only within the last few years, since botany has been studied from the biological side, that we have wakened up to understand what wonderful things plants really are - that we have made an effective study of their consciousness, their habits and their tendencies. Nothing can be more marked than their likes and dislikes; indeed, it is hardly an exaggeration to say that there is scarcely a virtue or a vice known to mankind which has not its counterpart among them. There was a time when flowers were regarded as created for the pleasure of man, but we have now realized that the life ensouling the plant adapts all its parts most wonderfully to the work which they have to do for the good of the organism as a whole. A plant or a tree may be said to be a colony of vegetable organisms. From the point of view of the plant, the flower, which seems to us the culmination and goal of the whole, is really an aborted and degraded leaf, though it also has its function to perform. We may say that the leaves act as accumulators of energy, for they gather carbon and liberate oxygen; the flowers, on the other hand, expend energy, for they require oxygen and liberate carbon dioxide. The leaves store up food materials in the tubers and the stem, while the flowers draw upon this account - never selfishly, be it understood, but always in the interest of the plant as a whole, and in the furtherance of its desire to found a family. They slowly and steadily store up energy, and then spend it all comparatively rapidly. The mouths of the leaves are on their under surfaces, and they are so tiny that a square inch of the ordinary lilac-leaf contains a quarter of a million of them. Forty-five million tons of carbon dioxide is thrown into the air daily by men and animals, and yet the whole of this is absorbed by those tiny mouths - or rather the carbon is extracted from it.

The adaptability of plants is wonderful. All climbing plants, for example, have acquired the power of climbing in order to reach the sunlight, and have developed whatever organs are necessary for this purpose - hooks or tendrils or extra roots, or sometimes simply the power of twining. Varieties of flowers develope in order to attract different types of insects, and many of the adaptations are wonderfully ingenious. Some flowers, for example, carefully provide a lip for the insect to alight upon, and arrange that the vibration which he communicates to the flower in doing so shall shake down pollen upon his back! Orchids cement their pollen, so that their insect messenger may not lose it fruitlessly by the way. The asclepiads defend themselves against the waste of their valuable material by catching and strangling flies which do not fertilize. Again, vegetable ingenuity is shown in the development of fruit in order to suit the various tastes and sizes of birds. The fruit remains acid and undesirable until the germ or stone within is fully developed and ready to be carried away to a distance. Then the fruit becomes sweet, the bird eats it, but is unable to digest the hard stone or pip, and drops it somewhere at a distance from the parent plant, so that it has a better opportunity to grow.

Some plants develope thorns in order to prevent themselves from being eaten by mammals; others, on the contrary, depend upon mammals for conveyance of their ripe seeds to a distance, as does the burdock or the goose-grass, which develope little hooks to cling to the coats of animals which pass by them. It may be remembered that when foreign wool was imported into Gloucestershire, it was found that plants from the Cape and from South America began to make their appearance in the neighbourhood where the wool was combed. Various plants trust to the wind for the dissemination of their seeds, as do the thistle, the cotton plant and the lime. The cocoanut palm trusts to tides or rivers to carry away its fruit, and therefore grows by preference on the very edge of the ocean. Another way in which the ingenuity of plants is displayed is in the methods which they adopt for their defence. Some develope bloom upon their fruit in order to shield it from the effects of rain and dew; others produce poisonous secretions to save themselves from marauding insects. Others grow woolly hairs for this purpose, as the mullein, while some endeavour to protect themselves from being eaten by developing spikes or thorns, as in many familiar plants, or by impregnating themselves with silica, as do the horse-tails. Many more instances of their curious cleverness might easily be given, but they may be found in the later books on botany, and we must pass on now to the next stage.

THE ANIMAL KINGDOM.

In the animal kingdom we observe the continuation of evolution along exactly the same lines. Here desire occupies a very prominent place, and there can be no doubt that the astral body is definitely beginning to function, though the animal has usually as yet but little that can be called consciousness in it apart from the physical vehicle. In the higher domestic animals, however, the astral body has sufficient development to persist after death for many days, and sometimes for months, while a certain amount of mental activity is distinctly beginning to show itself. This latter fact is indicated in our illustration by the green point which extends up into the lower part of the mental plane, while the fact that on the lowest sub-plane of the astral the band preserves its full width shows that the animal is capable to the fullest extent of the lower types of passion, emotion and desire. The rapid narrowing of the point as it approaches the higher astral level shows the kingdom as a whole to be capable only to a limited extent of the higher possibilities of the plane, though in some advanced individuals among the more developed domestic animals these possibilities are present to a very high degree. I remember that in the days of our youth we were told that reason was the distinguishing attribute of man alone, and that no animal possessed it. Any person who has ever kept a pet animal, and has made a friend of that animal, as he will have done if he was worthy of the honour of animal friendship, knows that this is untrue, for he is well aware that the animal does reason, although it may be only along certain narrow lines. Any book of stories of the sagacity of dogs, cats or horses is sure to contain plenty of evidence of the possession of reasoning power.

THE HUMAN KINGDOM.

When we come to the human kingdom we find that with the lower types of men desire is still emphatically the most prominent feature, though the mental development has also proceeded to some extent; during life the man has a dim consciousness in his astral vehicle while he is asleep, and after death he is fairly conscious and active in it, and his life in it endures for many years, though as yet he has practically nothing of the higher existence of the heaven world.

Coming to the ordinary cultured man of our own race, we find him showing high mental activity during life, and possessing qualities which give him the possibility of a very long existence in the heaven-world after death. He is fully conscious in his astral body during sleep, though not usually much in the habit of usefully employing that consciousness, and not generally able to carry through any connected memory from the one condition of existence to the other.

Examining the band of colour which represents humanity, we see that these various characteristics are indicated there. It retains its full width through the whole of the astral plane, and even to the lowest sub-plane of the mental, showing that man is capable of all varieties of desire to the fullest possible extent, the highest as well as the lowest, and that his reasoning faculty is fully developed as far as the selfish mentality of that lowest level is concerned. Higher than that the development is not yet perfect, though it is commencing. The dark blue point on the higher mental levels shows that he is a reincarnating ego, and possesses a causal body, though to represent the average man correctly the point should not rise above the third of those levels.

The cases of the comparatively few men who have as yet undertaken the task of self-development along occult lines show us that the future course of evolution simply means the unfolding of consciousness on higher and higher planes as humanity passes onward and becomes fit for such development. The band which appears at the extreme right of Diagram III. is emblematical of the spiritually-developed man - one who has trodden far upon the Path of Holiness.

It will be observed that in his case the broadest part of the band, which indicates always that part of the nature in which the consciousness is centred, and in which it works most readily, is no longer upon the physical or astral planes at all, but between the higher mental and the buddhic. The fact that he still retains his connection with the physical plane is indicated by the lower point; but it is only a point, because that is no longer the central part of his life - because he retains the physical body only in order that through it he may help his fellow-men. Both on the astral plane and on the mental his band is widest at the highest part, showing that to him the higher thoughts and higher feelings are those which come natural. His consciousness extends upward through the whole of the buddhic plane, and he has even a point which penetrates into Nirvana indicating thereby that he must have attained the level of the Arhat.

THE THIRD OUTPOURING.

The blue triangle which appears on the higher levels of the mental plane in the band which indicates the ordinary human kingdom in Diagram III. corresponds exactly to the white triangle in a circle in Diagram II. It is into the genesis of this triangle that we have now to enquire, for it is the result of the third great outpouring of divine life - that from the highest principle or Aspect of the Logos of the system, corresponding to the spirit in man, and holding the place filled in cosmic evolution by the first Logos, which has been called by Christianity God the Father.

An attempt has been made to indicate how the monadic essence in its upward course gradually unfolds consciousness, first in the physical plane, then in the astral, and then in the lower mental. But it is only when in the highest of the domestic animals it reaches this latter stage that the possibility of the third outpouring comes within measurable distance. For this third wave of divine life can descend of itself no lower than our buddhic plane, and there it seems as it were to hover, waiting for the development of fit vehicles to enable it to come down one step further and be the individual souls of men. The phrase sounds strange, but it is difficult to express accurately in human words the mysteries of the higher life.

Imagine (to use an Eastern simile) the sea of monadic essence steadily pressed upward into the mental plane by the force of evolution inherent in it, and this third outpouring hovering above that plane like a cloud, constantly attracting and attracted by the waves below. Anyone who has ever seen the formation of a water-spout in tropical seas will grasp the idea of this Oriental illustration - will understand how the downward-pointing cone of cloud from above and the upward-pointing cone of water from below draw nearer and nearer by mutual attraction, until a moment comes when they suddenly leap together, and the great column of mingled water and vapour is formed.

Similarly the blocks of animal monadic essence are constantly throwing parts of themselves into incarnation like temporary waves on the surface of the sea, and the process of differentiation goes on until at last a time comes when one of these waves rises high enough to enable the hovering cloud to effect a junction with it, and it is then drawn up into a new existence neither in the cloud nor in the sea, but between the two, and partaking of the nature of both; and so it is separated from the block of which it has hitherto formed a part, and falls back into the sea no more. That is to say, an animal belonging to one of the more advanced blocks of essence may by his love for and devotion to his master, and by the mental effort involved in the earnest endeavour to understand him and please him, so raise himself above his original level that he becomes a fit vehicle for this third outpouring, the reception of which breaks him away from his block and starts him on his career of immortality as an individual.

If we remember that the consciousness of the monadic essence has been developed up to the lower mental level, and that the hovering influence of the divine life has descended to the buddhic plane, we shall be prepared to look on the higher mental levels for the resultant combination; and that is truly the habitat of the causal body of man, the vehicle of the reincarnating ego.

But here we note that a curious change has taken place in the position of the monadic essence. All the way through its long line of evolution in all the previous kingdoms it has invariably been the ensouling and energizing principle, the force behind whatever forms it may have temporarily occupied. But now that which has hitherto been the ensouler becomes itself in turn the ensouled; from that monadic essence is formed the causal body - that resplendent sphere of living light into which the still more glorious light from above descends, and by means of which that divine spark is enabled to express itself as a human individuality.

Nor should any think that it is an unworthy goal to reach as the result of so long and weary an evolution, thus to become the vehicle of this last and grandest outpouring of the divine spirit; for it must be remembered that without the preparation of this vehicle to act as a connecting link the immortal individuality of man could never come into being, and that this upper triad thus formed becomes a transcendent unity - "not by conversion of the Godhead into flesh, but by taking of the manhood into God." So that no fragment of the work that has been done through all these ages is lost, and nothing has been useless; for without that work this final consummation could never have been reached, that man should become the equal of the Logos from whom he came forth, and that thus the very Logos Himself should be perfected, in that He has of His own offspring those equal to Himself upon whom that love which is the essence of His divine nature can for the first time be fully lavished.

Be it remembered also that it is only in the presence within him of this third outpouring of the divine life that man possesses an absolute guarantee of his immortality; for this is "the spirit of man that goeth upward" in contra-distinction to "the spirit of the beast that goeth downward" - that is to say, which flows back again at the death of the animal into the block of monadic essence from which it came.

A time will come, so we are told, though to our intellect it may well seem unthinkable - the time of the universal rest, called in the East the night of

Brahma - when "all things visible and invisible" will be re-absorbed into That from which they came; when even the Second and Third Logoi themselves, and all that is of their essence, must for the time sink into sleep and disappear. But even in that period of universal rest there is one Entity who remains unaffected; the First, the Unmanifested Logos, rests still, as ever, in the bosom of the Infinite. And since the direct essence of this, the divine Father of all, enters into the composition of the spirit of man, by that almighty power his immortality is absolutely assured.

How beautifully, how grandly these glorious conceptions are mirrored even in what is left to us of the Christian Creeds, I shall hope to show as we consider them clause by clause.

CHAPTER IV.
THE EXPOSITION OF THE CREEDS.

THE Apostles' and the Nicene Creeds so closely resemble one another that it will be the most convenient method for us to consider them together, taking for the present only occasional illustrations from the Athanasian, and leaving the more important clauses of the latter to be dealt with separately afterwards. It is evident that in these two shorter Creeds we have simply two different traditions of one original forma form already including reminiscences of the documents which we have called (a) and (b), and already tinged considerably by the influence of tendency (c).

The date at which this original form became fairly crystallized as regards its main outlines cannot yet be fixed with certainty, but we should probably not be far wrong in assigning it to the middle of the second century of our era - always bearing in mind that that era has nothing to do with the real time of the birth of the teacher called the Christ, and remembering also that in all likelihood no attempt was made to reduce the form to writing until a considerably later period. The two Creeds differ, as evidently the schools of thought which preserved them must have differed, the Nicene being always more metaphysical and less materialistic than the other, taking always a somewhat higher view, and therefore lending itself more readily to such an attempt to revive the original and only tenable interpretation as I wish to make.

THE FATHER.

"I believe in God the Father almighty, maker of heaven and earth." So runs the opening clause of the Apostles' Creed, referring evidently to the Logos of our solar system; the Nicaean symbol, taking an even wider range, is cast into a form equally applicable to the First Cause of all, and so it speaks of the one God, maker not only of heaven and earth, but "of all things visible and invisible." Well may the glorious title of "the Father" be given to That which is the first epiphany of the Infinite, for from Him all came, even the Second and Third Logoi themselves, and into Him one day all that came forth must return. Not to lose consciousness, be it observed, for that would be to throw away the result of all these aeons of evolution; but rather to become, in some way that to our finite minds is as yet unintelligible, a conscious part of that stupendous whole - a facet of that all - embracing Consciousness which is indeed the divine Father of all, "above all, and through all, and in you all." "Then shall the Son also himself be subject unto him that put all things under him, that God may be all in all."

The idea of "heaven and earth" seems to be a corruption of that more clearly expressed in the formula (a), in which the Christ indicates that the Logos called into existence "the scheme or system" (evidently our solar system) "yea, our world and all things therein, whether seen or unseen." Great confusion has been caused in the minds of many worthy people by the unfortunate (though etymologically natural) use of this word "heaven" in two totally distinct senses - first, the purely physical idea of the sky, the clouds, the sun and the stars, and secondly, the non-physical conception of the glorified state of intense bliss, which is the portion of man after his astral life is over. Probably this confusion is largely responsible for the degradation of heaven in the popular mind from a condition of consciousness through which all in turn must pass, into a physical location in space from which the majority of men are to be excluded.

The heads of the Essene community had inherited the Chaldaean and Egyptian knowledge of astronomy, and they were undoubtedly aware of the difference between the planets of our system and the fixed stars which are the suns of other systems, and would therefore appreciate the exact meaning of the teaching of the Christ; but it is not difficult to see how the ignorant section of the Church would blunder here, and include thousands of solar systems under the control of one Logos without even knowing what they were doing. Later still the yet more uncomprehending modern theologian imports the concept of the post-mortem home of bliss, and so all knowledge of the original shade of meaning completely disappears.

THE SON.

"And in one Lord Jesus Christ, the only-begotten Son of God, begotten of his Father before all worlds, God of God, Light of Light, very God of very God, begotten, not made, being of one substance with the Father; by whom all things were made; who for us men and for our salvation came down from heaven." With the exception of the first few words the whole of this is omitted from the Apostles' Creed, as we might perhaps expect that it would be in a form intended to apply to a somewhat less lofty level of the universe.

Here, in the insertion of the name Jesus Christ, we come upon the first trace of the materializing influence which we classified as (c), for the original formula (a) contains neither of these words. In the earliest copies written in Greek which have as yet been clairvoyantly seen by our investigators the words now rendered as ΙΗΣΟΥΝΧΡΙΣΤΟΝ and translated "Jesus Christ" appear either as ΙΗΤΡΟΝΑΡΙΣΤΟΝ, which would mean "the chiefest healer (or deliverer)," or as ΙΕΡΟΝΑΡΙΣΤΟΝ, which seems to mean simply "the most holy one." It is, however, of little use for us to speak of these various readings until some explorer on the physical plane discovers a manuscript containing them, for then only will the world of scholars be disposed to listen to the suggestions which naturally follow from them.

In any case the Greek form of the formula (a) is but a translation from an original given in an older tongue, so that to us as students it is more interesting to see the meaning attached to these words in the minds of those who had heard them spoken by the great Teacher than to follow out the details of their rendering into the corrupt and Hellenistic dialect of the period. Beyond all shadow of doubt that original conception refers exclusively to the Second Aspect of the Logos as manifesting Himself at different levels of the great descent into matter, and not in the slightest degree either to the Teacher or to any individual man at all.

THE ALONE-BORN.

The greater part of this poetic passage is an endeavour to make clear the position and functions of the Second Aspect of the Logos, and to guard so far as may be possible against various misconceptions of them. Great stress is laid upon the fact that naught else in the universe comes into existence in the same way as does this Second Person, called into being as He is by the mere action of the will of the First, working without intermediary; so that the old translator spoke truly enough in intention, however unfortunate he was in his choice of an expression, when he called Him "the only-begotten Son of God, begotten of His Father before all worlds, by whom all things were made"; since He is indeed the only direct manifestation of the First, the Unmanifested, and undoubtedly "without Him was not anything made which was made"; for the monadic essence which He pours forth is the ensouling and energizing principle at the back of all organic life of which we know anything.

The true meaning of the word μονογενης is very clearly stated by Mr. Mead in an article in *The Theosophical Review*, vol. xxi. p. 141, in which he remarks: "There is no longer any doubt that the term invariably translated 'only-begotten' means nothing of the kind, but 'created alone,' that is to say, created from one principle and not from a syzygy or pair."

It is obvious that this title is and can be truly given only to the Second Aspect of the Logos, for the manner in which He is emanated from the First must evidently differ from all other and later processes of generation, which are invariably the result of interaction.

It should also be borne in mind that "before all worlds," however true it may be as a statement referring to the emanation of the Christ, is a flagrant mistranslation of πρό πάυτων τῶυ αἰώυωυ, which can signify nothing but "before all the aeons." To any one who is even superficially familiar with Gnostic nomenclature this bears its meaning on its face, and tells us simply that the Second Person of the Logos is the first in time, as He is the greatest, of all the aeons or emanations from the eternal Father.

It will be well for us to note exactly the true meaning and derivation of this word *person*. It is compounded of the two Latin words *per* and *sona*, and therefore signifies "that through which the sound comes." On the Roman stage it seems that only the principal characters dressed for their parts as elaborately as actors do now. The supernumerary of the present day, who acts the part of a soldier in one scene, a policeman in another, and a countryman in a third, had his counterpart in Rome, but there, instead of changing his whole costume, he wore the ordinary dress of a peasant all the time, and changed only his mask and head-dress. He was provided with an assortment of these which indicated various minor parts, and that which he wore at a given moment showed the part he was then acting. This mask was called persona, because the sound of his voice came out through it. So we quite appropriately speak of the group of temporary lower vehicles which a soul assumes when he descends into incarnation as his "personality." Thus also these separate Aspects or manifestations of the One on different planes are rightly described as Persons.

Here also comes the emphatic and reiterated assertion that He is "of one substance with the Father," identical in every respect with Him from whom He came, save only that He has descended this one step further, and in thus becoming manifest has for the time limited the

full expression of that which yet He is in essence, so that He has a dual aspect - "equal to the Father as touching His Godhead, yet inferior to the Father as touching His manhood"; and yet through all rings the triumphant proclamation that the eternal unity is still maintained, "for although He be God and man, yet He is not two, but one Christ," now as ever "God of God, Light of Light, very God of very God."

Few grander protests against the doctrine of eternal duality - the God and the not-God - have ever been penned by mortal man; and in the later and more detailed Athanasian Creed we have the very proof of the essential unity adduced, in the statement of the power to bear back into the Highest all the fruit of the descent into matter, for we are told that He is "one, not by the conversion of the Godhead into flesh, but by the taking of the manhood into God."

HE CAME DOWN FROM HEAVEN.

Most truly and most beautifully also is it written of Him that "for us men and for our salvation He came down from heaven"; for though indeed it is true that the immortal spirit of man is of the nature of the Father Himself, yet but for the sacrifice of the Son, who poured forth of His substance as monadic essence into all the limitations of the lower kingdoms, the causal body could never have been, and without that as vehicle, as the vase to hold the elixir of life, heaven and earth could never have met together, nor this mortal have put on immortality. And so is the true Christ at once the creator and the saviour of man, for without Him the gap between spirit and matter could never be bridged over, and individuality could not be.

THE INCARNATION.

"And was incarnate by the Holy Ghost of the Virgin Mary." Here there seems for a moment to be a difficulty, for how can the birth of the Second Aspect of the Logos be due in any way to the action of the Third, who Himself holds to Him the relation of child rather than of father? Yet if we follow the original lines of thought we shall not be misled by the apparent contradiction, for we shall realize that what we are dealing with is simply a further stage of the great sacrifice of the descent into matter.

The English translator, or perhaps still more his Latin predecessor, has unfortunately confused the meaning by an entirely unwarranted change in one of the prepositions - a very remarkable mistranslation, so obvious and so astonishing that it could never have escaped the notice of scholars, were it not for the mist thrown round it by the initial misconception which blinded their eyes to the possibility of any but the grossest material interpretation of the whole sentence. Even in the latest Greek form there is but one preposition for the two nouns, and the phrase runs σαρκωέντα ἐκ πνεύματος ἁγίου καί Μαρίας της παρθένου - "and was incarnate of the Holy Ghost and the Virgin Mary." That is to say, the monadic essence, having already "come down from heaven," as mentioned in the previous clause, materializes itself by assuming a garment of the visible and tangible matter already prepared for its reception by the action of the Logos in His Third Aspect upon what without that action would have been virgin, or unproductive, matter.

This name "virgin" has frequently been applied to the atomic matter of the various planes, because when in this condition it does not of its own motion enter into any sort of combination, and so it remains, as it were, inert and unfruitful. But no sooner is it electrified by the outpouring of the Holy Ghost than it wakens into activity, combines into molecules, and rapidly generates the matter of the lower sub-planes, thus bringing into existence out of the atomic ether what chemists call the elements; and of this matter, thus vivified by that first outpouring, are composed the manifold forms which are ensouled by the monadic essence.

When this second outpouring reaches the physical plane in the shape of what we have sometimes called the mineral monad, it gives to these various chemical elements a further power of combination, and thus the way is prepared for the other and higher manifestations of life which are to follow in the later kingdoms. The Second Aspect of the Logos, therefore, takes form not of the "virgin" matter alone, but of matter which is already instinct and pulsating with the life of the Third, so that both the life and the matter surround Him as a vesture, and thus in very truth He is "incarnate of the Holy Ghost and the Virgin Mary."

Here again the materializing tendency has introduced a totally different idea by a very trifling alteration - in fact, by the insertion of a single letter, for in the earliest form the name was not Μαρία, but Μαία, meaning simply mother. It would be tempting to speculate as to whether there could possibly be any traditional connection between this strangely suggestive word and the Sanskrit Maya, which is so often used to express this same illusory veil of matter which the Logos draws round Him in His descent; but all that can be said at present is that no such connection has yet been traced.

Much controversy has raged round the question of the dogma of the Immaculate Conception - the difficulties being of course caused solely by the degrading materialization of the original idea. Behind this mystery there lie in reality three meanings: (1) the birth or appearance or manifestation of the Logos in matter through His Second Aspect; (2) the birth of the human soul, the ego, the individuality; and (3) the birth of the Christ-principle within the man at a later stage of his development.

The birth of the Logos into matter has already been described, and also the birth of that individuality which is so wonderfully made in His image. In this latter case we may think of the causal body as the mother, itself immaculately conceived by the action of the Logos in His Second Aspect upon matter prepared by the Third Person of the Tri-unity. Thirdly (after man has developed intellect), the Christ-principle, the intuitional Wisdom, is born in the soul, and when that buddhic consciousness is awakened, the soul becomes again, as it were, a little child, born into that higher life of the initiated which is in truth the kingdom of heaven.

As soon as the Creed is translated into Latin we are confronted by the obvious possibility of a play upon the word "Maria," and yet another suggestion of the true meaning of the descent into the "seas of virgin matter vivified by the Holy Ghost" is thrown in our way as though it were accidental.

"And was made man." The insertion of this clause is exceedingly significant, since it distinctly shows that the arrival of the monadic essence at the level of humanity was a stage separate from and later than the descent into matter, and that consequently the "taking flesh of the Holy Ghost and the Virgin Mary" previously mentioned did not and could not refer to a human birth. This clause is omitted from the Apostles' Creed, but duly appears in the draft made by the Council of Nicaea, where it is even more evidently intended to describe a later step in evolution, since the text runs "and was made flesh, and was made man," the assumption of the flesh clearly referring to the previous passage of the monadic essence through the animal kingdom. In the Apostles' Creed the influence of tendency (c) is predominant, for the whole process is described in the most grossly materialistic manner - "who was conceived by the Holy Ghost, born of the Virgin Mary."

PONTIUS PILATE.

"Suffered under Pontius Pilate." In this clause we have quite the most remarkable instance on record of the degrading and narrowing influence of the tendency which we have called (c), for by the insertion of the tiniest letter of the Greek alphabet (the iota, corresponding to the »jot" spoken of in the gospel) the original meaning has been not merely obscured, but absolutely lost and forgotten. The alteration is so simple and easy to make, and yet its effects are so extraordinary and so colossal, that those who discovered it could for some time scarcely believe their eyes, and when they had grasped the situation, they were unable to comprehend how it had been possible so long to overlook anything so exceedingly obvious.

Instead of ΠΟΝΤΙΟΥΠΙΛΑΤΟΥ, the earliest Greek manuscripts which the clairvoyant investigators have yet been able to find all read ΠΟΝΤΟΥΠΙΛΗΤΟΥ. Now the interchange of Α and Η is by no means infrequent in various Greek dialects, so that the only real alteration here is the insertion of the Ι, which changes πόντος, meaning a sea, into Πόντιος, which is a Roman proper name. I have no wish to suggest that this alteration, or either of the others which I have mentioned, was necessarily made with any deceitful object, or with intention to mislead; it may quite easily have been made under the impression that it was merely a correction of the unimportant mistake of some earlier copyist.

It was obvious to the investigators that the Essene monk who first translated the formula into Greek was by no means perfectly acquainted with that tongue, and the result was consequently anything but classical. Men into whose hands the manuscript (or copies of it) came at later periods amended here and there obvious errors in spelling or construction, and it is quite possible that one who approached its consideration with a mind incapable of appreciating its true mystical signification, and filled with the anthropomorphic interpretation, might suppose that in this case, for example, a letter must have been omitted by some ignorant scribe, and so might insert that letter without the least idea that he was thereby changing the entire meaning of the clause and introducing a conception absolutely foreign to the spirit of the whole document.

No doubt in ecclesiastical history there has been a large amount of direct, unblushing forgery, done "for the greater glory of God," which in the eyes of the monks simply meant the advancement of the interests of the Church; but we are fortunately not compelled to postulate dishonesty in this case, since we see that ignorance and prejudice may very easily have done quite innocently the fatal work of the utter materialization of conceptions originally so grand and so luminous.

It was no doubt with the same laudable though mistaken idea of polishing the diction that the preposition ἐπί was (much later) substituted for the earlier ὑπό, though after the theory of the proper name was once accepted the mischief was done, and this further alteration merely put the phrase into more elegant shape, and so lessened the probability of inquiry as to any other possible meaning than the apparent one. In the original translation the real intention of the writer was made even clearer still by the use of the dative case, thus indicating that the expression referred to a place, not a person; but this was almost immediately changed to the more usual genitive, even before the unfortunate insertion of the iota.

The words πόντος πιλητός, then, simply mean a compressed or densified sea - by no means a bad description of the lower part of the astral plane, which is so constantly typified by water. The clause usually translated "suffered under Pontius Pilate" should be rendered "He endured the dense sea" - that is to say, for us men and for our salvation he allowed himself to be for the time limited by, and imprisoned in, astral matter. We should note the exact order of the clauses here. Neither of the Creeds as they stand at present contains quite the whole of the original idea; for in the Apostles', though the order is accurate, several stages are omitted, and while the Nicene is fuller, there is a confusion in its arrangement. The first step mentioned is the assumption of the vesture of matter - "the incarnation"; then the taking of human form, though still in its higher principles only; then the "suffering under Pontius Pilate," or descent into the astral sea; and only after that the crucifixion on the cross of physical matter, in which he is graphically described as "dead and buried."

THE CRUCIFIXION.

"Was crucified, dead and buried." Here again we are face to face with an almost universal misunderstanding whose proportions have been colossal and its results most disastrous. The astonishing evolution of a perfectly reasonable allegory into an absolutely impossible biography has had a very sad influence upon the entire Christian Church and upon the faith which it has taught, and the enormous amount of devotional sympathy which has been poured forth through the centuries in connection with a story of physical suffering that is wholly imaginary is perhaps the most extraordinary and lamentable waste of psychic energy in the history of the world.

Once more we have to repeat that neither the Creed nor the gospels were originally intended to relate to the life-story of the great teacher Christ. But the gospel account as it stands now is so extraordinary a conglomerate, so inextricable an entanglement of the solar myth, the Christ-allegory of initiation common to almost all religions, and a tradition of the real story of part of the earth-life of Jesus, that it would be a task of no ordinary difficulty accurately to apportion its various incidents to their respective sources.

The crucifixion and the resurrection, however, clearly belong to the Christ-allegory; and that they do so ought to be evident to all students from the very fact that the date of their commemoration by the Church is not a fixed one, as would be the anniversary of any actual event, but is movable and dependent upon astronomical calculation. A reference to the Prayer-book will show that Easter is celebrated on the Sunday following the date of the next full moon after the vernal equinox.

Now this method of fixing a date would be grotesque if supposed to apply to a historical anniversary, and is reasonably explicable only upon some modification of the solar myth theory. Undoubtedly there has been a tendency of late years to run that idea to death, and

to see a solar myth in every fragment of prehistoric gossip which happens to have found a chronicler; but this must not blind us to the fact that there is a good deal of truth in the theory, especially when we recognize that the yearly course of the sun is itself used as an allegory to remind those who understand it of the great spiritual truths which it has so long been employed to symbolize.

The orthodox explanation of the arrangement of the commemoration of Easter is stated to be that a great point in the Jewish controversy turned on the crucifixion having taken place at the period of the Passover, and so being emphasized as the true Paschal sacrifice; and that since the Passover day moved with the moon, the celebration of Easter had to do so also. This is quite probable, but it in no way invalidates my contention that the mere fact that they are movable shows that neither the Passover nor the Easter festival can be intended to commemorate a definite historical event at all, otherwise they would be celebrated on a definite anniversary. On the contrary, it does very clearly show that the festival so fixed is an astronomical one, connected in some way with the worship of the heavenly bodies upon whose motion it depends.

As a matter of fact, the part of the Creed which we are now considering is simply quoted from the rubric of the old Egyptian initiation, which is in turn intended to illustrate the later stages of the descent of the monadic essence into matter. Let us consider first how this descent came to be symbolized as a crucifixion, and then how it was represented before the eyes of the neophytes in ancient Khem.

THE SYMBOL OF THE CROSS.

To understand this clearly we must first endeavour to ascertain what was the meaning attached to the emblem of the cross in the sacred mysteries of antiquity. Most of us were brought up in the belief that the cross was an exclusively Christian symbol, and it may be that there are still some people left who hold to that view. If so, it is of course simply because it has never occurred to them to investigate the question; for if they took up the matter and examined the evidence they could not fail to be struck with the remarkable universality of the use of this sign.

An exhaustive catalogue of the places in which the cross occurs before the Christian era would make a respectable book in itself, but in glancing over some of the modern works on the subject I see that evidence is adduced of its use in one or other of its forms in ancient Egypt, at Nineveh, among the Phoenicians at Gozzo, among the Etruscans and the prehistoric race who inhabited Italy before the Etruscans arrived, upon the pottery of the primitive lake-dwellers, amid the ruins of Palenque, in the earliest remains yet discovered of ancient Peru, India, China, Japan, Korea, Tibet, Babylonia, Assyria, Chaldaea, Persia, Phoenicia, Armenia, Algeria, Ashanti, Cyprus, Rhodes, and among the prehistoric inhabitants of Britain, France, Germany and America - a list which, partial and incomplete as it is, might well astonish the advocates of the exclusively Christian theory of the cross which prevailed in the days of our youth.

The only form of this symbol which is generally associated with Egypt is the *crux ansata*, or handled cross, but it is quite a mistake to suppose that the ancient inhabitants of Khem were unacquainted with the other varieties, for both Greek, Latin and Maltese crosses, as well as representations of the svastika, are to be found among the relics that they have left to us. I had the pleasure in 1884 of going over the museum of Egyptian antiquities at Boulak in the company of Madame Blavatsky and under the guidance of its learned curator, M. Maspero, and I well remember the interest with which I noticed among the contents of a case of trinkets attributed to one of the very earliest dynasties several beautifully cut cornelian representations of the cross rising out of the heart, exactly similar to the little charms of that shape which may be bought at a Catholic shop in London in the twentieth century.

The most widely spread of the derivatives of the simple cross is perhaps the svastika, which is to be found, I believe, in every one of the countries mentioned above. It has been generally supposed to be identical with the hammer of Thor, but there seems some reason to believe that the latter sign was originally made simply in the shape of the letter T. At any rate, it is certain that when, as King Olaf was keeping Christmas at Drontheim,

O'er his drinking-horn the sign

He made of the cross divine

As he drank, and muttered his prayers,

But the Berserks evermore

Made the sign of the hammer of Thor

Over theirs-

they were in reality using symbols practically identical. The svastika also appears occasionally in later Christian symbology; for example, it may be seen ornamenting the hem of the chasuble of a mediaeval bishop in a fine full-length figure sculptured upon one of the tombs in Winchester Cathedral.

The theosophical student should take care to avoid the mistake so often made by the more superficial observer, of confusing the meaning of all these various forms of the cross symbol. Each of them - the Greek, the Latin, the Maltese, the Tau, the Svastika - has its own particular signification, and is by no means to be confounded with any other, as will presently be seen.

THE DELUSION OF PHALLICISM.

There is one particularly gross delusion, unhappily widely prevalent in connection with this subject, from which we ought definitely to clear our minds before we can hope to consider it with profit - and that is the delusion of phallicism. Many writers appear to be absolutely obsessed by this unclean idea, and can see nothing but phallic emblems in all the holiest symbols of antiquity; whether it be the cross, the triangle, the circle, the pyramid, the obelisk, the dagoba, or the lotus, to their prurient imagination it can have but one obscene signification.

Happily occult investigation assures us (as indeed common-sense would naturally suggest even without such aid) that this unpleasant theory of the origin of all religion is absolutely devoid of foundation. In every case yet examined it has been found that in the earlier and purer stages of any faith none but the spiritual meaning was ever thought of in connection with its various symbols, and that where creation was suggested it was always the creation of ideas by the divine mind. Whenever, on the other hand, phallic emblems and ceremonies of an indecent nature are found to be associated with a religion, it may be taken as a sure sign of the degeneracy of that religion - an indication that, at any rate in the country where such emblems and practices may be seen, the pristine purity of the faith has been lost and its spiritual power is rapidly passing away.

Never under any circumstances are the phallicism and the indecency a part of the original conception of a great religion, and the modern theory - that all symbols had primarily some obscene meaning in the minds of the savages who invented them, and that, as in the course of ages a nation evolved to a higher level, it became ashamed of these cruder ideas and invented far-fetched spiritual interpretations to veil their immodesty - is exactly the reverse of the truth. The great spiritual truth always comes first, and it is only after long years, when that has been forgotten, that a degenerate race endeavours to attach a grosser signification to its symbols.

THE TRUE MEANING.

Putting aside, then, all later misrepresentations, what meaning was originally conveyed by the world-wide symbol of the cross? Part, at any rate, of the answer is given to us by Madame Blavatsky herself in the proem to *The Secret Doctrine*, when she describes the signs impressed upon the successive leaves of a certain archaic manuscript. It will be remembered that first of all there is the plain white circle which is understood to typify the Absolute; in that appears the central spot, the sign that the First Logos has entered upon a cycle of activity; the spot broadens into a line dividing the circle into two parts, thus symbolizing the dual aspect of the Second Logos as male-female, God-man, spirit-matter; and then, to show the next stage, this dividing line is crossed by another, and we have the hieroglyph of the Third Logos - God the Holy Ghost, the Lord, the Life-giver.

But all these symbols, be it noted, are still within the circle, and so are emblems of different stages in the unfolding of the Triple Logos - not as yet of His manifestation. When in the fulness of time He prepares for this further descent, the symbol changes, usually in one or other of two ways. Sometimes the circle falls away altogether, and we have then the even-armed Greek cross as the sign of the Third Aspect of the Logos at the commencement of a great cycle, with His creative power held in readiness for exercise, but not as yet exercised.

Along this line of symbolism the next step is the svastika, which always implies motion - the creative power in activity; for the lines added at right angles to the arms of the cross are supposed to represent flames streaming backwards as the cross whirls round, and thus they doubly indicate the eternal activity of the Universal Life, first by the ceaseless outpouring of the fire from the centre through the arms, and secondly by the rotation of the cross itself. Another method of expressing the same idea is seen in the Maltese cross, in which the arms, ever widening out as they recede from the centre, once more typify the divine energy spreading itself forth in every direction of space.

Sometimes, instead of dropping the circle altogether, the cross simply extends itself outside it. Then we get the equal-armed cross with the small circle in the midst of it, and in the next stage that circle blossoms forth into the rose - another well-known life-emblem - and so we have the familiar symbol from which the Rosicrucians take their name. Again, the cross not only bears the mystic rose in its centre, but itself becomes rosy in colour, showing that that which is poured out from it and through it is ever the fire of the divine love.

Naturally the great occult rule, "As above, so below," holds good in this connection also, and with very slight variation these symbols may be, and sometimes are, employed to indicate much lower stages of evolution; hence Madame Blavatsky's reference to the various races of men in her explanation of them. One can easily see how, out of a misunderstanding of this lower interpretation, and its association at one stage with the separation of the sexes, the unsavoury ideas of phallicism would take their rise. Indeed, the knowledge of the true meaning of the Greek cross seems to have been lost to public view at a very early period; its connection with the Third Aspect of the Logos has remained for ages known to occultists only, and superficial students have almost invariably confused it with the Latin cross of the Second Person, the derivation of which in reality is entirely different.

THE LATIN CROSS.

In tracing the symbolism of this Latin cross, or rather of the crucifix, back into the night of time, the investigators had expected to find the figure disappear, leaving behind what they supposed to be the earlier cross-emblem. As a matter of fact, exactly the reverse took place, and they were startled to find that eventually the cross drops away, leaving only the figure with uplifted arms. No longer is there any thought of pain or sorrow connected with that figure, though still it tells of sacrifice; rather is it now the symbol of the purest joy the world can hold - the joy of freely giving - for it typifies the Divine Man standing in space with arms upraised in blessing, casting abroad his gifts to all humanity, pouring forth freely of himself in all directions, descending into that "dense sea" of matter, to be cribbed, cabined and confined therein, in order that through that descent we may come into being.

A sacrifice, truly (at least from our point of view), yet with no thought of suffering, but only of transcendent joy. For that is the essence of the law of sacrifice - the law which moves the worlds even down here. So long as any thought of pain is connected with it, the sacrifice is not perfect; so long as a man is forcing himself to do that which he would rather not do, he is but on the way towards the fulfilling of the great law. But when he gives himself fully and freely because, having once seen the glory and the beauty of the Great Sacrifice, there is for him no other course possible in the three worlds but to join himself with it, however far away, however feebly and imperfectly; when he gives himself without ever thinking of pain or trouble - indeed, without any thought of himself at all, but only of that for which he is working; then, and then only, is his sacrifice perfect, for it is of the same nature as the sacrifice of the Logos, and partakes of the essence of that law of love which alone is the law of life eternal.

That even the early Christian Church had some tradition of all this seems to be shown by the fact that in the paintings in the catacombs at Rome we frequently find just such a figure as the one described, with arms uplifted in the peculiar manner indicated, standing in the midst of the twelve apostles, exactly where the figure of the Christ would naturally be expected. This is generally spoken of as the "orante" or praying figure: it has sometimes been supposed to be feminine, and has given rise, I believe, to considerable speculation among ecclesiastical archaeologists, but the most natural explanation of it appears to me to be that which I have suggested above.

We see, then, that the cross has been used from very early periods as the symbol of matter and manifestation - of the material world. It was therefore by no means unnatural that the further descent of the Divine Man into matter should be symbolized by the binding of the body to the cross, which also signified accurately enough the extreme limitation of the action of the Logos by such descent - the extent to which His expression of Himself was curtailed on this physical plane. Of course the nails, the blood, the wounds and all the ghastly horrors of the modern misrepresentation, are simply accretions due to the diseased imagination of the material-minded mediaeval monk, who had neither the intellect nor the education which could enable him to appreciate the beautiful meaning conveyed by the original allegory.

THE LIVING CHRIST UPON THE CROSS.

This much, at least, of the truth is now beginning to be understood by even the Christian investigators, for in an article by H. Marucchi, the well-known Catholic archeologist, in the new dictionary of the Abbe Vigoroux, the writer refers to the fifth-century gate of Santa Sabina at Rome and to an ivory of the same date in the British Museum as the oldest known examples of the crucifix, and says, "It is to be remarked that the Christ is here represented as still living, with the eyes open and without any mark of physical suffering."

He goes on to say that in the sixth century the crucifix is more frequent, but still the figure is always living and clothed in a long tunic, and that it is only in the twelfth century that "they cease to represent the Christ as living and triumphant on the cross." He seems to think that the new school of painting of Cimabue and Giotto is to a large extent responsible for the change. The gradual alteration is clearly shown in the examples of successive paintings of the crucifixion exhibited in the Uffizi Gallery at Florence.

We are not without other testimony which shows that there have been many who have to some extent comprehended the true signification of the cross. The description given in the Acts of Judas Thomas of the Christ standing in glory above the cross which separated the lower world from the higher, and that of the splendid vision of the cross of light, by looking into and through which all the manifested worlds were to be seen, while yet the aura of the Heavenly Man included all, interpenetrated all, and was the life of all these are sufficient to evidence that truth was not left entirely without its witnesses in the earlier ages of our era, and that its light was absolutely hidden only when the dense fog of

Christian superstition descended with all its weight upon Europe and stifled the whole of its intellectual life for close upon a thousand years.

It may be that there are some who will feel this wider presentation of the true meaning of the cross to be vaguer and colder than the very concrete form in which it had previously shaped itself to them - will feel that with the emancipation of their minds from the image of that nightmare tale of appalling physical suffering they have lost also some familiar sentimental associations which they can hardly help regretting.

If there be any such among my readers let me remind them that while we cannot but recoil with horror from all the terrible and indeed blasphemous ideas associated by the orthodox with the thought of crucifixion, we may yet gratefully recognize in the sign of the cross a constant reminder of the ineffable self-sacrifice of the Logos - of the enormous patience with which His almighty power bears with all limitations, in order that in the slow progress of their development these manifold forms which He takes may be gradually expanded and yet may not too soon be broken, so that each of them may be servicable to the uttermost.

It may serve to remind us also that man himself is thus crucified, if he did but know it; and that if he knows it not, it is because the living soul, the true Christ within him, is still blindly identifying himself with the cross of matter to which he is bound. It may help us to realize that our bodies, whether physical, astral or mental, are not ourselves, and that whenever we find, as it were, two selves warring within us, we have to remember that we are in truth the higher, and not the lower - the Christ, and not the cross.

And indeed this symbol of the cross may be to us as a touch-stone to distinguish the good from the evil in many of the difficulties of life. "Only those actions through which shines the light of the cross are worthy of the life of the disciple," says one of the verses in a book of occult maxims; and it is interpreted to mean that all that the aspirant does should be prompted by the fervour of self-sacrificing love. The same thought appears in a later verse: "When one enters the path, he lays his heart upon the cross; when the cross and the heart have become one, then hath he reached the goal." So, perchance, we may measure our progress by watching whether selfishness or self-sacrifice is dominant in our lives.

It should tell us, too, that all true sacrifice must be like that of the Logos - a willing sacrifice; that only when we give ourselves absolutely, fully and freely, can our sacrifice be one with His; then, and then only, have we truly signed ourselves with the sign of the cross of the eternal Christ.

THE EGYPTIAN RITUAL.

Now this great sacrifice-the descent of the Second Aspect of the Logos into matter in the form of monadic essence - was somewhat elaborately set forth in symbol in the ritual of the Egyptian form of that first of the great initiations which is called by the Buddhists the Sohan or Sotapatti; and, as before stated, the Christ had frequently used a description of the exoteric side of its ceremonies to illustrate and emphasize his teaching on the subject. He probably even recited to them the exact wording of the rubric, or direction given to the officiating hierophant, for this and the following passages of the Creed are curiously reminiscent of its form; indeed, almost the only change is that of mood, which of course was necessary to adapt the phrases to their new setting. The formula, handed down to the Egyptians from the exponents of Atlantean magic in far-distant ages, ran thus:

"Then shall the candidate be bound upon the wooden cross, he shall die, he shall be buried, and shall descend into the underworld; after the third day he shall be brought back from the dead, and shall be carried up into heaven to be the right hand of Him from Whom he came, having learnt to guide (or rule) the living and the dead."

The hall of initiation was often underground in an Egyptian temple - probably chiefly for the sake of convenience in keeping its situation secret, though the arrangement may also have been intended as part of the symbolism of the descent into matter which played so prominent a part in all these ancient mysteries. There may have been such a hall in or beneath the great Pyramid, for but a very small portion of its immense bulk has yet been investigated, or is ever likely to be.

In such a hall the ceremonies connected with this initiation used to take place. Putting aside the wearisome length of the earlier part, with which we have no concern at present, we come to the culmination where the candidate voluntarily laid himself down upon a huge wooden cross which was hollowed so as to receive and support the human figure. To this his arms were lightly bound, the end of the cord being carefully left loose in order to typify the entirely voluntary nature of the bondage.

The candidate then passed into a deep trance or, in other words, he left the physical body and for the time functioned entirely in the astral. While in this condition his body was borne away into a vault still lower down, beneath the floor of the hall of initiation, and was laid in an immense sarcophagus - a process which, as far as the physical body is concerned, was not at all inaptly symbolized as death and burial.

THE DESCENT INTO HELL.

"He descended into hell." But meantime, while the mere outer husk of the man was thus "dead and buried," he himself was fully alive and conscious elsewhere. Many and strange were the lessons which he had to learn, the experiences which he had to undergo, the tests through which he had to pass during his sojourn in that astral world; but they were all carefully calculated to familiarize him with this new sphere of action in which he found himself, to enable him to understand it, to give him confidence and self-reliance - in fact, so to train him that he could safely face all its perils, could use its powers with calmness and discretion, and could thus become a fitting instrument upon that plane in the hands of those who help the world.

This was the descent into the underworld - not, of course, into the hell of the gross Christian conception, but into Hades, the world of the departed, where it was undoubtedly the work of the initiate (among many other duties) to "preach to the spirits in prison," as the Christian tradition puts it - not, however, as that tradition ignorantly supposes, to the spirits of those who, having had the misfortune to live in times long past, could attain salvation only by thus after death hearing and accepting this particular form of faith - not to them, but to the spirits of those recently departed from this life, and still imprisoned and held down upon the astral plane by desires unexhausted and passions unsubdued.

To endeavour to help this vast army of unfortunates, by pointing out to them the true course of their evolution and the best method of hastening it, was one of the duties of the initiate then, as it is one of the duties of the Masters' pupils now; and therefore at this solemn ceremony, by which he was formally put into relation with the Great Brotherhood, he received his first lesson in what would thereafter form no inconsiderable portion of his work.

During this same "descent into hell" it was that, according to the Egyptian rite, the candidate had to pass through what used to be called "the tests of earth, water, air and fire" - unless indeed he had already experienced them at an earlier stage of his development. In other words, he had to learn with that absolute certainty that comes not by theory but by practical experience, that in his astral body none of these elements could by any possibility be hurtful to him - none could oppose any obstacle in the way of the work which he had to do.

When functioning in the physical body we are thoroughly convinced that fire will burn us, that water will drown us, that the solid rock forms an impassable barrier to our progress, that we cannot with safety launch ourselves unsupported into the ambient air. So deeply is this conviction ingrained in us that it costs most men a good deal of effort to overcome the instinctive action which follows from it, and to realize that in the astral body the densest rock offers no impediment to their freedom of motion, that they may leap with impunity from the highest cliff, and plunge with the most absolute confidence into the heart of the raging volcano or the deepest abysses of the fathomless ocean.

Yet until a man *knows* this - knows it sufficiently to act upon his knowledge instinctively and confidently - he is comparatively useless for astral work, since in emergencies that are constantly arising he would be perpetually paralyzed by imaginary disabilities. For this reason the candidate had to pass the tests of earth, water, air and fire thousands of years ago - for this reason he has to pass them to-day. For the same reason he has to go through many a strange experience - to meet face to face with calm courage the most terrifying apparitions amid the most loathsome surroundings - to show, in fact, that he can be trusted under any and all of the varied groups of circumstances in which he may at any moment find himself. This, then, is one among the many uses of the old rite of the "descent into hell."

THE RESURRECTION.

"The third day he rose again from the dead." It must surely have struck any thoughtful student of the received gospel narrative that to describe the interval between Friday evening and very early on Sunday morning as three complete days involves a certain amount of poetical license. It might be contended that such an interval was not inconsistent with the statement of the Creed that he rose again "on the third day"; but the person offering this somewhat disingenuous argument would have entirely to ignore the quite definite assertion attributed to Jesus that "the Son of Man shall remain three days and three nights in the heart of the earth."

The real explanation of these apparently bewildering discrepancies is clear enough when the true interpretation is adopted. In the later and degenerate days of the Mysteries, when attempts were made to minimize all requirements and to make entrance easy for less worthy candidates who were unable to pass into the trance, it was soon found that to spend in rigid seclusion upon the physical plane the seventy-seven hours originally so well occupied upon

the astral was to certain types of mind insufferably tedious; so the sycophantic hierophants of that later time conveniently discovered that seventy-seven was merely a clerical error for twenty-seven, and that the original form of the rubric "after the third day" really meant nothing more than "on the third day" - thus saving their noble patrons fully two days of what was practically solitary confinement.

This later and degraded form is accurately enough represented by the symbolism used in the gospels; but it could never have been adopted until the real meaning of the original ritual had been forgotten. Only after three clear days and nights and part of a fourth had passed was the still entranced candidate of more ancient days raised from the sarcophagus in which he had lain, and borne into the outer air at the eastern side of the pyramid or temple, so that the first rays of the rising sun might fall upon his face and awaken him from his long sleep. And when we remember that the whole of this ritual typifies the descent of the second great outpouring into matter, it will not be difficult for us to see why this particular period of time was chosen.

For three long journeys round our planetary chain and part of a fourth the monadic essence sinks deeper and ever deeper into the slough of dense matter, and only when in the fourth round the sun arises - when the Lords of the Flame appear upon earth - does that essence rise from the dead, and begin at last to enter upon that mighty sweep of its upward arc which in the end shall set it at the right hand of the Father.

THE ASCENSION.

"He ascended into heaven." It needs no explanation to show the meaning of this phrase with reference to the upward progress of the human soul; but the place which it fills in the old Egyptian ritual is worthy of our notice. For the lessons which the candidate had to learn at his initiation were not concluded with his experiences on the astral plane; it was necessary for him at this stage of his evolution to be brought into contact with something far higher and wider even than this. Those who have studied that section of Theosophical literature which treats of the Path of Holiness will remember that the Sotapanna, "the man who has entered upon the stream," receives as part of his initiation the first touch of awakening consciousness upon the buddhic plane.

This was of course the case in the Egyptian rite also, and it was this transcendent experience, changing as it did the man's entire conception of life and of evolution, which was spoken of as the ascent into heaven. By it the man for the first time realized in experience that great doctrine which is so familiar to us all as a theory - the spiritual brotherhood of man and the unity of all that lives. Yet so different is the holding of this merely as a theory from the knowing it absolutely as a fact in nature that, as has been said, this experience changes the man's whole life and attitude, so that never thereafter can he look upon anything in the world as he did before. Keen though his sympathy with suffering must be, yet his sorrow can never again be hopeless, for he knows that the sufferer also is a part of the one great life, and that therefore all must at last be well.

Sometimes also, along another line of symbolism, the ascent into heaven is taken to typify the attainment of the asekha level of initiation, when the Christ that has been born within the man becomes once more one with the Father. We may remember how the Christ prays for his disciples that they may all become one with him, even as he also is one with the Father.

TO GUIDE THE LIVING AND THE DEAD.

"And sitteth on the right hand of God the Father almighty, from whence he shall come to judge the quick and the dead." Here it will be seen that for the first time we come to a definite divergence of meaning between the wording of the Creed as we have it now and that of the Egyptian rubric. In the latter this clause is simply an extension of the former, and puts before us very clearly and beautifully the object of the whole vast course of evolution: "he shall be carried up into heaven to be the right hand of Him from Whom he came, having learnt to guide the living and the dead."

One trace at least which is accessible to ordinary scholarship is left to us to confirm the idea that this may have been the original reading, for in the Regula of Apelles, the disciple of Marcion, this clause runs, "the right hand of the Father, whence he hath come to rule the living and the dead." Thus all reference to the expected second advent of Christ is removed, and we have an important statement which not only emphasizes the great fact that the life which is poured forth returns in fullest measure to Him from whom it came, but also declares that the whole vast process was undertaken in order that mankind so returning should be the right hand of that Father almighty in His work of guiding the living and the dead. The great truth that all power which is gained is but held in trust, to be used as a means of helping others, has rarely been more clearly and more grandly set forth.

Not only has much misunderstanding been caused by the confusion which has been here introduced into the Creed, but this misunderstanding has been further accentuated by the use of the expression "to judge." Evidence is not wanting to show that in the English of the period when these documents were translated the significance of this word was a wider one than that usually assigned to it now, as we may see from such remarks as "Deborah judged Israel at that time" (Judges iv. 4), and "After him arose Jair, a Gileadite, and judged Israel twenty and two years " (Judges x. 3), etc., where it is obvious that to judge is simply synonymous with to rule - a meaning which brings us much nearer to the conception of guiding and helping conveyed in the Egyptian formula. Well may it be said, in the words added in the Nicaean symbol, of this magnificent conception of a ruler whose only object is to guide and to help: »His kingdom shall have no end."

THE HOLY GHOST.

"I believe in the Holy Ghost." In this clause - the final one of the original Creed drawn up by the Council of Nicaea - we return once more to the formula as given by the Christ. It has already been explained in the earlier part of this volume that the Holy Ghost corresponds to the Third Person of the Logos - the "Spirit of God which broods over the face of the waters" of space, and so brings into existence matter as we know it to-day. To His energy are due all the primary combinations of the ultimate atoms of our planes, so that the "atoms" with which modern chemistry deals are monuments of His work. His action brought them into existence in a certain definite order - an order which, so far as investigation into this subject has yet been carried, appears to correspond with that of their atomic weights, so that substances having high atomic weights, such as lead, gold or platinum, are of much later formation than elements of low atomic weight, such as hydrogen, helium or lithium.

At the Council of Constantinople in 381 A.D. the bare statement of the existence of the Holy Ghost, which was all that was contained either in the Apostles' Creed or in the original form of that of Nicaea, was considerably amplified, and the beautiful title of "the Life-giver" was then for the first time reinserted. The English version unfortunately lends itself here to a very common misunderstanding, and most people as they recite the Lord and Giver of Life" probably suppose it to mean - if they ever think of its meaning at all - the Lord of Life and the Giver of Life. A reference to the original Greek at once shows that such a construction is entirely unwarranted, and that the proper translation is simply "the Lord, the Life-giver."

Well might such a title be assigned to Him, not only because of the mighty work which He did when the solar system came into existence, not only because from Him comes all life of which we know anything (for the omnipresent vital fluid is but the manifestation of His activity upon these lower planes), but because of the equally stupendous work which He is doing even now. Whether the effect of that first great outpouring of energy is now complete, or whether chemical elements of a still more elaborate kind are still in process of production, we know not, though there is much to suggest that the latter hypothesis is the true one; but it is at least certain that all around us an evolution is going on upon a scale so vast in its totality, yet so infinitely minute in its method, that we live in the midst of it, yet in the most absolute unconsciousness of it.

Not the spiritual evolution of the immortal soul in man, for that is the work of our Logos in His First Aspect; not the evolution which science recognizes as ever in progress in the animal and vegetable kingdoms - the development of intelligence and faculty by means of repeated experiences, and the correspondential modification in outer forms which is the result of this; not even the evolution of the power of combination in the mineral kingdom, so that ever more and more complex chemical compounds are gradually coming into being - for all these are part of the wonderful activity of the Second Person of the Trinity; but within and behind all these is the evolution of the atom itself.

THE ATOM.

To explain the method of this evolution would take far more space than can be devoted to it here, and would also be somewhat outside the immediate scope of a treatise on the Creed; but an indication of the direction in which it works may readily be given to those who have read Mrs. Besant's article on "Occult Chemistry" in *Lucifer* for November, 1895, or have studied the information which she gives on this subject in *The Ancient Wisdom*. It will be remembered that, in the illustrations there given, the atom was shown as composed of a series of spiral tubes arranged in a certain order, and it was explained that these tubes themselves were in turn composed of finer tubes spirally coiled, and these finer tubes in turn of others still finer, and so on. These finer tubes have been called spirillae of the first, second and third orders respectively; and it is found that before we get back to the straight filament or line of astral atoms (for the physical atom is ultimately formed by the convolutions of ten such lines) we have to unwind seven series of the spirillae, each of which is wound at right angles to the one preceding it.

Now in the perfected physical atom, as it will be at the end of the seventh round, all of these orders of spirillae will be fully vitalized and active, each with a different order of force flowing through it; and thus this particular part of the work of the Holy Ghost will be accomplished. At present we are in the fourth round, and only four of these orders of spirillae; are as yet in activity, so that even the very physical matter in which we have to work is very far from having unfolded its full capacities. This mighty process of atomic evolution, which interpenetrates all else and yet moves on its way absolutely independent of all conditions, is ever being carried steadily on by the wonderful impulse of that first outpouring from the Third Aspect of the Logos.

A GLIMPSE OF A MIGHTY PLAN.

It seems clear that all this marvellous activity is and has ever been steadily tending towards differentiation - individualization, as it were; while it is equally evident that the action of the second great outpouring gives all sorts of new powers of combination which appear to be tending back again towards a kind of higher unity, so that we have here what looks at first sight like an opposition between the working of these two mighty forces.

Now, as I have said before, it is obvious that with such exceedingly fragmentary knowledge of all these wonderful operations as we at present possess, and with the further disadvantage of looking at them all from so low a plane-examining all their action, as it were, from below instead of from above - any ideas which even the wisest of us may form as to the real working of the great scheme must necessarily be so incomplete that they may well be hopelessly misleading, and unless put forward with due reservation and modesty they would be only too likely to be blasphemous as well. Yet it seems to me that, even in such examination as is possible for us of this marvellous complexity of evolution, we do get here and there glimpses of a part of its plan - hints which we can test by applying them to different levels of this process of development.

Here, for example, we seem to see clearly in action the broad principle of first of all generating a certain set of elements, and endowing them with so much of stability, and, as it were, individuality, that under all ordinary conditions of temperature and pressure they maintain their position as separate entities; while, as a later and distinctly higher stage of their evolution, there is developed within them the capability of and the desire for union. It is impossible not to be reminded, by this rough outline of evolution in the mineral kingdom, of the statement that the Logos Himself has become manifest only in order that from Him might emanate an immense multitude of individuals who, when they have become sufficiently separated to be each a living and powerful centre, shall rise again towards perfect union and realize their oneness in Him.

Even when we turn to examine the individual development of man, we may still see the same principle working. After man as an individual with a causal body has definitely come into existence, the whole force of his environment seems to be directed to the evolution in him of mind, the discriminative and separative faculty, which in him as the microcosm distinctly corresponds with Mahat, the universal Mind or the Holy Spirit in the macrocosm. Much later comes the development of the intuitional wisdom, the faculty of combining and unifying, which may be taken as in many ways corresponding with the Second Aspect of the Logos in the wider world.

For the old text which tells us that man is made in the image of God is wonderfully and beautifully true, as may be seen by comparing in Diagram I. the triad of the human soul with the Trinity in manifestation above it. It will be found that the one reproduces the other with marvellous exactness. Just as Three Aspects of the Divine are seen upon the seventh plane, so the Divine Spark of the spirit in man is seen to be triple in its appearance on plane five. In both cases the Second Aspect is able to descend one plane lower and to clothe itself in the matter of that plane; in both cases the Third Aspect is able to descend two planes and repeat the process. So in both cases there is a Trinity in Unity, separate in its manifestations, yet one in the reality behind.

Indeed, incomprehensible though the statement may be, hopeless as would be any effort to explain it, it is in reality true that the principles in man which we call spirit, intuition, intellect, are not merely correspondences, not merely even reflections or rays of the Three Great Persons of the Logos, but are somehow in very truth themselves those glorious entities, uncreate, incomprehensible, the Father, the Son, and the Holy Ghost.

In the stages of world-evolution also we find the same general law holding good. In it also

so far the action has been chiefly creative and separative, chiefly concerned with the development of intellect, and we have scarcely as yet even the dawn of the unfolding of the intuitional wisdom, the great unifying power which is truly the Christ in man.

Here and there we see, one man who shows a little of its influence - here and there faint indications of what is to come may be discerned by those who know how to read the signs of the times. Nay, it may even be that some of the most terrible features of our social condition, evil though they are in their results, evil in their organization because so hopelessly marred by the selfishness and ignorance (and blind hatred of every one wiser and better than themselves) which are always shown by their promoters, may yet in all their iniquity have this much dim reflection of a hope behind them, that they may perchance be the first manifestation that there is a force pressing behind - the first blundering, misdirected gropings of the uninstructed after the true unity that is one day to come, though by means the very opposite to those which are now employed.

We must remember that after all we have but just passed the turning-point of the whole system of evolution - but just entered upon the mighty upward sweep which is to end in divinity. We are still in the fourth journey round the planetary chain - the round, properly speaking, devoted to the development of the astral body and the fact that we find ourselves possessed of intellect at all at this stage of the proceedings is due almost entirely to the help and stimulation given to our humanity by the advent of the great Lords of the Flame at a period which is after all comparatively recent. The full development of intellect even is not due until the next round, so that surely the merest foretaste of the stupendous power of the intuitional wisdom is all that we can expect for a very long time yet.

Still, nature is slowly moving forward towards that stage, and the future is with those who even now will recognize that fact and work for it - who will strive in every possible way to help forward the unifying principle, to break down the barriers of distrust and hatred which unfortunately so often exist between class, and class, between nation and nation. That indeed is truly Theosophical work -

the work of our Masters - work in which it is the greatest of privileges to be allowed to join, to however small an extent, in however humble a capacity.

THE PROCESSION OF THE HOLY GHOST.

"Who proceedeth from the Father and the Son." It was nominally with reference to this

doctrine of the procession of the Holy Ghost from the Son as well as from the Father that there occurred the greatest schism which has yet rent the Christian Church - the division between the Eastern and Western (or as we now call them, the Greek and the Roman) Churches, which took place in the eleventh century. It is, however, probable that this question was merely a pretext, since the Greek Church did not discover the heinousness of this heresy for more than four hundred years. The progressive centralization of the Western Church under the see of Rome was becoming exceedingly inconvenient to the Oriental patriarchs, and strained relations had been existing for some time; while the final determining cause of the secession seems to have been the transfer of their allegiance by the Bulgarians from the patriarchs to the popes. Still its use even as a pretext in so important an event in Church history has invested this "filioque" clause with an interest which is perhaps greater than its intrinsic importance would warrant.

The question at issue was whether the Third Person of the Trinity came forth from the First alone, or from the First and the Second. Looking as we are doing at the esoteric meaning of the symbol, we see that the Western Church in no way added to or corrupted the original doctrine by inserting its celebrated "filioque" clause, but only expressed in words what must have been obvious from the first to any one who read behind the mere letter of the formula; and yet there was a very real meaning in the protest of the Eastern Church.

If we turn to Diagram I. we shall readily grasp the point of contention, and we shall be able to see that in a very real sense both the disputants were right. Since the manifestation of the eternal Father takes place on the seventh plane, and that of the Holy Ghost on the fifth, it is clear that, if the latter comes forth from the former, it can do so only by passing through the intermediate level of the sixth plane, upon which is the manifestation of the Son. Resting itself upon that obvious fact, the Roman Church inserted its "filioque." The Greek Church, however, misunderstood this apparently harmless addition, and supposed it to indicate a confusion of the functions and manifestation of the separate Persons or Aspects. To use the symbolism of our diagram, they feared that an attempt was being made to draw through the First, Second and Third Manifestations just such a diagonal line as is drawn in the lower or human Trinity, connecting Spirit, Intuition, and Intelligence; and they quite rightly protested against any such theory of the procession as that would typify. It was certainly not from the manifested Person of the Father through the manifested Person of the Son that the Holy Ghost came forth. The dotted line on the right of the diagram, showing how the Third Aspect descends from the seventh plane through the sixth, and finally manifests on the fifth, is the key to the true line of procession, and the absolute harmony of the two conflicting ideas. It is clear that if the disputants had honestly desired to reach an agreement, and if they had had such a grasp of the truth behind the symbols as Theosophy gives to its students, there need have been no schism at all.

Of all the suggested renderings the nearest to the truth is that of St. John Damascene: "Who proceedeth from the Father through the Son" (*De Hymno Trisag.*, n. 28); yet it seems as though it would have been better still if in the original document the words used to express the coming forth of the Second and Third Aspects had been interchanged - if it had been written that the Son proceeded from the Father, and that the Holy Ghost was begotten of the Son. It has been already explained that the real meaning of *μονογενής* is "coming forth from one alone," and not from the interaction of a pair. Everything else in nature of which we know is produced by the interaction of two factors, whether these factors are separate entities, as they usually are, or merely two poles included within the same organism, as in the case of the parthenogenetic reproduction of the alternate generations of aphides.

What is commonly called the procession of the Holy Ghost is in no sense an exception to this rule, for the duality of the Second Person of the Trinity has always been clearly recognized, and although in the modern Christian system the two poles or aspects are expressed only as divinity and humanity, in older faiths and even in the Gnostic traditions they were often considered as male and female respectively, and the Second Person was frequently spoken of as containing within Himself the characteristics of both the sexes, and was even called "The Father-Mother."

"Who with the Father and the Son together is worshipped and glorified." This simply means that the Three Aspects of the Logos are to be regarded as equally worthy of the deepest reverence, as equally standing apart from all else within the system to which they have given birth - that "in this Trinity none is afore or after other, none is greater or less than another, but the whole three persons are coeternal together and coequal," as far at any rate as this aeon is concerned - all equally to be glorified by man, since his debt of gratitude, for the labour and stupendous sacrifice involved in his evolution, is due to all three alike.

"WHO MANIFESTETH THROUGH HIS ANGELS."

"Who spake by the prophets." This clause, which is one of those first incorporated in the Creed at the Council of Constantinople, embodies a very early misconception for which it is not difficult to account, and though it does not directly refer to the story of Jesus, it must none the less be attributed to the tendency which we have called (c). The meaning of the original expression which it represents can perhaps be best rendered into English as "Who manifesteth through His angels"; and when we remember that in Greek the words "angel" and "messenger" are identical, we shall easily see how in the mind of a Jewish translator eagerly anxious to emphasize the continuity of the newer teaching with that of his own religion, what to him would seem an obscure passage referring to "manifestation through His messengers," came to be interpreted as indicating the inspiration of the Hebrew prophets.

The Jewish faith, corrupt and grossly material as it was, had still some tradition of the messengers through whom the Logos manifested Himself in matter - the seven great archangels, later called "the seven spirits before the throne of God" - the seven lesser Logoi (lesser only in comparison with the ineffable splendour of the Trinity) who are the first emanation of the Godhead. But it was manifestly impossible that the reference to them in the passage under consideration should be understood by a mind already obsessed with the idea that all that was said of the Second Person of the Trinity was to be taken as descriptive only of a human teacher. If the Second Person were but a man, and the Third a vague influence proceeding from him, then the messengers through whom that influence had previously manifested must obviously be men also, and it was quite natural that the supposed inspiration of his own prophets should at once occur to the mind of an Israelite. The grandeur of the true conception was far above out of his sight; he had already coarsened and degraded it beyond the power of words to express, and so he saw nothing incongruous in regarding the itinerant preachers of his own petty tribe as directly controlled by the influence of the Supreme.

That this "manifestation through the angels" is a vivid reality every student of occultism knows. On every plane he finds the seven great types, not only of matter, but of life or energy. On the astral plane, for example, he finds that all the multitudinous varieties of the elemental essence may be grouped under seven great classes - not those which energize the matter of the seven sub-planes, but another division quite apart from that, and crossing it at right angles, as it were. He finds that through all astral matter these great divisions run - that the energy ensouling every astral element belongs to one or other of these classes. Out of these seven, therefore, is every astral form built, even the astral body of the plant, of the animal, or of the man; and according to the preponderance of one or other of these types of essence in their astral bodies, men may be classified into temperaments - the sanguine, the lymphatic, etc. - or arranged under planets, as is done by the astrologer, who speaks constantly of a Venus man or a Mars man, a Jupiter man, and so on.

The student of occultism, seeking for the reason that lies behind all this, finds it in the fact that the Divine Life came forth in seven mighty parallel streams through seven great living Channels, which, though assuredly separate entities, are nevertheless in a very real sense centres of energy in the Logos himself. Each of these great Channels has left its ineffaceable mark on all that has passed through it, and has impressed an individual character on the life-stream as it poured it forth into the lower planes. Furthermore, he realizes that each of these great Channels or specializers is a glorious living Spirit, and that the life poured out through each remains his life, a very part of him. Therefore, again it follows that man's astral body, which he has thought to be his own, in reality belongs also to these Great Ones, since the life of each one of them is ever pulsating through it. Thus verily and thus vividly is the Divine Life ever manifesting not only without us, but within us, yet always »through His angels," those wondrous living lights which yet are centres in that still greater, Light which knows no setting, but shines for evermore.

"THE HOLY CHURCH THROUGHOUT ALL THE WORLD."

"The holy catholic Church." This clause appears in the Nicene Creed as the "one catholic and apostolic Church," and has always been understood to signify the body of faithful believers all over the world - the word catholic simply meaning universal. This is in effect a statement of the brotherhood of man, for it proclaims how community of interest in spiritual things draws together men out of every nation, "without distinction of race, creed, caste, sex or colour," as the first object of the Theosophical Society puts it. If we will but put aside the misinterpretations which later sectarianism has accumulated round these words, and think what they really mean, we shall see at once how beautifully expressive they are.

The Church is the ἐκκλησία - the body of those who are "called out" of the ordinary worldly life of misdirected energy by the common knowledge which they possess of the great facts underlying nature - the men who, because they know the relative importance of each, have "set their affection on things above, and not on things of the earth," no matter to what nation they may belong, nor by what name they may choose to call their faith in spiritual things.

That by no means all of them yet recognize their brotherhood, that many of them distrust and misunderstand one another, sad though it is, in no way alters the great fact that because they regard things spiritual rather than things temporal, because they have definitely ranged themselves on the side of good instead of evil, of evolution instead of retardation, they have a bond between them of community of aim which is stronger far than any of the external divisions that separate them - stronger because it is spiritual, and belongs to a higher plane than this.

This is the true Church of the Christ, and it is catholic because among its numbers there are men of every race and creed under heaven - "of all nations and kindred and peoples and tongues"; it is holy, because its members are striving to make their lives holier and better; it is apostolic, for in very truth all its members are apostles - "men sent forth" (though many of them know it not) by the great Power who is guiding all, that they may be His expression in the earth - His emissaries to help their more ignorant brethren, by precept and example, to learn the all-important lesson which they have already made part of their own lives. And whatever its outward divisions may be, this Church is fundamentally one - "elect from every nation, yet one o'er all the earth" - one in essence, though it may be many a century yet before all its members realize their spiritual unity.

For the truth is that there are only two classes of men in the whole world - the few who have already realized the mighty Divine scheme, and the vast mass who as yet know it not. The latter live for themselves, and are largely the slaves of their passions; the former live for God and for the evolution which is His will, whether they call themselves Buddhist or Hindu, Moslem or Christian, Freethinker or Jew. And these men are the salt of the earth, the holy Church throughout all the world which always acknowledges its Head, though it may call Him by many names and image Him under many forms.

THE GREAT WHITE BROTHERHOOD.

"The communion of saints." This is interpreted in two ways by modern orthodoxy. The first takes it merely as an extension of the previous clause, "the holy catholic Church (which is) the communion of the saints." That is to say that the Church consists of the fellowship of the holy ones in every land, very much as has just been explained - except that of course in the orthodox system none but the Christians of every nation are recognized as brothers! The other method of interpretation gives a somewhat more mystical sense to the word communion, and explains the clause as pointing out the intimate association between Christians on earth and those who have passed away - the blessed dead, more especially those of transcendent virtue, who are usually called the saints.

As is so often the case, the truth includes both hypotheses, and yet is grander far than either of them, for the true meaning of the expression of belief in the communion of the saints is the recognition of the existence and the functions of the Great Brotherhood of Adepts which is in charge of so much of the evolution of mankind. Thus it is truly an extension of the idea of the brotherhood of man implied in the belief in the holy catholic Church; yet it also involves the closest possible association and even communication with the noblest of those who have gone before us. But it is much more than all this; for to those who really grasp it and begin even dimly to understand what it means, it gives a sense of absolute peace and security which passes all understanding - which can never be shaken or lost through any of the changes and chances of this mortal life.

When once this is realized by any man, however keen may be his sympathy with the manifold sufferings of humanity - however he may fail to understand much of what he sees in the world around him - the element of hopelessness, which before made it all so terrible, is gone, and gone for ever. For though he feels that dread mysteries, as yet but partially explained, underlie many an act in the great drama of the world's history - though questions may sometimes arise within him to which man can give no answer, and to which the higher powers have given none thus far, yet he knows, with the absolute certainty born of experience, that the power, the wisdom, and the love which guide the evolution of which he is part, are far more than strong enough to carry it through to a glorious end. He knows that no human sympathy can be as great as theirs who stand behind; none can love man as they do - they who are sacrificing themselves for man. Yet they know all, from the beginning to the end; and they are satisfied.

EMANCIPATION FROM SIN.

"The forgiveness of sins "; or, as the Greek may be more literally rendered, "the emancipation from sins." For the more mystical side of the idea symbolized in the ecclesiastical doctrine of the so-called forgiveness of sins, the reader may be referred to Mrs. Besant's article in *The Theosophical Review* for November 1891, or to the chapter on the subject in *Esoteric Christianity*. Here, however, we have to deal, not with the later developments of dogma, but rather with the meaning attached to this clause in the original formula, which was a comparatively simple one.

No idea even remotely resembling that suggested by the modern word "forgiveness" was in any way connected with it; it was a straightforward declaration that the candidate acknowledged the necessity of setting himself free from the dominion of all his sins before attempting to enter upon the path of occult progress, and its spirit would be far more accurately rendered by an expression of belief in the demission of sins rather than their remission. It was primarily intended to be a definite reminder of the principle which requires moral development as an absolute pre-requisite to advancement, and a warning against the danger of the method of the darker magical schools which did not exact morality as a necessary qualification for membership.

But it had also another and an inner meaning, referring to a higher stage in man's development, and this is more clearly brought out in the form assumed by this clause in the Nicaean symbol, "I acknowledge one baptism for the remission of sins." Again, of course, we must substitute the idea of emancipation for that of forgiveness, and remembering that baptism has always been the symbol of initiation, we have before us a conception which might be expressed in the Buddhist phraseology with which students of Theosophical literature are more familiar: "I acknowledge, one initiation for the casting-off of the fetters." The candidate proclaims by this statement that he has definitely set before him as his goal the initiation which sets his foot upon the Path of Holiness - *one* initiation, given only by the one Brotherhood in the name of the Great Initiator - in and through which he gains power entirely to cast off the three fetters of doubt, superstition, and the delusion of self. (See *Invisible Helpers*, chapter xvi.)

THE TRUE BAPTISM.

He gains power, I say advisedly, for however clear his intellectual convictions on these points may have been previously, he does not attain the certainty which comes from definite knowledge until he has experienced that touch of buddhic consciousness which is part of the ritual of that first initiation - the portal of the Path of Holiness. And in that touch, momentary though it may be, not only does he obtain this vast increase of knowledge which puts a new face for him upon the whole of nature, but he also enters for the moment into a relation with his Master far more intimate than anything he has ever before comprehended. And in that flash of contact he receives a very real baptism, for there pours into his soul such a rush of power, of wisdom, and of love, that he is at once strengthened for effort which before would have seemed inconceivable to him. Not that the Master's feeling or attitude has in any way changed, but that by the development of this new faculty the pupil has become capable of seeing more of what He is, and so of receiving more from Him.

In a very true sense, then, is this first great initiation "a baptism for the emancipation from sins," and the baptism administered to infants soon after their birth was but a symbol and a prophecy of this - a ceremony intended as a kind of dedication of the young life to the effort to enter upon the Path. Very soon after the materializing tendency set in the true meaning of all this was obscured, and then it became necessary to invent some reason for the baptismal ceremony. Some tradition of its connection with the putting away of sins still survived, and as it was obvious, even to a Church father, that a baby could hardly have committed any serious offences, the extraordinary doctrine of "original sin" was invented, and did much harm in the world.

REINCARNATION.

"The resurrection of the body." Here again is a case similar to the last - a case where a doctrine, perfectly simple and reasonable in itself, falls gradually into oblivion and misconstruction among the ignorant, until a monstrous and absurd dogma is erected to take the place of the forgotten truth. What numbers of books have been written and sermons preached in defence of this scientifically impossible teaching of the resurrection of the physical body - the "agenrisyng of fleish," as it is called in an English Creed of about the date 1400 - when all the time the clause meant nothing more nor less than an affirmation of the doctrine of reincarnation!

This, which in more enlightened times was a universal belief, had gradually dropped out of popular knowledge in later Egypt and in classical Greece and Rome, though of course it was never lost sight of in the teaching of the Mysteries. It was quite plainly mentioned in the original formula given by the Christ to his disciples, where a reference occurs to "the wheel of birth and death"; and it was only the gross ignorance of later days which perverted the simple explanation, that after death man would again appear upon the earth in bodily form, into a theory that he would at some future time collect the very particles of which his physical vehicle had been constructed at the moment of death, and once more build up that corpse into the semblance which it then wore.

In the Nicene Creed the clause now appears in the more comprehensible form, "I look for the resurrection of the dead," though in some of its earlier variants it also speaks of the resurrection of the flesh. Yet the simple idea that what was meant was resurrection in a body, not resurrection of that same body, was not suggested by any of these renderings. Looking at the subject impartially, it certainly seems that nothing else could satisfy the requirements of the teaching given. Reason leads us to suppose that the corruptible body cannot rise again; therefore that which rises must be the incorruptible soul. Since this soul is to rise in a body, it must rise in a fresh body - that is, in the body of an infant.

Evidence also is not wanting even on this physical plane in support of the theory (which we from other sources know to be true) that this belief in reincarnation was held by many at the alleged time of Christ, and was also held and taught by him. A metempsychosis of souls was a distinctive feature of the Jewish Kabala, and we have the testimony of Josephus that the Pharisees believed in the return to earth of the souls of the just in other bodies.

Jerome and Lactantius both bear witness to the fact that a belief in metempsychosis existed in the early Church. Origen not only expressed his belief in it, but was careful to state that his ideas on the subject were not drawn from Plato, but that he was instructed by Clemens of Alexandria, who had studied under Pantaenus, a disciple of apostolic men. Indeed, it seems by no means improbable that this doctrine of reincarnation formed one of the "mysteries" of the early Church, taught fully only to those who were found worthy to hear.

But few references to it now remain in the canon of scripture as at present accepted, but there are some which are unmistakable. One of these occurs in the story of the man who was born blind, and was brought to the Christ to be cured. The disciples inquired, "Master, who did sin, this man or his parents, that he was born blind?" This question clearly implies belief in a large proportion of the Theosophical doctrine in the minds of those who asked it. We note that they definitely understood the idea of cause and effect, and of Divine justice. Here was the case of a man born blind - a terrible affliction, of course, both for the child himself and the parents. The disciples realized that this must be the result of some sin or folly; and their question is as to whose sin it was that had brought about this deplorable result. Was it that the father had been so wicked that he deserved to have the sorrow of a blind son? Or was it that in some previous state of existence the man himself had sinned, and so brought upon himself this pitiable fate? Obviously if the latter were the true solution, the sins which deserved this punishment must have been committed before he was born - that is to say, in a previous life; so that in fact both the great fundamentals of Theosophical teaching are clearly implied in this one question. The answer of the Christ is very noteworthy. We know that on other occasions he was by no means backward in commenting vigorously upon inaccurate doctrine or practice; he spoke very strongly on many occasions to the Scribes and Pharisees and others. If, therefore, reincarnation and the idea of Divine justice were false and foolish beliefs, we should certainly expect to find him taking this opportunity to rebuke his disciples for holding them; yet we notice that he does nothing of the kind. He simply accepts their suggestions as entirely matters of course; he does not rebuke them in any way, but simply explains that neither of the hypotheses which they suggest is the true cause of the affliction in this particular case: "Neither hath this man sinned, nor his parents; but that the works of God should be made manifest in him."

There is one clear definite statement by Christ himself, which of course must settle the question once for all for anyone who believes in the gospel history and in the inspiration of the scriptures. When he has been speaking of John the Baptist, and inquiring what opinions were generally held about him, he terminates the conversation by the emphatic pronouncement, "If ye will receive it, this is Elias which was for to come." I am quite aware that the orthodox theologian thinks that Christ did not mean what he said in this case, and wishes us to believe that he was endeavouring to explain that Elias had been a type of John the Baptist. But in reply to such a disingenuous plea it will be sufficient to ask what would be thought of anyone who in ordinary life tried to explain away a statement in so clumsy a fashion. Christ knew perfectly well what was the popular opinion with reference to such matters; he knew quite well that he himself was supposed by the common people to be a reincarnation, sometimes of Elijah, sometimes of Jeremiah, and sometimes of some of the other prophets; and he was well aware that the return of Elijah had been prophesied, and that all the common people were in constant expectation of his advent. Consequently, in making a direct statement such as this, he must have known perfectly well how all his hearers would understand him. "If you will receive it"

- that is to say, if you can believe it - "this is the very Elijah whom you are expecting." That is an absolutely unequivocal statement, and to suppose that when Christ said that, he did not mean it, but instead intended to express something vague and symbolical, is simply to accuse him of wilfully misleading the people by giving to them a direct statement which he must have known perfectly well that they could take only in one way. Either Christ said this, or he did not say it; if he did not say it, what becomes of the inspiration of the gospel? If he did say it, then reincarnation is a fact. The passage will be found in Matthew xi. 14.

Another and much higher meaning is sometimes attached to this phrase, "the resurrection of the dead," as is evidenced by the fact that in the third chapter of his epistle to the Philippians we find St Paul describing himself as "striving if by any means he might attain unto the resurrection of the dead." What can this resurrection have been to which he, the great Apostle, found it necessary to strive in order that he might attain? Clearly it could not be what is ordinarily understood by that term, for the rising again from the dead at the last day is to happen to all people, good and bad alike; there could be no necessity to strive in order to gain that. What he is striving to attain is undoubtedly that initiation which liberates the man from life and death alike, which raises him above the necessity of further incarnation upon earth. We shall notice that a few verses further on he urges "as many as be perfect" to strive as he is striving; he does not give this advice to the ordinary member of the church, because he knows that for him this is not yet possible.

To rise from the dead, then, is sometimes merely to reincarnate, sometimes to take the first great initiation according to the Egyptian rite, and sometimes to take that far higher one which permits the man to escape altogether from the wheel of birth and death - the samsara, as the Buddhistcalls it.

"And the life everlasting." The semi-poetical form into which our translators have thrown this clause has led the orthodox to see in it a reference to eternal life in heaven, but in reality it bears no such signification; it is merely a straightforward statement of the immortality of the human soul. In the Celtic Creed the form is simpler still, "I believe in life after death," while the Nicaean symbol expresses it as "the life of the world to come," or, to translate more accurately, "the life of the coming age."

CHAPTER V.
THE ATHANASIAN CREED.

HAVING now glanced through the various clauses of the Nicene and the Apostles' Creeds, it remains for us only to take up such points in the Athanasian Creed as have not already been dealt with in the consideration of the earlier symbols.

The Athanasian Creed is admittedly a much later production than the others. Of course everyone is aware that it is not in any way connected with Athanasius, and bears his name only because its compilers wished it to be considered as an expression of the doctrines which he had so stoutly upheld centuries before. Part of it at any rate has been attributed to Hilary, Bishop of Arles, and part also appears in the Profession of Denebert, though it is noticeable that in all these earlier fragments what are called the damnatory clauses are conspicuous by their absence. But as a Creed it was certainly unknown even at the very end of the eighth century, for at the Council of Friuli, held in 796, the need of just such an amplification of the earlier Confession of Faith was deplored, and indeed it was very probably in consequence of the discussion which then took place on the subject that the Athanasian Creed appeared in its present form. There is some evidence to show that the two parts into which it so obviously divides itself - the first dealing with the doctrine of the Trinity, the second with that of the Incarnation - existed separately some few years before, but it seems certain that they were not publicly used in the combined and amplified form earlier than the year 800.

Nevertheless, and in spite of the decision of the critics, clairvoyant examination shows that as a matter of fact both the parts were penned by the same hand in the sea-girt monastery of Lerins at a date considerably prior to this, though it is certainly true that the writing was not made public.

I append it here in the form in which it appears in the Prayer-book of the Church of England to-day.

QUICUNQUE VULT.

Whosoever will be saved: before all things it is necessary that he hold the Catholick Faith.

Which Faith except everyone do keep whole and undefiled, without doubt he shall perish everlastingly.

And the Catholic Faith is this, That we worship one God in Trinity, and Trinity in Unity.

Neither confounding the Persons, nor dividing the Substance.

For there is one person of the Father, another of the Son, and another of the Holy Ghost.

But the Godhead of the Father, of the Son, and of the Holy Ghost, is all one: the Glory equal, the Majesty co-eternal.

Such as the Father is, such is the Son, and such is the Holy Ghost.

The Father uncreate, the Son uncreate, and the Holy Ghost uncreate.

The Father incomprehensible, the Son incomprehensible, and the Holy Ghost incomprehensible.

The Father eternal, the Son eternal, and the Holy Ghost eternal.

And yet they are not three eternals, but one eternal.

As also there are not three incomprehensibles, nor three uncreated, but one uncreated, and one incomprehensible.

So likewise the Father is Almighty, the Son Almighty, and the Holy Ghost Almighty.

And yet they are not three Almighties, but one Almighty.

So the Father is God, the Son is God, and the Holy Ghost is God.

And yet they are not three Gods, but one God.

So likewise the Father is Lord, the Son is Lord, and the Holy Ghost Lord.

And yet not three Lords, but one Lord.

For like as we are compelled by the Christian verity to acknowledge every Person by himself to be God and Lord;

So are we forbidden by the Catholic religion to say, There be three Gods, or three Lords.

The Father is made of none; neither created nor begotten.

The Son is of the Father alone, not made, nor created, but begotten.

The Holy Ghost is of the Father and of the Son, neither made, nor created, nor begotten, but proceeding.

So there is one Father, not three Fathers; one Son, not three Sons; one Holy Ghost, not three Holy Ghosts.

And in this Trinity none is afore or after other, none is greater or less than another;

But the whole three Persons are co-eternal together, and co-equal.

So that in all things, as is aforesaid, the Unity in Trinity and the Trinity in Unity is to be worshipped.

He therefore that will be saved must thus think of the Trinity.

Furthermore, it is necessary to everlasting salvation that he also believe rightly the Incarnation of our Lord Jesus Christ.

For the right Faith is, that we believe and confess that our Lord Jesus Christ, the Son of God, is God and man.

God, of the Substance of the Father, begotten before the worlds, and Man, of the substance of his Mother, born in the world;

Perfect God and perfect Man, of a reasonable soul and human flesh subsisting;

Equal to the Father, as touching his Godhead, and inferior to the Father, as touching his Manhood.

Who, although he be God and Man, yet he is not two, but one Christ;

One; not by conversion of the Godhead into flesh, but by taking of the Manhood into God. One altogether; not by confusion of Substance, but by unity of Person.

For as the reasonable soul and flesh is one man, so God and Man is one Christ;

Who suffered for our salvation, descended into hell, rose again the third day from the dead.

He ascended into heaven, he sitteth on the right hand of the Father, God Almighty, from whence he shall come to judge the quick and the dead;

At whose coming all men shall rise again with their bodies, and shall give account for their own works.

And they that have done good shall go into life everlasting, and they that have done evil into everlasting fire.

This is the Catholic Faith, which except a man believe faithfully, he cannot be saved.

———————

The Athanasian Creed is usually regarded as little more than an expansion of the earlier formulae, and, as has already been stated, criticism fixes the date of its composition comparatively late. Much obloquy has been cast upon it in recent years in consequence of what have been called its damnatory clauses, and many people who naturally enough entirely misunderstood their real meaning, have on this account regarded the whole Creed with horror indeed some of our most enlightened clergy, in open defiance of the directions of the rubric, have declined to allow its recitation in their churches. Had the meaning ordinarily attached to those clauses been the true one, such a refusal would have been far more than justified, yet to the mind of the Theosophical student they are entirely unobjectionable, for he sees in them not a blasphemous proclamation of the inability of the Logos to carry through the evolution which He has commenced, but merely the statement of a well-known fact in nature.

Let us take up the examination of the Quicunque vult, omitting, of course, such parts of its explanation as would be mere repetitions of what has already been said, and confining ourselves to the points in which this Creed is fuller than the other two.

THE ATTAINMENT OF SAFETY.

In the ordinary interpretation of the opening words, "Whosoever will be saved," we at once encounter a misconception of the most glaring character, for they are commonly supposed to embody some such blasphemous idea as "saved from eternal damnation," or "saved from the wrath of god" (I really cannot honour with a capital letter any being who is supposed to be capable in his anger of committing so unspeakable an atrocity as the infliction of endless torture!). A far more accurate translation, and one much less likely to be misunderstood, would have been "Whoever wishes to be safe," and when it is put in this form any student of occultism will at once see exactly what is meant.

We have all read in early Theosophical literature about the critical period of the fifth round, and we thus understand that a period will then be reached when a considerable portion of humanity will have to drop out for the time from our scheme of evolution, simply because they have not yet developed themselves enough to be able to take advantage of the opportunities which will then be opening before mankind because under the conditions then prevailing no incarnations of a sufficiently unadvanced type to suit them will be available.

Thus we shall come to a definite division - a kind of day of judgment upon which will take place the separation of the sheep from the goats, after which these shall pass on into aeonian life, and those into aeonian death - or at least into a condition of comparatively suspended evolution. AEonian, we observe; that is, age-long, lasting throughout this age or dispensation; but not for a moment to be looked upon as eternal. Those who thus fall out of the current of progress for the time will take up the work again in the next chain of globes exactly where they had to leave it in this; and though they lose such place as they have held in this evolution, yet it is only because the evolution has passed beyond them, and it would have been a mere waste of time for them to attempt to stay in it any longer. Their position is exactly that of children who have to be put back from their class into a lower one, because they are not yet thoroughly grounded in what that lower class has to teach, and so they are unable to go on along with their former classmates.

It will be remembered that when a pupil has been so happy as to pass successfully through all the difficulties of the probationary period, and has taken that first initiation which is the gateway to the Path Proper, he is spoken of as the Sotapanna - "he who has entered upon the stream." The meaning of this is that he as an individual has already passed the critical period to which we have referred; he has already reached the point of spiritual development which Nature requires as a passport to the later stages of the scheme of evolution of which we form a part. He has entered upon the stream of that evolution, now sweeping along its upward arc, and though he may still retard or accelerate his progress - may even, if he act foolishly, waste a very great deal of valuable time - he cannot again turn aside permanently from that stream, but is carried steadily along by it towards the goal appointed for humanity.

He is thus safe from the greatest of the dangers which menace mankind during this age the danger of dropping out of the current of its evolution; and so he is often spoken of as "the saved" or "the elect." It is in this sense, and in this sense only, that we can take the words of this first clause of the Athanasian Creed, "Whosoever will be saved, before all things it is necessary that he hold the Catholic Faith."

THE TRUE CATHOLIC FAITH.

Nor need we let ourselves fall into the vulgar error as to the real meaning of this last statement. The word catholic means simply universal, and that faith which is truly universal is not the form into which truth is cast by any one of the great Teachers, but the truth itself which underlies all form - the Wisdom Religion, of which all the exoteric religions are only partial expressions. So that this clause, when properly understood, simply conveys to us the undeniable statement that for any man who wishes to carry out his evolution to its appointed end, the most important thing is rightly to understand the great occult teaching as to the origin of all things and the descent of spirit into matter.

It has been objected that this statement is inaccurate, and the objectors remark that surely the most important teaching to any man is that which educates him morally - which tells him, not what he must believe, but w hat he must do. Now of course that is quite true; but such objectors ignore or forget the fact that the fullest moral development is always taken for granted in all religions before even the possibility of attaining a true grasp of any sort of high occult knowledge is admitted. They also forget that it is only by this occult knowledge that either the commands or the sanctions of their moral code can be explained, or indeed that any reason can be shown for the very existence of a moral code at all.

In addition to all this it has to be clearly recognized that though morality is absolutely necessary as a pre-requisite to real progress, it is by no means all that is required. Unintelligent goodness will save a man much pain and trouble in the course of his upward path, but it can never carry him beyond a certain point in it; there comes a period when in order to progress it is absolutely imperative that a man should know. And this is at once the explanation and the justification of the second verse of the Creed, around which such heated controversy has raged - "Which faith except every one do keep whole and undefiled, without doubt he shall perish everlastingly" - the last word being of course not taken in the unphilosophical and metaphysically impossible orthodox sense, but understood as before to signify aeonially, as far as this age or chain of worlds is concerned.

There is no halo of special antiquity surrounding this particular form of words, for in the Profession of Denebert, which is the oldest form we have of this earlier part of the Creed, they do not appear. It is probable that the original writer used them and that Denebert, misunderstanding them, omitted them; but whether that is so or not, there is no need to be afraid of them or to attempt to explain away their obvious meaning; this clause is after all merely the converse of the last one, and simply states somewhat more emphatically that, since a grasp of certain great facts is most important and indeed necessary in order to pass the critical period, those who do not acquire that grasp will certainly fail to pass it. A serious statement, truly, and well worthy of our closest attention, but surely in no sense a dreadful one; for when a man has once got beyond the stage in which he "faintly trusts the larger hope" to that further stage where he knows that it is not a hope but a certainty - in other words, when he has for the first time discovered something of what evolution really means - he can never again feel that awful sense of helpless horror which was born of hopelessness.

THE TRINITY IN UNITY.

Our author then very carefully proceeds to inform us what these great facts are whose comprehension (in so far as our very finite minds may at present comprehend them) is so essential to our hope of progress.

"And the Catholic faith is this, that we worship one God in Trinity, and Trinity in Unity, neither confounding the persons, nor dividing the substance." Perhaps the great mystery of the Logos could hardly be better put into words for our physical understanding; we can scarcely better express the eternal Oneness which is yet ever threefold in Its aspect. And assuredly the final caution is most emphatically necessary, for never will the student be able even to approach the comprehension of the origin of the solar system to which he belongs - never by consequence will be in the least understand the wonderful trinity of spirit, intuitional wisdom, and intellect, which is himself, unless he takes the most scrupulous care to keep clear in his mind the different functions of the Three Great Aspects of the One, while never for one moment running the risk of "dividing the substance " by losing sight of the eternal underlying Unity.

It is obviously impossible to picture this divine manifestation in any way, for it is necessarily entirely beyond our power either of representation or comprehension, yet a small part of its action may perhaps to some extent be brought within our grasp by the employment of certain simple symbols, such as those adopted in Diagram I. It will be seen that on the seventh or highest plane of our system the triple manifestation of our Logos is imaged by three circles, representing His three aspects. Each of these aspects appears to have its own quality and power. In the First Aspect He does not manifest Himself on any plane below the highest, but in the Second He descends to the sixth plane, and draws round Himself a garment of its matter, this making a quite separate and lower expression of Him. In the Third Aspect He descends to the upper portion of the fifth plane and draws round Himself matter of that level, thus making a third manifestation. It will be observed that these three manifestations on their respective planes are entirely distinct one from the other, and yet we have only to follow up the dotted lines to see that these separate persons are nevertheless in truth but aspects of the one. Quite separate, when regarded as persons, each on his own plane - quite unconnected diagonally, as it were, yet each having his perpendicular connection with himself at the level where these three are one.

Most certainly "there is one person of the Father, another of the Son, and another of the Holy Ghost," for persona is nothing in the world but a mask, an *aspect*; yet again beyond all shadow of doubt or question "the Godhead of the Father, of the Son, and of the Holy Ghost is all *one* - the glory equal, the majesty co-eternal," since all are equally manifestations of the ineffable splendour of Him in whom our whole system lives and moves and has its being.

"Uncreate" indeed are each of these aspects as regards their own system, and differing thereby from every other force or power within its limits, since all these others are called into existence by them and in them; "incomprehensible" indeed, not only in the modern sense of "non-understandable," but in the much older one of "uncontainable," since nothing on these far lower planes (which alone we know) can ever be more than the most partial and incomplete manifestation of their unshadowed glory; "eternal" certainly, in that they all endure as long as their system endures, and probably through many thousands of systems; "and yet they are not three eternals, but one eternal; not three uncreated, nor three incomprehensibles, but one uncreated, and one incomprehensible," for that in them which is uncreated, incomprehensible and eternal, is not the aspect, but ever the underlying Unity which is one with the All.

"For like as we are compelled by the Christian verity to acknowledge every person by himself to be God and Lord" (that is, to recognize the almighty power of the Logos as working

equally in each of these His aspects)," so are we forbidden by the Catholic religion to say there be three Gods or three Lords" - that is, to set up the three aspects in any sense against or apart from each other - to regard them in any way disproportionately, or as separate entities. How often these aspects of the Divine have been divided, and worshipped separately as gods or goddesses of wisdom, of love, or of power, and with what disastrous results of partial or one-sided development in their followers, the pages of history will reveal to us. Here, at any rate, the warning against such a fatal mistake is sufficiently emphatic.

Again, in the Athanasian Creed we see evidence of the same careful endeavour to make clear as far as may be the difference of genesis of the Three Aspects of the Logos which we found so prominent in the wording of the Nicene Creed. "The Father is made of none, neither created nor begotten; the Son is of the Father alone, not made, nor created, but begotten; the Holy Ghost is of the Father and of the Son, neither made, nor created, nor begotten, but proceeding."

We need not here go over again the ground already traversed in connection with the corresponding clauses in the Nicene Creed, further than to point out that in the words "the Son is of the Father alone," we have once more an emphatic statement of the true meaning of the term usually so grossly mistranslated as "only-begotten."

THE EQUALITY OF THE ASPECTS.

Yet again does our writer recur to the vast question of the equality of the three great aspects, for he continues: "And in this Trinity none is afore or after other, none is greater or less than another, but the whole three persons are co-eternal together and co-equal." It has been objected that philosophically this must be untrue, since that which had a beginning in time must have an end in time; that since the Son comes forth from the Father, and the Holy Ghost from the Father and the Son, a time must come when these later manifestations, however glorious, must cease to be; that, in point of fact (to put the objection in the form so familiar fifteen hundred years ago), "Though great is the only-begotten, yet greater is he that begat."

This suggestion seems at first sight to be countenanced by much that we read in Theosophical

teachings as to what is to occur at that far-distant period in the future when all that exists shall once more be merged in the infinite - when even "the Son himself shall become subject to Him that put all things under him, that God may be all in all." Of that great consummation of the ages it is obvious that in reality we know, and can know, nothing; yet if, remembering the well-known occult aphorism, "As above, so below," we endeavour to lift our minds in its direction by the help of analogies in microcosmic history which are less hopelessly beyond our grasp, we are not without some evidence that, even taken in this highest and sublimest sense, the confident words of our Creed may still be justified, as we shall presently see.

But it is evident that this utterance, like all the rest of the document, is primarily to be interpreted as referring to our own solar system and those Three Aspects of its Logos which to us represent the Three Great Logoi; and assuredly they may be regarded as aeonially eternal, for, so far as we know, they existed as separate aspects for countless ages before our system came into being, and will so exist for countless ages after it has passed away.

And after all he would be but a superficial thinker to whom it would be necessary to prove that as regards the work of the evolution of man, at any rate, "in this Trinity none is greater or less than another"; for though it is true that the spirit of man is directly the gift of the Father, since it comes to him in that third outpouring which is of the essence of the First Aspect of the Logos, yet it is also true that no individual vehicle could ever have been evolved to receive that spirit without the long process of the descent into matter of the monadic essence, which is the outpouring of the Second Aspect, the Son; and assuredly that descent could never have taken place unless the way had been prepared for it by the wonderful vivifying action of the Third Aspect, the Holy Ghost, upon the virgin matter of the cosmos, which alone made it possible that, for us men and for our salvation, He should become "incarnate of the Holy Ghost and the Virgin Mary."

CO-ETERNAL AND CO-EQUAL.

So that all three of the forms of action were equally necessary to the evolution of humanity, and thus it is that we are so clearly taught to recognize that among them "none is afore or after other," either in point of time or of importance, since all must equally be acting all the while in order that the intended result may be brought about; thus it is that we are equally bound to all by ties of deepest gratitude, and that to us therefore it remains true that "the whole three Persons are co-eternal together and co-equal," the upper triad which forms the Individuality of the Solar Logos Himself.

I said that there seemed some evidence to show that, even in the highest and remotest sense, this glorious Trinity would remain co-eternal together. For undoubtedly the principles in man which correspond to its Three Persons are those which we have been in the habit of calling atma, buddhi, manas - the spirit, the intuition, and the intellect. Whether those Sanskrit names were wisely chosen, whether their real meaning in the East is at all identical with that which we have learnt to attach to them, I am not concerned to discuss now. I am using them simply as they have always been used in our literature, to indicate certain well-known and distinguishable principles. And I say that, although we know nothing whatever (of our own knowledge) about the universal cessation of manifestation when all that is has been once more withdrawn into its central point, we have some small amount of direct evidence as to the corresponding process of withdrawal towards the centre in the case of the microcosm, man.

AS ABOVE, SO BELOW.

We know how after each incarnation a partial withdrawal takes place, and how, though each personality in turn seems entirely to disappear, the essence and. outcome of all that is gained in each of them is not lost, but persists through the ages in a higher form. That higher form, the individuality, the reincarnating ego, seems to us the one thing really permanent amidst all the fleeting phantasmagoria of our lives; yet at a certain rather more advanced stage of our evolution our faith in its permanence *as we have known it* will receive a severe and sudden shock.

After a man has passed far enough upon his way to have raised his consciousness fully and definitely into that ego, so as to identify himself entirely with it, and not with any of the transient personalities upon whose long line he can then look back as mere days of his higher life, he begins gradually but increasingly to obtain glimpses of the possibilities of a still subtler and more glorious vehicle - the buddhic body.

At last there comes a time when that body in turn is fully developed - when in full consciousness he is able to rise into it and use it as before he used his causal body. But when, in his enjoyment of such extended consciousness, he turns to look down from outside upon what has for so long been the highest expression of him, he is startled beyond measure to find that it has disappeared. This that he had thought of as the most permanent thing about him has vanished like a mist-wreath; he has not left it behind him to resume at will, as it has long been his custom to leave his mind-body, his astral body, and his physical encasement; it has simply to all appearance ceased to exist.

Yet he has lost nothing; he is still himself, still the same individuality, with all the powers and faculties and memories of that vanished body - and how much more! He soon realizes that though he may have transcended that particular aspect of himself, he has yet not lost it; for not only is its whole essence and reality still a part of himself, but the moment he descends in thought to its plane once more, it flashes into existence again as the expression of him upon that plane - not the same body technically, for the particles which composed the former one are dissipated beyond recall, yet one absolutely identical with it in every respect, but newly called into objective existence simply by the turning of his attention in its direction.

Now to say that in such a man the intellect was lost would indeed be a marvel of misrepresentation; it is in existence as definitely as ever, even though it has been spiritualized and raised to the buddhic plane. And when at a still later stage his consciousness transcends even the buddhic plane, can we doubt that all the powers both of intuitional wisdom and intellect will still be at his command, even though an infinity be added to them?

Perhaps it may be somewhere along the line of thought which is thus suggested that it will be found possible to harmonize these apparently contradictory ideas - that all which exists must one day cease to be, and yet that "the whole Three Persons are co-eternal together and coequal, so that in all things, as is aforesaid, the Unity in Trinity and the Trinity in Unity is to be worshipped."

And so this first half of the Athanasian Creed ends as it began, with a clear straightforward statement which leaves nothing to be desired: "He therefore that will be saved must thus think of the Trinity."

THE DOCTRINE OF THE DESCENT.

We then pass on, just as in the other Creeds, to a further elaboration of the doctrine of the descent of the Second Person of the Logos into matter, which is also declared to be a prerequisite for aeonian progress: "Furthermore, it is necessary to everlasting salvation that he also believe rightly the incarnation of our Lord Jesus Christ."

Then our writer proceeds carefully and methodically to define his position in this important matter: " For the right faith is, that we believe and confess that our Lord Jesus Christ, the Son of God, is God and man; God, of the substance of the Father, begotten before the worlds, and man, of the substance of his mother, born in the world."

This part of the subject was so fully considered in the earlier part of this volume when dealing with the Nicaean symbol that it is hardly necessary to dwell much upon it here, since this is simply a fuller and more explicit form of the statement of the dual aspect of the Christ, showing how He, the alone-born, the first of all the aeons or emanations from the Father, was absolutely of one substance with the Eternal and identical with Him in every respect, while yet in his later form He had just as truly and really taken upon himself the vesture of this lower matter, and so was "incarnate of the Holy Ghost and the Virgin Mary," as has been previously explained. And in this latter form it is particularized that He had not existed" before the worlds" or ages began, but was "born in the world" - that is, that his descent into incarnation had taken place at a definite and comparatively recent period within this age - that is to say, within the life of the solar system. The Latin word *saeculum* does not, of course, mean "world" at all, but "world-period" or "age."

As we know from the accounts which are called by courtesy the "history" of the Christian Church, there had been those to whom this idea of duality had been a stumbling-block - who had deemed it impossible that conditions differing so widely and entirely could both be manifestations of the same great power; and so our Creed insists with emphasis upon the actual identity and indivisibility of the Christos. We are told that He is "perfect God and perfect man, of a reasonable soul and human flesh subsisting "that is, consisting of the intellect as well as of the lower principles; that He is" equal to the Father as touching His Godhead, yet inferior to the Father as touching His manhood" -

equal to Him in every way, save only that He has descended this one step further, and in thus becoming manifest has for the time limited the full expression of that which yet He is in essence all the while.

THE UNDERLYING UNITY.

Yet in all our consideration of this never must we for a moment lose sight of the underlying unity; "for although He be God and man, yet He is not two, but one Christ; one, not by the conversion of the Godhead into flesh, but by the taking of the manhood into God." However deeply involved in matter the Christ-principle may become, it remains the Christ-principle still, just as the lower self in man is ever fundamentally one with and an aspect of the higher, however wide apart from it it may sometimes seem when looked at from below; and the writer further makes clear to us that this is to be regarded as finally and absolutely proved not chiefly because its origin is one, as though the Godhead has been brought down to the human level, but rather by the even more glorious fact that in the future they will once again become consciously one, when all the true essence of the lower and all the quality that it has developed from latency into action shall be borne back triumphantly into the higher, and thus shall be achieved the grandest conception that any doctrine has ever given us - the true and full at-one-ment," the taking of the manhood into God."

Fundamentally, essentially one are they, "one altogether, not by confusion" (that, is commingling or melting together)" of substance, but by unity of person" - a unity which has been a fact in Nature all the time, if we could but have seen it just as, once more, the lower and the higher self are one, just as the physical body is one with the soul within it, because it is after all an expression and an aspect of it, however defective - "for as the reasonable soul and flesh is one man, so God and man is one Christ."

"Who suffered for our salvation, descended into hell, rose again the third day from the dead; he ascended into heaven, he sitteth on the right hand of the Father, God Almighty, from whence he shall come to judge the quick and the dead." These clauses call for no special notice here, since they are simply a reproduction of those upon which we have already so fully commented in writing of the earlier Creeds, though we may just observe in passing that here we have no mention of the myths of Pontius Pilate and the crucifixion.

Indeed on the whole this, the longest and perhaps latest of the Creeds, is remarkably free from the corrupting influence of the tendency which we have called (c); the only really bad instance of it occurs in the neat clauses, which are obviously a blundering reference to the critical period of the fifth round. "At whose coming all men shall rise again with their bodies, and shall give account for their own works; and they that have done good shall go into life everlasting" (that is, as usual, aeonian), "and they that have done evil into everlasting fire."

The writer is quite accurate in supposing that the judgment in the fifth round will be passed upon men when they rise again with their bodies - that is, when they reincarnate; but he is in error in associating this with the messianic myth of the return of a personal Christ. Again, he is right in asserting that life for the rest of the aeon awaits those who successfully pass the tests, but wrong in dooming those who fail to the crucible of the aeonian fire - a fate reserved solely for those personalities which have been definitely severed from their egos.

These unhappy entities (if entities they may still be called) pass into the eighth sphere, and are there resolved into their constituent elements, which are then ready for the use of worthier egos in a future age. This may not inaptly be described as falling into aeonian fire; but more accurate knowledge would have shown the writer that this could happen only to lost personalities - never to individualities; and that the fate of those who are rejected in the fifth round will be aeonian delay only, and not aeonian fire, since they will remain in a subjective but by no means unhappy condition until nature offers another opportunity of a kind by which they are capable of profiting.

Our Creed ends with a repetition of the statement with which it commenced: "This is the Catholic faith, which except a man believe faithfully he cannot be saved." The Treves edition of the *Quicunque* gives us a much modified form of this verse; but, as we have said before, when we recognize definitely what it really means, we have no reason to shirk the most positive statement of what we see to be an important truth in nature.

And so we take our leave of these time-honoured formulae of the Christian Church, hoping that such fragmentary exposition as it has here been possible to make of them may have at least this much result, that if it happens in the future to any of our readers to hear or to take part in their recitation, they may bring to them a deeper interest and a fuller comprehension, and so derive from them a greater profit than ever before.

The End

BOOK THREE

THE LIFE AFTER DEATH

AND HOW THEOSOPHY UNVEILS IT

CHAPTER I.

IS THERE ANY CERTAIN KNOWLEDGE?

This subject of life after death is one of great interest to all of us, not only because we ourselves must certainly one day die, but far more because there can scarcely be any one among us, except perhaps the very young, who has not lost (as we call it) by death some one or more of those who are near and dear to us. So if there be any information available with regard to the life after death, we are naturally very anxious to have it.

But the first thought which arises in the mind of the man who sees such a title as this is usually "Can anything be certainly known as to life after death?" We have all had various theories put before us on the subject by the various religious bodies, and yet even the most devoted followers of these sects seem hardly to believe their teachings about this matter, for they still speak of death as *the king of terrors," and seem to regard the whole question as surrounded by mystery and horror. They may use the term falling asleep in Jesus," but they still employ the black dresses and plumes, the horrible crepe and the odious black-edged note-paper, they still surround death with all the trappings of woe, and with everything calculated to make it seem darker and more terrible. We have an evil heredity behind us in this matter; we have inherited these funereal horrors from our forefathers, and so we are used to them, and do not see the absurdity and monstrosity of it all. The ancients were in this respect wiser than we, for they did not associate all these nightmares of gloom with the death of the body—partly perhaps because they had a so much more rational method of disposing of the body—a method which was not only infinitely better for the dead man and more healthy for the living, but was also free from the gruesome suggestions connected with slow decay. They knew much more about death in those days, and because they knew more they mourned less.

The first thing that we must realize about death is that it is a perfectly natural incident in the course of our life. That ought to be obvious to us from the first, because if we believe at all in a God who is a loving Father we should know that a fate which, like death, comes to all alike, cannot have in it aught of evil to any, and that whether we are in this world or the next we must be equally safe in His hands. This consideration alone should have shown us that death is not something to be dreaded, but simply a necessary step in our evolution. It ought not to be necessary for Theosophy to come among Christian nations and teach that death is a friend and not an enemy, and it would not be necessary if Christianity had not so largely forgotten its own best traditions. It has come to regard the grave as "the bourne from which no traveller returns,' and the passage into it as a leap in the dark, into some awful unknown void. On this point, as on many others, Theosophy has a gospel for the western world; it has to announce that there is no gloomy impenetrable abyss beyond the grave, but instead a world of light and life, which may be known to us as clearly and fully and accurately as the streets of our own city. We have created the gloom and the horror for ourselves, like children who frighten themselves with ghastly stories, and we have only to study the facts of the case, and all these artificial clouds will roll away at once. Death is no darksome king of terrors, no skeleton with a scythe to cut short the thread of life, but rather an angel bearing a golden key, with which he unlocks for us the door into a fuller and higher life than this.

But men will naturally say This is very beautiful and poetical, but how can we certainly know that it is really so?" You may know it in many ways; there is plenty of evidence ready to the hand of any one who will take the trouble to gather it together. Shakespeare's statement is really a remarkable one when we consider that ever since the dawn of history, and in every country of which we know anything, travellers have always been returning from that bourne, and showing themselves to their fellow-men. There is any amount of evidence for such apparitions, as they have been called. At one time it was fashionable to ridicule all such stories; now it is no longer so, since scientific men like Sir William Crookes, the discoverer of the metal thallium and the inventor of Crooke's radiometer; and Sir Oliver Lodge, the great electrician, and eminent public men like Mr. Balfour, the late Premier of England, have joined and actively worked with a society instituted for the investigation of such phenomena. Read the reports of the work of that Society for Psychical Research, and you will see something of the testimony which exists as to the return of the dead. Read books like Mr. Stead's "Real Ghost Stories," or Camille Flammarion's L'lnconnu," and you will find there plenty of accounts of apparitions, showing themselves not centuries ago in some far-away land, but here and now among ourselves, to persons still living, who can be questioned and can testify to the reality of their experiences.

Another line of testimony to the life after death is the study of Modern Spiritualism. I know that many people think that there is nothing to be found along that line but fraud and deception; but I can myself bear personal witness that this is not so. Fraud and deception there may have been—nay, there has been—in certain cases; but nevertheless I fearlessly assert that there are great truths behind, which may be discovered by any man who is willing to devote the necessary time and patience to their unfolding. Here again there is a vast literature to be studied, or the man who prefers it may make his investigations for himself at first-hand as I did.

Many men may not be willing to take that trouble or to devote so much time; very well, that is their affair, but unless they will examine, they have no right to scoff at those who have seen, and therefore know that these things are true.

A third line of evidence, which is the one most con-mending itself to Theosophical students, is that of direct investigation. Every man has within himself latent faculties, undeveloped senses, by means of which the unseen world can be directly cognized, and to any one who will take the trouble to evolve these powers the whole world beyond the grave will lie open as the day. A good many Theosophical students have already unfolded these inner senses, and it is the evidence thus obtained that I wish to lay before you. I know very well that this is a considerable claim to make—a claim which would not be made by any minister of any church when he gave you his version of the states after death. He will say, ' The church teaches this," or * The Bible tells us so," but he will never say, I who speak to you, I myself have seen this, and know it to be true." But in Theosophy we are able to say to you quite definitely that many of us know personally that of which we speak, for we are dealing with a definite series of facts which we have investigated, and which you yourselves may investigate in turn. "We offer you what we know, yet we say to you Unless this commends itself to you as utterly reasonable, do not rest contented with our assertion; look into these things for yourselves as fully as you can, and then you will be in a position to speak to others as authoritatively as we do," But what are the facts which are disclosed to us by these investigations?

CHAPTER II.

THE TRUE FACTS.

The state of affairs found as actually existing is much more rational than most of the current theories. It is not found that any sudden change takes place in man at death, or that he is spirited away to some heaven beyond the stars. On the contrary man remains after death exactly what he was before it—the same in inteEect, the same in his qualities and powers; and the conditions in which he finds himself are those which his own thoughts and desires have already created for him. There is no reward or punishment from outside, but only the actual result of what the man himself has done and said and thought while here on earth. In fact, the man makes his bed during earth-life and afterwards he has to lie on it.

This is the first and most prominent fact—that we have not here a strange new life, but a continuation of the present one. We are not separated from the dead, for they are here about us all the time. The only separation is the limitation of our consciousness, so that we have lost, not our loved ones, but the power to see them. It is quite possible for us so to raise our consciousness, that we can see them and talk with them as before, and all of us constantly do that, though we only rarely remember it fully. A man may learn to focus his consciousness in his astral body while his physical body is still awake, but that needs special development, and in the case of the average man would take much time. But during the sleep of his physical body every man uses his astral vehicle to a greater or less extent, and in that way we are daily with our departed friends. Sometimes we have a partial remembrance of meeting them, and then we say we have dreamt of them; more frequently we have no recollection of such encounters and remain ignorant that they have taken place. Yet it is a definite fact that the ties of affection are still as strong as ever, and so the moment the man is freed from the chains of his physical encasement he naturally seeks the company of those whom he loves. So that in truth the only change is that he spends the night with them instead of the day, and he is conscious of them astrally instead of physically.

The bringing through of the memory from the astral plane to the physical is another and quite separate consideration, which in no way affects our consciousness on that other plane, nor our ability to function upon it with perfect ease and freedom. Whether you recollect them or not, they are still living their life close to you, and the only difference is that they have taken off this robe of flesh which we call the body. That makes no change in them, any more than it makes a change in your personality when you remove your overcoat. You are somewhat freer, indeed, because you have less weight to carry, and precisely the same is the case with them. The man's passions, affections, emotions, and intellect are not in the least affected when he died, for none of these belong to the physical body which he has laid aside. He has dropped this vesture and is living in another, but he is still able to think and to feel just as before.

I know how difficult it is for the average mind to grasp the reality of that which we cannot see with our physical eyes. It is very hard for us to realize how very partial our sight is—to understand that we are living in a vast world of which we see only a tiny part. Yet science tells us with no uncertain voice that this is so, for it describes to us whole worlds of minute life of whose very existence we should be entirely ignorant as far as our senses are concerned. Nor are the creatures of those worlds unimportant because minute, for upon a knowledge of the condition and habits of some of those microbes depends our ability to preserve health, and in many cases life itself. But our senses are limited in another direction. We cannot see the very air that surrounds us; our senses would give us no indication of its existence, except that when it is in motion we are aware of it by the sense of touch. Yet in it there is a force that can wreck our mightiest vessels and throw down our strongest buildings. You see how all about us there are mighty forces which yet elude our poor and partial senses; so obviously we must beware of falling into the fatally common error of supposing that what we see is all there is to see.

We are, as it were, shut up in a tower, and our senses are tiny windows opening out in certain directions. In many other directions we are entirely shut in, but clairvoyance or astral sight opens for us one or two additional windows, and so enlarges our prospect, and spreads before us a new and wider world, which is yet part of the old one, though before we did not know of it.

Looking out into this new world, what should we first see? Supposing that one of us transferred his consciousness to the astral plane, what changes would be the first to strike him? To the first glance there would probably be very little difference, and he would suppose himself to be looking upon the same world as before. Let me explain, to you why this is so—partially at least, for to explain fully would need a whole treatise upon astral physics. Just as we have different conditions of matter here, the solid, the liquid, the gaseous, so are there different conditions or degrees of density of astral matter, and each degree is attracted by and corresponds to that which is similar to it on the physical plane. So that your friend would still see the walls and the furniture to which he was accustomed, for though the physical matter of which they are composed would no longer be visible to him, the densest type of astral matter would still outline them for him as clearly as ever. True, if Fuller details on this may be found in my "The Other Side of Death.". he examined the object closely he would perceive that all the particles were visibly in rapid motion, instead of only invisibly, as is the case on this plane; but very few men do observe closely, and so a man who dies often does not know at first that any change has come over him.

He looks about him, and sees the same rooms with which he is familiar, people still by those whom he has known and loved—for they also have astral bodies, which are within the range of his new vision. Only by degrees does he realize that in some ways there is a difference. For example, he soon finds that for him all pain and fatigue have passed away. If you can at all realize what that means, you will begin to have some idea of what the higher life truly is. Think of it, you who have scarcely ever a comfortable moment, you who in the stress of your busy life can hardly remember when you last felt free from fatigue; what would it be to you never again to know the meaning of the words weariness and pain? We have so mismanaged our teaching in these western countries on the subject of immortality that usually a dead man finds it difficult to believe that he is dead, simply because he still sees and hears, thinks and feels. I am not dead," he will often say, "I am alive as much as ever, and better than I ever was before." Of course he is; but that is exactly what he ought to have expected, if he had been properly taught.

Realization may perhaps come to him in this way. He sees his friends about him, but he soon discovers that he cannot always communicate with them. Sometimes he speaks to them, and they do not seem to hear; he tries to touch them, and finds that he can make no impression upon them. Even then, for some time he persuades himself that he is dreaming, and will presently awake, for at other times (when they are what we call asleep) his friends are perfectly conscious of him, and talk with him as of old. But gradually he discovers the fact that he is after all dead, and then he usually begins to become uneasy. Why? Again because of the defective teaching which he has received. He does not understand where he is, or what has happened, since his situation is not what he expected from the orthodox standpoint. As an English general once said on this occasion, "But if I am dead, where am I? If this is heaven I don't think much of it; and if it is hell, it is better than I expected!"

CHAPTER III.

PURGATORY.

A great deal of totally unnecessary uneasiness and even acute suffering has been caused by those who still continue to teach the world silly fables about non-existent bugbears instead of using reason and common sense. The baseless and blasphemous hell-fire theory has done more harm than even its promoters know, for it has worked evil beyond the grave as well as on this side. But presently the *dead' man will meet with some other dead person who has been more sensibly instructed, and will learn from him that there is no cause for fear, and that there is a rational life to be lived in this new world just as there was in the old one.

He will find by degrees that there is very much that is new as well as much that is a counterpart of that which he already knows; for in this astral world thoughts and desires express themselves in visible forms, though these are composed mostly of the finer matter of the plane. As his astral life proceeds, these become more and more prominent, for we must remember that he is all the while steadily withdrawing further and further into himself. The entire period of an incarnation is in reality occupied by the ego in first putting himself forth into matter, and then in drawing back again with the results of his effort. If the ordinary man were asked to draw a line symbolical of life, he would probably make it a straight one, beginning at birth and ending at death; but the Theosophical student should rather represent the life as a great ellipse, starting from the ego on the higher mental level and returning to him. The line would descend into the lower part of the mental plane, and then into the astral. A very small portion, comparatively, at the bottom of the ellipse, would be upon the physical plane, and the line would very soon reascend into the astral and mental planes. The physical life would therefore be represented only by that small portion of the curve which lay below the line which indicated the boundary between the astral and physical planes, and birth and death would simply be the points at which the curve crossed that line—obviously by no means the most important points of the whole.

The real central point would clearly be that furthest removed from the ego—the turning point, as it were— what in astronomy we should call the aphelion. That is neither birth nor death, but should be a middle point in the physical life, when the force from the ego has expended its outward rush, and turns to begin the long process of withdrawal. Gradually his thoughts should turn upward, he cares less and less for merely physical matters, and presently he drops the dense body altogether. His life on the astral plane commences, but during the whole of it the process of withdrawal continues. The result of this is that as time passes he pays less and less attention to the lower matter of which counterparts of physical objects are composed, and is more and more occupied with that higher matter of which thought-forms are built—so far, that is, as thought-forms appear on the astral plane at all. So his life becomes more and more a life in a world of thought, and the counterpart of the world which he has left fades from his view, not that he has changed his location in space, but that his interest is shifting its center. His desires still persist, and the forms surrounding him will be very largely the expression of these desires, and whether his life is one of happiness or discomfort will depend chiefly upon the nature of these.

A study of this astral life shows us very clearly the reason for many ethical precepts. Most men recognize that sins which injure others are definitely and obviously wrong; but they sometimes wonder why it should be said to be wrong for them to feel jealousy, or hatred, or ambition, so long as they do not allow themselves to manifest these feelings outwardly in deed or in speech. A glimpse at this after-world shows us exactly how such feelings injure the man who harbors them, and how they would cause him suffering of the most acute character after his death. We shall understand this better if we examine a few typical cases of astral life, and see what their principal characteristics will be.

Let us think first of the ordinary colorless man, who is neither specially good, nor specially bad, nor indeed specially anything in particular. The man is in no way changed, so colorlessness will remain his principal characteristic (if we can call it one) after his death. He will have no special suffering and no special joy, and may very probably find astral life rather dull, because he has not during his time on earth developed any rational interests. If he has had no ideas beyond gossip or what is called sport, or nothing beyond his business or his dress, he is likely to find time hang heavy on his hands when all such things are no longer possible. But the case of a man who has had strong desires of a low material type, such as could be satisfied only on the physical plane, is an even worse one. Think of the case of the drunkard or the sensualist. He has been the slave of overmastering craving during earth-life, and it still remains undiminished after death—rather, it is stronger than ever, since its vibrations have no longer the heavy physical particles to set in motion. But the possibility of gratifying this terrible thirst is for ever removed, because the body, through which alone it could be satisfied, is gone. We see that the fires of purgatory are no inapt symbols for the vibrations of such a torturing desire as this. It may endure for a quite long time, since it passes only by gradually wearing itself out, and the man's fate is undoubtedly a terrible one. Yet there are two points that we should bear in mind in considering it.

First, the man has made it absolutely for himself, and determined the exact degree of its power and its duration. If he had controlled that desire during life there would have been just so much the less of it to trouble him after death. Secondly, it is the only way in which he can get rid of the vice. If he could pass from a life of sensuality and drunkenness directly into his next incarnation, he would be born a slave to his vice —it would dominate him from the beginning, and there would be for him no possibility of escape. But now that the desire has worn itself out, he will begin his new career without that burden, and the soul, having had so severe a lesson, will make every possible effort to restrain its lower vehicles from repeating such a mistake. All this was known to the world even as lately as classical times. "We see it clearly imaged for us in the myth of Tantalus, who suffered always with raging thirst, yet was doomed for ever to see the water recede just as it was about to touch his lips. Many another sin produces its result in a manner just as gruesome, although each is peculiar to itself. See how the miser will suffer when he can no longer hoard his gold, when he perhaps knows that it is being spent by alien hands. Think how the jealous man will continue to suffer from his jealousy, knowing that he has now no power to interfere upon the physical plane, yet feeling more strongly than ever. Remember the fate of Sisyphus in Greek myth—how he was condemned forever to roll a heavy rock up to the summit of a mountain, only to see it roll down again the moment that success seemed within his reach. See how exactly this typified the after-life of the man of worldly ambition. He has all his life been in the habit of forming selfish plans, and therefore he continues to do so in the astral world; he carefully builds up his plot until it is perfect in his mind, and only then realizes that he has lost the physical body which is necessary for its achievement. Down fall his hopes; yet so ingrained is the habit that he continues again and again to roll the same stone up the same mountain of ambition, until the vice is worn out. Then at last he realizes that he need not roll his rock, and lets it rest in peace at the bottom of the hill.

.We have considered the case of the ordinary man, and of the man who dii3Pers from the ordinary because of his gross and selfish desires. Now let us examine the case of the man who differs from the ordinary in the other direction—who has some interests of a rational nature. In order to understand how the after-life appears to him, we must bear in mind that the majority of men spend the greater part of their waking life and most of their strength in work that they do not really like, that they would not do at all if it were not necessary in order to earn their living, or support those who are dependent upon them. Realize the condition of the man when all necessity for this grinding toil is over, when it is no longer needful to earn a living, since the astral body requires no food nor clothing nor lodging. Then for the first time since earliest childhood that man is free to do precisely what he likes, and can devote his whole time to whatever may be his chosen occupation— so long, that is, as it is of such a nature as to be capable of realization without physical matter. Suppose that a man's greatest delight is in music; upon the astral plane he has the opportunity of listening to all the grandest music that earth can produce, and is even able under these new conditions to hear far more in it than before, since here other and fuller harmonies than our dull ears can grasp are now within his reach. The man whose delight is in art, who loves beauty in form and color, has all the loveliness of this higher world before him from which to choose. If his delight is in beauty in Nature, he has unequalled possibilities for indulging it; for he can readily and rapidly move from place to place, and enjoy in quick succession wonders of Nature which the physical man would need years to visit. If his fancy turns towards science or history, the libraries and the laboratories of the world are at his disposal, and his comprehension of processes in chemistry and biology would be far fuller than ever before, for now he could see the inner as well as the outer workings, and many of the causes as well as the effects. And in all these cases there is the wonderful additional delight that no fatigue is possible. Here we know how constantly, when we are making some progress in our studies or our experiments, we are unable to carry them on because our brain will not bear more than a certain amount of strain; outside of the physical no fatigue seems to exist, for it is in reality the brain and not the mind that tires.

All this time I have been speaking of mere selfish gratification, even though it be of the rational and intellectual kind. But there are those among us who would not be satisfied without something higher than this— whose greatest joy in any life would consist in serving their fellow-men. What has the astral life in store for them? They will pursue their philanthropy more vigorously than ever, and under better conditions than on this lower plane. There are thousands whom they can help, and with far greater certainty of really being able to do good than we usually attain in this life. Some devote themselves thus to the general good; some are especially occupied with cases among their own family or friends, either living or dead. It is a strange inversion of the facts, this employment of those words living and dead; for surely we are the dead, we who are buried in these gross, cramping physical bodies; and they are truly the living, who are so much freer and more capable, because less hampered. Often the mother who has passed into that higher life will still watch over her child, and be to him a veritable guardian angel; often the 'dead' husband still remains within reach, and in touch with his sorrowing wife, thankful if even now and then he is able to make her feel that he lives in strength and love beside her as of yore.

If all this be so, you may think, then surely the sooner we die the better; such knowledge seems almost to place a premium on suicide! If you are thinking solely of yourself and of your pleasure, then emphatically that would be so. But if you think of your duty towards God and towards your fellows, then you will at once see that this consideration is negatived. You are here for a purpose—a purpose which can only be attained upon this physical plane. The soul has to take much trouble to go through much limitation, in order to gain this earthly incarnation, and therefore its efforts must not be thrown away unnecessarily.

The instinct of self-preservation is divinely implanted in our breasts, and it is our duty to make the most of this earthly life which is ours, and to retain it as long as circumstances permit. There are lessons to be learnt on this plane which cannot be learnt anywhere else, and the sooner we learn them the sooner we shall be free for ever from the need of return to this lower and more limited life. So none must dare to die until his time comes, though when it does come he may well rejoice, for indeed he is about to pass from labor to refreshment. Yet all this which I have told you now is insignificant beside the glory of the life which follows it—the life of the heaven-world. This is the purgatory—that is the endless bliss of which monks have dreamed and poets sung—not a dream after all, but a living and glorious reality. The astral life is happy for some, unhappy for others, according to the preparation they have made for it; but what follows it is perfect happiness for all, and exactly suited to the needs of each.

Before closing this chapter let us consider one or two questions which are perpetually recurring to the minds of those who seek information about the next life. Shall we be able to make progress there, some will ask? Undoubtedly, for progress is the rule of the Divine Scheme. It is possible to us just in proportion to our development. The man who is a slave to desire can only progress by wearing out his desire; still, that is the best that is possible at his stage. But the man who is kindly and helpful learns much in many ways through the work which he is able to do in that astral life; he will return to earth with many additional powers and qualities because of the practice he has had in unselfish effort. So we need have no fear as to this question of progress.

Another point often raised is, shall we recognize our loved ones who have passed on before us ? Assuredly we shall, for neither they nor we shall be changed; why,, then, should we not recognize them? The attraction is still there, and will act as a magnet to draw together those who feel it, more readily and more surely there than here. True, that if the loved one has left this earth very long ago, he may have already passed beyond the astral plane, and entered the heaven-life; in that case we must wait until we also reach that level before we can rejoin him, but when that is gained we shall possess our friend more perfectly than in this prison-house we can ever realize. But of this be sure, that those whom you have loved are not lost; if they have died recently, then you will find them on the astral plane; if they have died long ago, you will find them in the heaven-life, but in any case the reunion is sure where the affection exists. For love is one of the mightiest powers of the universe, whether it be in life or in death.

There is an infinity of interesting information to be given about this higher life. You should read the literature; read Mrs. Besant's 'Death an d After," and my own books on The AstraLi'lane," and "The Other Side of Deat h." It is very well worth your while to study tliis subject, for the knowledge of the truth takes away all fear of death, and makes life easier to live, because we understand its object and its end. Death brings no suffering, but only joy, for those who live the true, the unselfish life. The old Latin saying is literally true— Mors janua vitae —death is the gate of life. That is exactly what it is—a gate into a fuller and higher life. On the other side of the grave, as well as on this, prevails; the great law of Divine Justice, and we can trust as im-plicity there as here to the action of that law, with regard both to ourselves and to those we love.

CHAPTER IV.

THE HEAVEN-WORLD

All religions agree in declaring the existence of heaven, and in stating that the enjoyment of its bliss follows upon a well-spent earthly life. Christianity and Mohammedanism speak of it as a reward assigned by God to those who have pleased Him, but most other faiths describe it rather as the necessary result of the good life, exactly as we should from the Theosophical point of view. Yet though all religions agree in painting this happy life in glowing terms, none of them have succeeded in producing an impression of reality in their descriptions. All that is written about heaven is so absolutely unlike anything that we have known, that many of the descriptions seem almost grotesque to us. We should hesitate to admit this with regard to the legends familiar to us from our infancy, but if the stories of one of the other great religions were read to us, we should see it readily enough. In Buddhist or Hindu books you will find magniloquent accounts of interminable gardens, in which the trees are all of gold and silver, and their fruits of various kinds of jewels, and you might be tempted to smile, unless the thought occurred to you that after all, to the Buddhist or Hindu our tales of streets of gold and gates of pearl might in truth seem quite as improbable. The fact is that the ridiculous element is imported into these accounts only when we take them literally, and fail to realize that each scribe is trying the same task from his point of view, and that all alike are failing because the great truth behind it all is; utterly indescribable. The Hindu writer had no doubt seen some of the gorgeous gardens of the Indian kings, where just such decorations as he describes are commonly employed. The Jewish scribe had no familiarity with such things, but he dwelt in a great and magnificent city— probably Alexandria; and so his conception of splendor was a city, but made unlike anything on earth by the costliness of its material and its decorations. So each is trying to paint a truth which is too grand for words by employing such similes as are familiar to his mind.

There have been those since that day who have seen the glory of heaven, and have tried in their feeble way to describe it. Some of our own students have been among these, and in the Theosophical Manual No. 6* you may find an effort of my own in that direction.

* 'The Devachanic Plane, or the Heaven-World.

We do not speak now of gold and silver, of rubies and diamonds, when we wish to convey the idea of the greatest possible refinement and beauty of color and form; we draw our similes rather from the colors of the sunset, and from all the glories of sea and sky, because to us these are the more heavenly. Yet those of us who have seen the truth know well that in all our attempts at description we have failed as utterly as the Oriental scribes to convey any idea of a reality which no words can ever picture, though every man one day shall see it and know it for himself.

For this heaven is not a dream; it is a radiant reality; but to comprehend anything of it we must first change one of our initial ideas on the subject. Heaven is not a place, but a state of consciousness. If you ask me 'Where is heaven?" I must answer you that it is here—round you at this very moment, near to you as the air you breathe. The light is all about you, as the Buddha said so long ago; you have only to cast the bandage from your eyes and look. But what is this casting away of a bandage? Of what is it symbolical? It is simply a question of raising the consciousness to a higher level, of learning to focus it in the vehicle of finer matter. I have already spoken of the possibility of doing this with regard to the astral body, thereby seeing the astral world; this needs simply a further stage of the same process, the raising of the consciousness to the mental plane, for man has a body for that level also, through which he may receive its vibrations, and so live in the glowing splendor of heaven while still possessing a physical body—though indeed after such an experience he will have little relish for the return to the latter.

The ordinary man reaches this state of bliss only after death, and not immediately after it except in very rare cases. I have explained how after death the Ego steadily withdrew into himself. The whole astral life is in fact a constant process of withdrawal, and when in course of time the soul reaches the limit of that plane, he dies to it in just the same way as he did to the physical plane. That is to say, he casts off the body of that plane, and leaves it behind him while he passes on to higher and still fuller life. No pain or suffering of any kind precedes this second death, but just as with the first, there is usually a period of unconsciousness, from which the man awakes gradually. Some years ago I wrote a book called The Devachanic Plane," in which I endeavored to some extent to describe what he would see, and to tabulate as far as I could the various subdivisions of this glorious Land of Light, giving instances which had been observed in the course of our investigations in connection with this heaven-life. For the moment I shall try to put the matter before you from another point of view, and those who wish may supplement the information by reading the book as well.

Perhaps the most comprehensive opening statement is that this is the plane of the Divine mind, that here we are in the very realm of thought itself, and that everything that man possibly could think is here in vivid living reality. We labor under a great disadvantage from our habit of regarding material things as real, and those which are not material as dream-like and therefore unreal; whereas the fact is that everything which is material is buried and hidden in this matter, and so whatever of reality it may possess is far less obvious and recognizable than it would be when regarded from a higher standpoint. So that when we hear of a world of thought, we immediately think of an unreal world, built out of such stuff as dreams are made of," as the poet says.

Try to realize that when a man leaves his physical body and opens his consciousness to astral life, his first sensation is of the intense vividness and reality of that life, so that he thinks "Now for the first time I know what it is to live." But when in turn he leaves that life for the higher one, he exactly repeats the same experience, for this life is in turn so much fuller and wider and more intense than the astral that once more no comparison is possible. And yet there is another life yet, beyond all this, unto which even this is but as moonlight unto sunlight; but it is useless at present to think of that.

There may be many to whom it sounds absurd that a realm of thought should be more real than the physical world; well, it must remain so for them until they have some experience of a life higher than this, and then in one moment they will know far more than any words can ever tell them.

On this plane, then, we find existing the infinite fulness of the Divine Mind, open in all its limitless affluence to every soul, just in proportion as that soul has qualified himself to receive. If man had already completed his destined evolution, if he had fully realized and unfolded the divinity whose germ is within him, the whole of this glory would be within his reach; but since none of us has yet done that, since we are only gradually rising towards that splendid consummation, it comes that none as yet can grasp that entirely, but each draws from it and cognizes only so much as he has by previous effort prepared himself to take. Different individuals bring very different capabilities; as the Eastern simile has it, each man brings his own cup, and some of the cups are large and some are small, but, small or large, every cup is filled to its utmost capacity; the sea of bliss holds far more than enough for all.

All religions have spoken of this bliss of heaven, yet few of them have put before us with sufficient clearness and precision this leading idea which alone explains rationally how for all alike such bliss is possible—which is, indeed, the key-note of the conception—the fact that each man makes his own heaven by selection from the ineffable splendors of the Thought of God Himself. A man decides for himself both the length and character of his heaven-life by the causes which he himself generates during his earth-life; therefore he cannot but have exactly the amount which he has deserved, and exactly the quality of joy which is best suited to his idiosyncrasies, for this is a world in which every being must, from the very fact of his consciousness there, be enjoying the highest spiritual bliss of which he is capable—a world whose power of response to his aspirations is limited only by his capacity to aspire.

He had made himself an astral body by his desires and passions during earth-life, and he had to live in it during his astral existence, and that time was happy or miserable for him according to its character. Now this time of purgatory is over, for that lower part of his nature has burnt itself away; now there remain only the higher and more refined thoughts, the noble and unselfish aspirations that he poured out during earth-life. These cluster round him, and make a sort of shell about him, through the medium of which he is able to respond to certain types of vibration in this refined matter. These thoughts which surround him are the powers by which he draws upon the wealth of the heaven-world, and he finds it to be a storehouse of infinite extent upon which he is able to draw just according to the power of those thoughts and aspirations which he generated in the physical and astral life. All the highest of his affection and his devotion is now producing its results, for there is nothing else left; all that was selfish or grasping has been left behind in the plane of desire.

For there are two kinds of affection. There is one, hardly worthy of so sublime a name, which thinks always of how much love it is receiving in return for its investment of attachment, which is ever worrying as to the exact amount of affection which the other person is showing for it, and so is constantly entangled in the evil meshes of jealousy and suspicion. Such feeling, grasping and full of greed, will work out its results of doubt and misery upon the plane of desire, to which it so clearly belongs. But there is another kind of love, which never stays to think how much it is loved, but has only the one object of pouring itself out unreservedly at the feet of the object of its affection, and considers only how best it can express in action the feeling which fills its heart so utterly. Here there is no limitation, because there is no grasping, no drawing towards the self, no thought of return, and just because of that there is a tremendous outpouring of force, which no astral matter could express, nor could the dimensions of the astral plane contain it. It needs the finer matter and the wider space of the higher level, and so the energy generated belongs to the mental world. Just so there is a religious devotion which thinks mainly of what it will get for its prayers, and lowers its worship into a species of bargaining ; while there is also a genuine devotion, which forgets itself absolutely in the contemplation of its deity. We all know well that in our highest devotion there is something which has never yet been satisfied, that our grandest aspirations have never yet been realized, that when we really love unselfishly, our feeling is far beyond all power of expression on this physical plane, that the profound emotion stirred within our hearts by the noblest music or the most perfect art reaches to heights and depths unknown to this dull earth. Yet all this is a wondrous force of power beyond our calculation, and it must produce its result somewhere, somehow, for the law of the conservation of energy holds good upon the higher planes of thought and aspiration just as surely as in ordinary mechanics. But since it must react upon him who set it in motion, and yet it cannot work upon the physical plane because of its narrowness and comparative grossness of matter, how and when can it produce its inevitable result? It simply waits for the man until it reaches its level; it remains as so much stored-up energy until its opportunity arrives. While this consciousness is focussed upon the physical and astral planes it cannot react upon him, but as soon as he transfers himself entirely to the mental it is ready for him, its floodgates are opened, and its action commences. So perfect justice is done, and nothing is ever lost, even though to us in this lower world it seems to have missed its aim and come to nothing.

CHAPTER V.
MANY MANSIONS.

The key-note of the conception is the comprehension of how man makes his own heaven. Here upon this plane of the Divine Mind exists, as we have said, all beauty and glory conceivable; but the man can look out upon it all only through the windows he himself has made. Every one of his thought-forms is such a window, through which response may come to him from the forces without. If he has chiefly regarded physical things during his earth-life, then he has made for himself but few windows through which this higher glory can shine in upon him. Yet every man will have had some touch of pure, unselfish feeling, even if it were but once in all his life, and that will be a window for him now. Every man, except the utter savage at a very early stage, will surely have something of this wonderful time of bliss. Instead of saying, as orthodoxy does, that some men will go to heaven and some to hell, it would be far more correct to say that all men will have their share of both states (if we are to call even the lowest astral life by so horrible a name as hell), and it is only their relative proportions which differ. It must be borne in mind that the soul of the ordinary man is as yet but at an early stage of his development. He has learnt to use his physical vehicle with comparative ease, and he can also function tolerably freely in his astral body, though he is rarely able to carry through the memory of its activities to his physical brain; but his mental body is not yet in any true sense a vehicle at all, since he cannot utilize it as he does those lower bodies, cannot travel about in it, nor employ its senses for the reception of information in the normal way.

We must not think of him, therefore, as in a condition of any great activity, or as able to move about freely, as he did upon the astral levels. His condition here is chiefly receptive, and his communication with the world outside him is only through his own windows, and therefore exceedingly limited. The man who can put forth full activity there is already almost more than man, for he must be a glorified spirit, a great and highly-evolved entity. He would have full consciousness there, and would use his mental vehicle as freely as the ordinary man employs his physical body, and through it vast fields of higher knowledge would lie open to him.

But we are thinking of one as yet less developed than this—one who has his windows, and sees only through them. In order to understand his heaven we must consider two points: His relation to the plane itself, and his relation to his friends. The question of his relation to his surroundings upon the plane divides itself into two parts, for we have to think first of the matter of the plane as moulded by his thought, and secondly of the forces of the plane as evoked in answer to his aspirations.

I have mentioned how man surrounds himself with thought-forms; here on this plane we are in the very home of thought, so naturally those forms are all-important in connection with both these considerations. There are living forces about him, mighty angelic inhabitants of the plane, and many of their orders are very sensitive to certain aspirations of man, and readily respond to them. But naturally both his thoughts and his aspirations are only along the lines which he has already prepared during earth-life. It might seem that when he was transferred to a plane of such transcendent force and vitality, he might well be stirred up to entirely new activities along hitherto unwonted lines; but this is not possible. His mind-body is not in by any means the same order as his lower vehicles, and is by no means so fully under his control. All through a past of many lives, it has been accustomed to receive its impressions and incitements to action from below, through the lower vehicles, chiefly from the physical body, and sometimes from the astral; it has done very little in the way of receiving direct mental vibrations at its own level, and it cannot suddenly begin to accept and respond to them. Practically, then, the man does not initiate any new thoughts, but those which he has already form the windows through which he looks out on his new world.

With regard to these windows there are two possibilities of variation—the direction in which they look, and the kind of glass of which they are composed. There are very many directions which the higher thought may take. Some of these, such as affection and devotion, are so generally of a personal character that it is perhaps better to consider them in connection with the man's relation to other people; let us rather take first an example where that element does not come in—where we have to deal only with the influence of his surroundings. Suppose that one of his windows into heaven is that of music. Here we have a very mighty force; you know how wonderfully music can uplift a man, can make him for the time a new being in a new world; if you have ever experienced its effect you will realize that here we are in the presence of the stupendous power. The man that has no music in his soul has no window open in that direction; but a man who has a musical window will receive through it three entirely distinct sets of impressions, all of which, however, will be modified by the kind of glass he has in his window. It is obvious that his glass may be a great limitation to his view; it may be colored, and so admit only certain rays of light, or it may be of poor material, and so distort and darken all the rays as they enter. For example, one man may have been able while on earth to appreciate only one class of music, and so on. But suppose his musical window to be a good one, what will he receive through it?

First, he will sense that music which is the expression of the ordered movement of the forces of the plane. There was a definite fact behind the poetic idea of the music of the spheres, for on these higher planes all movement and action of any kind produces glorious harmonies both of sound and color. All thought expresses itself in this way—his own as well as that of others—in a lovely yet indescribable series of ever-changing chords, as of a thousand Aeolian harps. This musical manifestation of the vivid and glowing life of heaven would be for him a kind of ever-present and ever-delightful background to all his other experiences.

Secondly, there is among the inhabitants of the plane one class of entities— one great order of angels, as our Christian friends would call them, who are specially devoted to music, and habitually express themselves by its means to a far fuller extent than the rest. They are spoken of in old Hindu books under the name of Gandharvas.

The man whose soul is in tune with music will certainly attract their attention, and will draw himself into connection with some of them, and so will learn with ever-increasing enjoyment all the marvellous new combinations which they employ. Thirdly, he will be a keenly appreciative listener to the music made by his fellow-men in the heaven-world. Think how many great composers have preceded him: Bach, Beethoven, Mendelssohn, Handel, Mozart, Rossini— all are there, not dead but full of vigorous life, and ever pouring forth far grander strains, far more glorious harmonies, than any which they knew on earth. Each of these is indeed a fountain of wondrous melody, and many an inspiration of our earthly musicians is in reality but a faint and far-off echo of the sweetness of their song.

Very far more than we realize of the genius of this lower world is naught but a reflection of the untrammelled powers of those who have gone before us; oftener than we think the man who is receptive here can catch some thought from them, and reproduce it, so far as may be possible, in this lower sphere. Great masters of music have told us how they sometimes hear the whole of some grand oratorio, some stately march, some noble chorus in one resounding chord; how it is in this way that the inspiration comes to them, though when they try to write it down in notes, many pages of music may be necessary to express it. That exactly expresses the manner in which the heavenly music differs from that which we know here; one mighty chord there will convey what here would take hours to render far less effectively.

Very similar would be the experiences of the man whose window was art. He also would have the same three possibilities of delight, for the order of the plane expresses itself in color as well as in sound, and all Theosophical students are familiar with the fact that there is a color language of the Devas—an order of spirits whose very communication one with another is by flashings of splendid color. Again, all the great artists of mediaeval times are working still— not with brush and canvas, but with the far easier, yet infinitely more satisfactory moulding of mental matter by the power of thought. Every artist knows how far below the conception in his mind is the most successful expression of it upon paper or canvas; but here to think is to realize, and disappointment is impossible. The same thing is true of all directions of thought, so that there is in truth an infinity to enjoy and to learn, far beyond all that our limited minds can grasp down here.

CHAPTER VI.

OUR FRIENDS IN HEAVEN.

But let us turn to the second part of our subject, the question of the man's relations with persons whom he loves, or with those for whom he feels devotion or adoration. Again and again people ask us whether they will meet and know their loved ones in this grander life, whether amid all this unimaginable splendor they will look in vain for the familiar faces without which all would for them seem vanity. Happily to this question 1 the answer is clear and unqualified; the friends will j be there without the least shadow of doubt, and far more fully, far more really, than ever they have been with us ! yet.

Yet again, men often ask "what of our friends already in the enjoyment of the heaven-life; can they see us here below? Are they watching us and waiting for us?" Hardly; for there would be difficulties in the way of either of these theories. How could the dead be happy if he looked back and saw those whom he loved in sorrow or suffering, or, far worse still, in the commission of sin? And if we adopt the other alternative, that he does not see, but is waiting, the case is scarcely better. For then the man will have a long and wearisome period of waiting, a painful time of suspense, often extending over many years, while the friend would in many cases arrive so much changed as to be no longer sympathetic. On the system so wisely provided for us by nature all these difficulties are avoided; those whom the man loves most he has ever with him, and always at their noblest and best, while no shadow of discord or change can ever

come between them, since he receives from them all the time exactly what he wishes. The arrangement is infinitely superior to anything which the imagination of man has been able to offer us in its place—as indeed we might have expected—for all those speculations were man's idea of what is best, but the truth is God's idea. Let me try to explain it.

Whenever we love a person very deeply we form a strong mental image of him, and he is often present in our mind. Inevitably we take his mental image into the heaven-world with us, because it is to that level of matter that it naturally belongs. But the love which forms and retains such an image is a very powerful force—a force which is strong enough to reach and act upon the soul of that friend, the real man whom we love. That soul at once and eagerly responds, and pours himself into the thought-form which we have made for him, and in that way we find our friend truly present with us, more vividly than ever before. Remember, it is the soul we love, not the body; and it is the soul that we have with us here. It may be said, "Yes, that would be so if the friend were also dead; but suppose he is still alive; he cannot be in two places at once."

The fact is that, as far as this is concerned, he can be in two places at once, and often many more than two; and whether he is what we commonly call living, or what we commonly call dead, makes not the slightest difference. Let us try to understand what a soul really is, and. we shall see better how this may be.

The soul belongs to a higher plane, and is a much greater and grander thing "than any manifestation of it can be. Its relation to its manifestations is that of one dimension to another—that of a line to a square, or a square to a cube. No number of squares could ever make a cube, because the square has only two dimensions, while the cube has three. So no number of expressions on any lower plane can ever exhaust the fulness of the soul, since he stands upon an altogether higher level . He puts down a small portion of himself into a physical body in order to acquire experience which can only be had on this plane; he can take only one such body at a time, for that is the law; but if he could take a thousand, they would not be sufficient to express what he really is. He may have only one physical body, but if he has evoked such love from a friend, that that friend has a strong mental image of him always present in his thought, then he is able to respond to that love by pouring into that thought-form his own life, and so vivifying it into a real expression of him on this level which is two whole planes higher than the physical, and therefore so much the better able to express his qualities.

If it still seems difficult to realize how his consciousness can be active in that manifestation as well as in this, compare with this an ordinary physical experience. Each of us, as he sits in his chair, is conscious at the same instant of several physical contacts. He touches the seat of the chair, his feet rest on the ground, his hands feel the arms of the chair, or perhaps hold a book; and yet his brain had no difficulty in realizing all these contacts at once; why, then should it be harder for the soul, which is so much greater than the mere physical consciousness, to be conscious simultaneously in more than one of these manifestations on planes so entirely below him ? It is really the one man who feels all those different contacts; it is really the one man who feels all these different thought-images, and is real, living and loving in all of them. You have him there always at his best, for this is a far fuller expression than the physical plane could ever give, even under the best of circumstances.

Will this affect the evolution of the friend in any way, it may be asked? Certainly it will, for it allows him an additional opportunity of manifestation. If he has a physical body he is already learning physical lessons through it, but this enables him at the very same time to develop the quality of affection much more rapidly through the form on the mental plane which you have given him. So your love for him is doing great things for him. As we have said, the soul may manifest in many images if he is fortunate enough to have them made for him. One who is much loved by many people may have part in many heavens simultaneously, and so may evolve with far greater rapidity; but this vast additional opportunity is the direct result and reward of those lovable qualities which drew towards him the affectionate regard of so many of his fellowmen. So not only does he receive love from all these, but through that receiving he himself grows in love, whether these friends be living or dead.

We should observe, however, that there are two possible limitations to the perfection of this intercourse. First, your image of your friend may be partial and imperfect, so that many of his higher qualities may not be represented, and may therefore be unable to show themselves forth through it. Then, secondly, there may be some difficulty from your friend's side. You may have formed a conception somewhat inaccurately; if your friend be as yet not a highly evolved soul, it is possible that you may even have overrated him in some direction, and in that case there might be some aspect of your thought image which he could not completely fill. This, however, is unlikely, and could only take place when a quite unworthy object had been unwisely idolized. Even then the man who made the image would not find any change or lack in his friend, for the latter is at least better able to fulfil his ideal than he has ever been during physical life. Being undeveloped, he may not be perfect, but at least he is better than ever before, so nothing is wanting to the joy of the dweller in heaven. Your friend can fill hundreds of images with those qualities which he possesses, but when a quality is as yet undeveloped in him, he does not suddenly evolve it because you have supposed him already to have attained it.

Here is the enormous advantage which those have who form images only of those who cannot disappoint them— or, since there could be no disappointment, we should rather say, of those capable of rising above even the highest conception that the lower mind can form of them. The Theosophist who forms in his mind the image of the Master knows that all the inadequacy will be on his own side, for he is drawing there upon a depth of love and power which his mental plummet can never sound.

But, it may be asked, since the soul spends so large a proportion of his time in the enjoyment of the bliss of this heaven-world, what are his opportunities of development during his stay there ? They may be divided into three classes, though of each there may be many varieties. First, through certain qualities in himself he has opened certain windows into this heaven-world; by the continued exercise of those qualities through so long a time he will greatly strengthen them, and will return to earth for his next incarnation very richly dowered in that respect. All thoughts are intensified by reiteration, and the man who spends a thousand years principally in pouring forth unselfish affection will assuredly at the end of that period know how to love strongly and well.

Secondly, if through his window he pours forth an aspiration which brings him into contact with one of the great orders of spirits, he will certainly acquire much from his intercourse with them. In music they will use all kinds of overtones and variants which were previously unknown to him; in art they are familiar with a thousand types of which he has had no conception. But all of these will gradually impress themselves upon him, and in this way also he will come out of that glorious heaven-life richer far than he entered it.

Thirdly, he will gain additional information through the mental images which he has made, if these people themselves are sufficiently developed to be able to teach him. Once more, the Theosophist who has made the image of a Master will obtain very definite teaching and help through it, and in a lesser degree this is possible with lesser people.

Above and beyond all this comes the life of the soul or ego in his own causal body—the vehicle which he carries on with him from life to life, unchanging except for its gradual evolution. There comes an end even to that glorious heaven-life, and then the mental body in its turn drops away as the others have done, and the life in the causal begins. Here the soul needs no windows, for this is his true home, and here all his walls have fallen away. The majority of men have as yet but very little consciousness at such a height as this: they rest, dreamily unobservant and scarcely awake, but such vision as they have is true, however limited by their lack of development. Still, every time they return these limitations will be smaller, and they themselves will be greater, so that this truest life will be wider and fuller " for them. As the improvement continues, this causal life grows longer and longer, assuming an ever larger proportion, as compared to the existence at lower levels. And as he grows the man becomes capable not only of receiving, but of giving. Then, indeed, is his triumph approaching, for he is learning the lesson of the Christ, learning the crowning glory of sacrifice, the supreme delight of pouring out all his life for the helping of his fellow-men, the devotion of the self to the all, of celestial strength to human service, of all these splendid heavenly forces to the aid of struggling sons of earth. That is part of the life that lies before us; these are some of the steps which even we, who are as yet at the very bottom of the golden ladder, may see rising above us, so that we may report them to you who have not seen them yet, in order that you, too, may open your eyes to the unimaginable splendor which surrounds you here and now in this dull daily life. This is part of the gospel which Theosophy brings to you—the certainty of this sublime future for all. It is certain because it is here already, because to inherit it we have only to fit ourselves for it.

CHAPTER VII.

GUARDIAN ANGELS.

To my mind it is one of the most beautiful points about our Theosophical teaching that it gives back to a man all the most useful and helpful beliefs of the religions which he has outgrown. There are many who, though they feel that they cannot bring themselves to accept much that they used to take as a matter of course, nevertheless look back with a certain amount of regret to some of the prettier ideas of their mental childhood. They have come up out of the twilight into fuller light, and they are thankful for the fact, and they could not return into their former attitude if they would; yet some of the dreams of the twilight were lovely, and the fuller light seems sometimes a little hard in comparison with its softer tints. Theosophy comes to their rescue here, and shows them that all the glory and the beauty and the poetry, glimpses of which they used dimly to catch in their twilight, exists as a living reality, and that instead of disappearing before the noonday glow, its splendor will be only the more vividly displayed thereby. But our teaching gives them back their poetry on quite a new basis—a basis of scientific fact instead of uncertain tradition. A very good example of such a belief is to be found under our title of "Guardian Angels." There are many graceful traditions of spiritual guardianship and angelic intervention which we should all very much like to believe if we could only see our way to accept them rationally, and I hope to explain that to a very large extent we may do this.

The belief in such intervention is a very old one. Among the earliest Indian legends we find accounts of the occasional appearances of minor deities at critical points in human affairs; the Greek epics are full of similar stories, and in the history of Rome itself we read how the heavenly twins. Castor and Pollux, led the armies of the infant republic at the battle of Lake Regillus. In mediaeval days St. James is recorded to have led the Spanish troops to victory, and there are many tales of angels who watched over the pious wayfarer, or interfered at the right moment to protect him from harm. *Merely a popular superstition,' the superior person will say; perhaps, but wherever we encounter a popular superstition which is widely-spread and persistent, we almost invariably find some kernal of truth behind it— distorted and exaggerated often, yet a truth still. And this is a case in point.

Most religions speak to men of guardian angels, who stand by them in times of sorrow and trouble; and Christianity was no exception to this rule. But for its sins there came upon Christendom the blight which by an extraordinary inversion of truth was called the Reformation, and in that ghastly upheaval very much was lost that for the majority of us has not even yet been regained. That terrible abuses existed, and that a reform was needed in the church I should be the last to deny: yet surely the Reformation was a very heavy judgment for the sins which had preceded it. What is called Protestantism has emptied and darkened the world for its votaries, for among many strange and gloomy falsehoods it has endeavored to propagate the theory that nothing exists to occupy the infinity of stages between the divine and the human. It offers us the amazing conception of a constant capricious interference by the Ruler of the universe with the working of His own laws and the result of His own decrees, and this usually at the request of His creatures, who are apparently supposed to know better than He what is good for them. It would be impossible, if one could ever come to believe this, to divest one's mind of the idea that such interference might be and indeed must be, partial and unjust. In Theosophy we have no such thought, for we hold the belief in perfect Divine justice, and therefore we recognize that there can be no intervention unless the person involved has deserved such help. Even then, it would come to him through agents, and never by direct Divine interposition. We know from our study, and many of us from our experience also, that many intermediate stages exist between the human and the Divine. The old belief in angels and archangels is justified by the facts, for just as there are various kingdoms below humanity, so there are also kingdoms above it in evolution. We find next above us, holding much the same position with regard to us that we in turn hold to the animal kingdom, the great kingdom of the devas or angels, and above them again an evolution which has been called that of the Dhyan Chohans, or archangels (though the names given to these orders matter little), and so onward and upward to the very feet of Divinity. All is one graduated life, from God Himself to the very dust beneath our feet—one long ladder, of which humanity occupies only one of the steps. There are many steps below us and above us, and every one of them is occupied. It would indeed be absurd for us to suppose that we constitute the highest possible form of development—the ultimate achievement of evolution. The occasional appearance among humanity of men much further advanced shows us our next stage, and furnishes us with an example to follow. Men such as the Buddha and the Christ, and many other lesser teachers, exhibit before our eyes a grand ideal towards which we may work, however far from its attainment we may find ourselves at the present moment.

If special interventions in human affairs occasionally take place, is it then to the angelic hosts that we may look as the probable agents employed in them? Perhaps sometimes, but very rarely, for these higher beings have their own work to do, connected with their place in the mighty scheme of things, and they are little likely either to notice or to interfere with us. Man is unconsciously so extraordinarily conceited that he is prone to think that all the greater powers in the universe ought to be watching over him, and ready to help him whenever he suffers through his own folly or ignorance. He forgets that he is not engaged in acting as a beneficent providence to the kingdoms below him, or going out of his way to look after and help the wild animals. Sometimes he plays to them the part of the orthodox devil, and breaks into their innocent and harmless lives with torture and wanton destruction, merely to gratify his own degraded lust of cruelty, which he chooses to denominate "sport"; sometimes he holds animals in bondage, and takes a certain amount of care of them, but it is only that they may work for him—not that he may forward their evolution in the abstract. How can he expect from those above him a type of supervision which he is so very far from giving to those below him? It may well be that the angelic kingdom goes about its own business, taking little more notice of us than we take of the sparrows in the trees. It may now and then happen that an angel becomes aware of some human sorrow or difficulty which moves his pity, and he may try to help us, just as we might try to assist an animal in distress; but certainly his wider vision would recognize the fact that at the present stage of evolution such interpositions would in the vast majority of cases be productive of infinitely more harm than good. In the far-distant past man was frequently assisted by these non-human agencies because then there were none as yet among our infant humanity capable of taking the lead as teachers; but now that we are attaining our adolescence, we are supposed to have arrived at a stage when we can provide leaders and helpers from among our own ranks.

There is another kingdom of nature of which little is known—that of nature-spirits or fairies. Here again popular tradition has preserved a trace of the existence of an order of beings unknown to science. They have been spoken of under many names—pixies, gnomes, ko-bolds, brownies, sylphs, undines, good people, etc., and there are few lands in whose folk-lore they do not play a part. They are beings possessing either astral or etheric bodies, and consequently it is only rarely and under peculiar circumstances that they become visible to man. They usually avoid his neighborhood, for they dislike his wild outbursts of passion and desire, so that when they are seen it is generally in some lonely spot, and by some mountaineer or shepherd whose work takes him far from the busy haunts of the crowd. It has sometimes happened that one of these creatures has become attached to some human being, and devoted himself to his service, as will be found in stories of the Scottish Highlands; but as a rule intelligent assistance is hardly to be expected from entities of this class.

Then there are the great adepts, the Masters of Wisdom—men like ourselves, yet so much more highly evolved that to us they seem as gods in power, in wisdom and in compassion. Their whole life is devoted to the work of helping evolution; would they therefore be likely to intervene sometimes in human affairs? Possibly occasionally, but only very rarely, because they have other and far greater work to do. The ignorant sometimes have suggested that the Adepts ought to come down into our great towns and succor the poor—the ignorant, I say, because only one who is exceedingly ignorant and incredibly presumptuous ever ventures to criticize thus the action of those so infinitely wiser and greater than himself. The sensible and modest man realizes that what they do they must have good reason for doing, and that for him to blame them would be the height of stupidity and ingratitude. They have their own work, on planes far higher than we can reach; they deal directly with the souls of men, and shine upon them as sunlight upon a flower, drawing them upwards and onwards, and filling them with power and life; and that is a grander work by far than healing or caring for or feeding their bodies, good though this also may be in its place. To employ them in working on the physical plane would be a waste of force infinitely greater than it would be to set our most learned men of science to the labor of breaking stones upon the road, upon the plea that that was a physical work for the good of all, while scientific work was not immediately profitable to the poor! It is not from the Adept that physical intervention is likely to come, for he is far more usefully employed.

CHAPTER VIII.

HUMAN WORKERS IN THE UNSEEN.

There are two classes from whom intervention in human affairs may come, and in both cases they are men like ourselves, and not far removed from our own level. The first class consists of those whom we call the dead. We think of them as far away, but that Is a delusion; they are very near us, and though in their new life they cannot usually see our physical bodies, they can and do see our astral vehicles, and therefore they know all our feelings and emotions. So they know when we are in trouble, and when we need help, and it sometimes happens that they are able to give it. Here, then, we have an enormous number of possible helpers, who may occasionally intervene in human affairs. (Occasionally, but not very often; for the dead man is all the while steadily withdrawing into himself, and therefore passing rapidly out of touch with earthly things; and the most highly developed, and therefore the most helpful of men, are precisely those who must pass away from earth most quickly.) Still there are undoubted cases in which the dead have intervened in human affairs; indeed, perhaps such cases are more numerous than we imagine, for in very many of them the work done is only the putting of a suggestion into the mind of some person still living on the physical plane, and he often remains unconscious of the source of his happy inspiration. Sometimes it is necessary for the dead man's purpose that he should show himself, and it is only then that we who are so blind are aware of his loving thought for us. Besides, he cannot always show himself at will; there may be many times when he tries to help, but is unable to do so, and we all the time know nothing of his offer. Still there are such cases, and some of them will be found recounted in my book on The Other Side of Death,

The second class among which helpers may be found consists of those who are able to function consciously upon the astral plane while still living—or perhaps we had better say, while still in the physical body, for the words "living" and "dead" are in reality ludicrously misapplied in ordinary parlance.

It is we, immeshed as we are in this physical matter, buried in the dark and noisome mist of earth-life, blinded by the heavy veil that shuts out from us so much of the light and the glory that are shining around us—it is surely we who are the dead; not those who, having cast off for the time the burden of the flesh, stand amongst us radiant, rejoicing, strong, so much freer, so much more capable than we.

These who, while still in the physical world, have learnt to use their astral bodies, and in some cases their mental bodies also, are usually the pupils of the great Adepts before-mentioned. They cannot do the work which the Master does, for their powers are not developed; they cannot yet function freely on those lofty planes where He can produce such magnificent results; but they can do something at lower levels, and they are thankful to serve in whatever way He thinks best for them, and to undertake such work as is within their power. So sometimes it happens that they see some human trouble or suffering which they are able to alleviate, and they gladly try to do what they can. They are often able to help both the living and the dead, but it must always be remembered that they work under conditions. When such power and such training are given to a man, they are given to him under restrictions. He must never use them selfishly, never display them to gratify curiosity, never employ them to pry into the business of others, never give what at Spiritualistic seances are called tests— that is to say, he must never do anything which can be proved as a phenomenon on the physical plane. He might if he chose take a message to a dead man, but it would be beyond his province to bring back a reply from the dead to the living, unless it were under direct instructions from the Master. Thus the band of invisible helpers does not constitute itself into a detective office, nor into an astral information bureau, but it simply and quietly does such work as is given to it to do, or as comes in its way.

HUMAN WORKERS IN THE UNSEEN.

Let us see how a man is able to do such work and give such help as we have described, so that we may understand what are the limits of this power, and see how we ourselves may to some extent attain it. We must first think how a man leaves his body in sleep. He abandons the physical body, in order that it may have complete rest; but he himself, the soul, needs no rest, for he feels no fatigue. It is only the physical body that ever becomes tired. When we speak of mental fatigue it is in reality a misnomer, for it is the brain and not the mind that is tired. In sleep, then, the man is simply using his astral body instead of his physical, and it is only that body that is asleep, not the man himself. If we examine a sleeping savage with clairvoyant sight, indeed, we shall probably find that he is nearly as much asleep as his body—that he has very little definite consciousness in the astral vehicle which he is inhabiting. He is unable to move away from the immediate neighborhood of the sleeping physical body, and if an attempt were made to draw him away he would wake in terror. If we examine a more civilized man, as for example one of ourselves, we shall find a very great difference. In this case the man in his astral body is by no means unconscious, but quite actively thinking. Nevertheless, he may be taking very little more notice of his surroundings than the savage, though not at all for the same reason. The savage is incapable of seeing; the civilized man is so wrapped up in his own thought that he does not see, though he could. He has behind him the immemorial custom of a long series of lives in which the astral faculties have not been used, for these faculties have been gradually growing inside a shell, something as a chicken grows inside the egg. The shell is composed of the great mass of self-centered thought in which the ordinary man is so hopelessly entombed.) Whatever may have been the thoughts chiefly engaging his mind during the past day, he usually continues them when falling asleep, and he is thus surrounded by so dense a wall of his own making that he practically knows nothing of what is going on outside. Occasionally some violent impact from without, or some strong desire of his own from within, may tear aside this curtain of mist for the moment and permit him to receive some definite impression; but even then the fog closes in again almost immediately, and he dreams on unobservantly as before. Can he be awakened, you will say? Yes, that may happen to him in four different ways. First in the far-distant future the slow but sure evolution of the man will undoubtedly gradually dissipate the curtain of the mist; Secondly, the man himself, having learnt the facts of the case, may by steady and persistent effort clear away the mist from within, and by degrees overcome the inertia resulting from ages of inactivity. He may resolve before going to sleep to try when he leaves his body to awaken himself and see something. This is merely a hastening of the natural process, and there will be no harm in it if the man has previously developed common sense and the moral qualities. If these are defective, he may come very sadly to grief, for he runs the double danger of misusing such powers as he may acquire, and of being overwhelmed by fear in the presence of forces which he can neither understand nor control. Thirdly, it has sometimes happened that some accident, or some unlawful use of magical ceremonies, has so rent the veil that it can never wholly be closed again. In such a case the man may be left in the terrible condition so well described by Madame Blavatsky in her story of A Bewitched Life, or by Lord Lytton in his powerful novel Zanoni. Fourthly, some friend who knows the man thoroughly, and believes him capable of facing the dangers of the astral plane and doing good unselfish work there, may act upon this cloud-shell from without and gradually arouse the man to his higher possibilities. But he will never do this unless he feels absolutely sure of him, of his courage and devotion, and of his possession of the necessary qualifications for good work. If in all these ways he is judged satisfactory, he may thus be invited and enabled to join the band of helpers.

Now, as to the work such helpers can do. I have given many illustrations of this in the little book which I have written, bearing the title of Invisible Helpers, so I will not repeat those stories now, but rather give you a few leading ideas as to the different types of work which are most usually done. Naturally it is of varied kinds, and most of it is not in any way physical; perhaps it may best be divided into work with the living, and work with the dead.

The giving of comfort and consolation in sorrow or sickness at once suggests itself as a comparatively easy task, and one that can constantly be performed without anyone knowing who does it.

Often efforts are made to patch up quarrels—to effect a reconciliation between those who long have been separated by some difference of opinions or of interests. Sometimes it has been possible to warn men of some great danger which impended over their heads, and thus to avert an accident. There have been cases in which this has been done even with regard to a purely physical matter, though more generally it is against moral danger that such warnings are given. Occasionally it has been permissible to offer a solemn warning to one who was leading an immoral life, and so to help him back into the path of rectitude. If the helpers happen to know of a time of special trouble for a friend, they will endeavor to stand by him through it, and to give him strength and comfort.

In great catastrophes, too, there is often much that can be done by those whose work is unrecognized by the outer world. Sometimes it may be permitted that some one or two persons may be saved; and so it comes that in accounts of terrible wholesale destruction we hear now and then of escapes which are esteemed miraculous. But this is only when among those who are in danger there is one who is not to die in that way—one who owes to the Divine law no debt that can be paid in that fashion. In the great majority of cases all that can be done is to make some effort to impart strength and courage to face what must happen, and then afterwards to meet the souls as they arrive upon the astral plane, and welcome and assist them there.

CHAPTER IX.
HELPING THE DEAD.

This brings us to the consideration of what is by far the greatest and most important part of the work—the helping of the dead. Before we can understand this we must throw aside altogether the ordinary clumsy and erroneous ideas about death and the condition of the dead. They are not far away from us, they are not suddenly entirely changed, they have not become angels or demons. They are just human beings, exactly such as ey were before, neither better nor worse, and they stand close by us still, sensitive to our feelings and our thoughts even more than of yore. That is why uncontrolled grief for the dead is so wrong as well as so selfish. The dead man feels every emotion which passes through the heart of his loved ones, and if they uncomprehendingly give way to sorrow, that throws a corresponding cloud of depression over him, and makes his way harder than it need be if his friends had been better taught.

So there is much help that may be given to the dead in very many ways. First of all, many of them—indeed, most of them—need much explanation with regard to the new world in which they find themselves. Their religion ought to have taught them what to expect, and how to live amid these new conditions; but in most cases it has not done anything of the kind. So it comes that very many of them are in a condition of considerable uneasiness, and others of positive terror. They need to be soothed and comforted, for when they encounter the dreadful thought-forms which they and their kind have been making for centuries—thoughts of a personal devil and an angry and cruel deity—they are often reduced to a pitiable state of fear, which is not only exceedingly unpleasant, but very bad for their evolution; and it often costs the helper much time and trouble to bring them into a more reasonable frame of mind.

There are men to whom this entry into a new life seems to give for the first time an opportunity to see themselves as they really are, and some of them are therefore filled with remorse. Here again the helper's services are needed to explain that what is past is past, and that the only effective repentance is the resolve to do this thing no more-l-that whatever the dead man may have done, he is not a lost soul, but that he must simply begin from where he finds himself, and try to live the true life for the future. " Some of them cling passionately to earth, where all their thoughts and interests have been fixed, and they suffer much when they find themselves losing hold and sight of it.) Others are earth-bound by the thought of crimes that they have committed, or duties that they have left undone, while others in turn are worried about the condition of those whom they have left behind. All these are cases which need explanation, and sometimes it is also necessary for the helper to take steps on the physical plane in order to carry out the wishes of the dead man, and so leave him free and untroubled to pass on to higher matters. People are inclined to look at the dark side of Spiritualism; but we must never forget that it has done an enormous amount of good in this sort of work—in giving to the dead an opportunity to arrange their affairs after a sudden and unexpected departure.

I (It is surely a happy thought that the time of much-needed repose for the body is not necessarily a period of inactivity for the true man within.', I used at one time to feel that the time given to sleep was sadly wasted time; now I understand that Nature does not so mismanage her affairs as to lose one-third of the man's life. Of course there are qualifications required for this work; but I have given them so carefully and at length in my little book on the subject, Invisible Helpers, that I need only just mention them here. First, he must be one-pointed, and the work of helping others must be ever the first and highest duty for him. Secondly, he must have perfect self-control— control over his temper and his nerves. He must never allow his emotions to interfere with his work in the slightest degree; he must be above anger, and above fear. Thirdly, he must have perfect calmness, serenity and joyousness. Men subject to depression and worry are useless, for one great part of the work is to soothe and to calm others, and how can they do that if they are all the time in a whirl of excitement or worry themselves? Fourthly, the man must have knowledge; he must have already learnt down here on this plane all that he can about the other, for he cannot expect that men there will waste valuable time in teaching him what he might have acquired for himself. Fifthly, he must be perfectly unselfish. He must be above the foolishness of wounded feelings, and must think not of himself but of the work that he has to do, so that he will be glad to take the humblest duty or the greatest duty without envy on the one hand or conceit on the other. Sixthly, he must have a heart filled with love-—not sentimentalism, but the intense desire to serve, to become a channel for that love of God which, like the peace of God, passeth man's understanding.

You may think that this is an impossible standard; on the contrary, it is attainable by every man. It will take time to reach it, but assuredly it will be time well spent. Do not turn away disheartened, but set to work here and now, and strive to become fit for this glorious task, and while we are striving, do not let us wait idly, but try to undertake some little piece of work along the same lines. Every one knows some case of sorrow or distress, whether among the living or the dead does not matter; if you know such a case, take it into your mind when you lie down to sleep, and resolve as soon as you are free from this body to go to that person and endeavor to comfort him. You may not be conscious of the result, you may not remember anything of it in the morning; but be well assured that your resolve will not be fruitless, and that whether you remember what you have done or not, you will be quite sure to have done something. Some day sooner or later you will find evidence that you have been successful. Remember that as we help, we can be helped; remember that from the lowest to the highest we are bound together by one long chain of mutual service, and that although we stand on the lower steps of the ladder, it reaches up above these earthly mists to where the light of God is always shining.

CHAPTER X.

THOUGHTS ARE THINGS.

Reference has been made to the fact that thought and emotion, besides the effect which they produce upon the physical body, cause vibration in the subtler bodies appropriate to them—the astral and mental bodies by which each human being is surrounded. The following passages from an article by Mrs. Besant, which appeared in 1896, will help to make the matter clearer, when read in conjunction with the illustrations reproduced in this booklet (for a fuller account of these researches see "Thought Forms," by Annie Besant and C. W. Leadbeater).

The pictures of thought-forms herewith presented were obtained as follows; two clairvoyant Theosophists observed the forms caused by definite thoughts thrown out by one of them, and also watched the forms projected by other persons under the influence of various emotions. They described these as fully and accurately as they could to an artist who sat with them, and he made sketches and mixed colors, till some approximation to the objects was made. Unfortunately the clairvoyants could not draw and the artist could not see, so the arrangement was a little like that of the blind and lame men—the blind men having good legs carried the lame ones, and the lame men having good eyes guided the blind. The artist at his leisure painted the forms, and then another committee was held and sat upon the paintings and in the light of the criticisms then made our long-suffering brother painted an almost entirely new set—the most successful attempt that has hitherto been made to present these elusive shapes in the dull pigments of earth.

All students know that what is called the Aura of man is the outer part of the cloud-like substance of his higher bodies, interpenetrating each other, and extending beyond the confines of his physical body, the smallest of all. They know also that two of these bodies, the mental and desire bodies, are those chiefly concerned with the appearance of what are called thought-forms. But in order that the matter may be made clear for all, and not only for students already acquainted with Theosophical teachings, a recapitulation of the main facts will not be out of place.

Man, the Thinker, is clothed in a body composed of innumerable combinations of the subtle matter of the mental plane, this body being more or less refined in its constituents and organized more or less fully for its functions, according to the stage of intellectual development at which the man himself has arrived. The mental body is an object of great beauty the delicacy and rapid motion of its particles giving it an aspect of living iridescent light, and this beauty becomes an extraordinarily radiant and entrancing loveliness as the intellect becomes' more highly evolved and is employed chiefly on pure and sublime topics. Every thought gives rise to a set of correlated vibrations in the matter of this body, accompanied with a marvellous play of color, like that in the spray of a waterfall as the sunlight strikes it, raised to the n degree of color and vivid delicacy. The body under this impulse throws off a vibrating portion of itself, shaped by the nature of the vibrations—as figures are made by sand on a disk vibrating to a musical note— and this gathers from the surrounding atmosphere matter like itself in fineness from the elemental essence of the mental world. We have then a thought-form pure and simple, and it is a living entity of intense activity animated by the one idea that generated it. If made of the finer kinds of matter, it will be of great power and energy, and may be used as a most potent agent when directed by a strong and steady will. Into the details of such use we will enter later. Such a thought-form, if directed to affect any object or person on the astral world, will take to itself a covering of astral materials, of fineness correlated to its own, from the elemental essence of the astral world.

When the man's energy flows outwards towards external objects of desire, or is occupied in passional and emotional activities, this energy works in a less subtle order of matter than the mental, in that of the astral world. What is called his desire-body is composed of this matter, and it forms the most prominent part of the aura in the undeveloped man. Where the man is of a gross type, the desire-body is of the denser matter of the astral plane, and is dull in hue, browns and dirty greens and reds playing a great part in it. Through this will flash various characteristic colors, as his passions are excited. A man of higher type has his desire-body composed of the finer qualities of astral matter, with the colors rippling over and flashing through it fine and clear in hue. While less delicate and less radiant than the mental body, it forms a beautiful object and as selfishness is eliminated all the duller and heavier shades disappear;

Three general principles underlie the production of all thought-forms:

1. Quality of thought determines color.

2. Nature of thought determines form.

3. Definiteness of thought determines clearness of outline. Color. Colors depend on the number of vibrations that take place in a second, and this is true in the astral and mental worlds as well as in the physical. If the astral and mental bodies are vibrating under the influence of devotion the aura will be suffused with blue, more or less intense, beautiful and pure according to the depth, elevation and purity of the feeling. In a church, such thought-forms may be seen rising, for the most part not very definitely outlined, but rolling masses of blue clouds (Fig. 2). Too often the color is dulled by the intermixture of selfish feelings, when the blue is mixed with browns and thus loses its pure brilliancy. But the devotional thought of an unselfish heart is very lovely in color, like the

deep blue of a summer sky. Through such clouds of blue will often shine out golden stars of great brilliancy, darting upwards like a shower of sparks.

Anger gives rise to red, of all shades from lurid brick-red to brilliant scarlet; brutal anger will show as flashes of lurid dull red from dark-brown clouds, while the anger of "noble indignation' is a vivid scarlet, by no means unbeautiful to look at though it gives an unpleasant thrill.

Affection, love, sends out clouds of rosy hue varying from dull crimson, where the love is animal in its nature, rose-red mingled with brown when selfish, or with dull green when jealous, to the most exquisite shades of delicate rose like the early flushes of the dawning, as the love becomes more purified from all selfish elements, and flows out in wider and wider circles of generous impersonal tenderness and compassion to all who are in need.

Intellect produces yellow thought-forms (Fig. 6), the pure reason directed to spiritual ends giving rise to a very beautiful delicate yellow, while used for more selfish ends or mingled with ambition it yields deep shades of orange, clear and intense (Fig. 7).

Form. According to the nature of the thought will be the form it generates. In the thought-forms of devotion the flower which is figured was a thought of pure devotion offered to One worshipped by the thinker, a thought of self-surrender, of sacrifice (Fig. 3).

Such thoughts constantly assume flower-like forms, exceedingly beautiful, varying much in outline but characterized by curved upward-pointing petals like azure flames. It is this flower-like characteristic of devotion that may have led to the direction, by those who saw, of offering flowers as part of religious worship, figuring in suggestive material forms that which was visible in the astral world, hinting at things unseen by things seen, and influencing the mind by an appropriate symbology. A beam of blue light, like a pencil of rays, shot upwards towards the sky, was a thought of loving devotion to the Christ from the mind of a Christian. The five-pointed star (Fig. 1, Frontispiece), was a thought directed towards the Deity, a devotional aspiration to be in harmony with cosmic law, as the expression of His nature, and it was these latter elements which gave it its geometrical form, while the mental constituents added the yellow rays. Thoughts which assume geometrical shapes, such as the circle, cube, pyramid, triangle, pentacle, double triangle, and the like, are thoughts concerned with cosmic order, or they are metaphysical concepts. Thus if this star were yellow, it would be a thought directed intellectually to the working of law, in connection with the Diety or with rational man.

Among the thought-forms of affection Fig. 4 is very good—a thought of love, clearly defined and definitely directed towards its object. Fig. 5 is a thought which is loving but appropriative, seeking to draw to itself and to hold.

Fig. 7 is a characteristic form of a strong and ambitious thought; it was taken from the aura of a man of keen intellect and noble character, who was ambitious (and worthy) to wield power, and whose thoughts were turned to the public good. The ambitious element contributes the hooked extensions, just as the grasping love in Fig. 5 causes similar protrusions.

Clearness of outline. This depends entirely on the definiteness of the thought, and is a comparatively rare thing. Contrast Figs. 1, 2 and 3. Vague, dreamy devotion yields the cloudy mass of Fig. 2 and comparatively few worshippers show anything but this. So the great majority of people when thinking send out such clouds as Fig. 6:3 The creator of Fig. 3 knew just what he meant, and so did the creator of Fig. 1. There was no drifting, no "wobbling," clear, pure and strong were the thoughts of these devotees. So again the person who generated the form represented by Fig. 4 had a very clear and definite love directed towards a specific object, and the maker of Fig. 7 meant to carry out the thought there outlined.

A thought of love and of desire to protect directed strongly towards some beloved object creates a form which goes to the person thought of and remains in his aura as a shielding and protecting agent; it will seek all opportunities to serve; and all opportunities to defend, not by a conscious and deliberate action, but by a blind following out of the impulse impressed upon it, and it will strengthen friendly forces that impinge on the aura and weaken unfriendly ones. Thus may we create and maintain veritable guardian angels round those we love, and many a mother's prayer for a distant child thus circles round him, though she knows not the method by which her "prayer is answered."

The End

BOOK FOUR

AN OUTLINE OF THEOSOPHY

CHAPTER I. INTRODUCTORY.

WHAT IT IS.

For many a year men have been discussing, arguing, enquiring about certain great basic truths—about the existence and the nature of God, about His relation to man, and about the past and future of humanity. So radically have they differed upon these points, and so bitterly have they assailed and ridiculed one another's beliefs, that there has come to be a firmly-rooted popular opinion that with regard to all these matters there is no certainty available—nothing but vague speculation amid a cloud of unsound deductions drawn from ill-established premises. And this in spite of the very definite, though frequently incredible, assertions made on these subjects on behalf of the various religions.

This popular opinion, though not unnatural under the circumstances, is entirely untrue. There are definite facts available—plenty of them. Theosophy gives them to us; but it offers them not (as the religions do) as matters of faith, but as subjects for study. It is not itself a religion, but it bears to the religions the same relation as did the ancient philosophies. It does not contradict them, but explains them. Whatever in any of them is unreasonable it rejects as necessarily unworthy of the Deity and derogatory to Him; whatever is reasonable in each and all of them it takes up, explains and emphasizes, and thus combines all into one harmonious whole.

It holds that truth on all these most important points is attainable—that there is a great body of knowledge about them already existing. It considers all the various religions as statements of that truth from different points of view; since, though they differ much as to nomenclature and as to articles of belief, they all agree as to the only matters which are of real importance—the kind of life which a good man should lead, the qualities which he must develop, the vices which he must avoid. On these practical points the teaching is identical in Hinduism and Buddhism, in Zoroastrianism and Muhammadanism, in Judaism and Christianity.

Theosophy may be described to the outside world as an intelligent theory of the universe. ; Yet for those who have studied it, it is not theory, but fact; for it is a definite science, capable of being studied, and its teachings are verifiable by investigation and experiment for those who are willing to take the trouble to apply themselves for such enquiry, [it is a statement of the great facts of Nature so far as they are known—an outline of the scheme of our corner of the universe.

HOW IT IS KNOWN.

How did this scheme become known, some may ask; by whom was it discovered ? We cannot speak of it as discovered, for in truth it has always been known to mankind, though sometimes temporarily forgotten in certain parts of the world. There has always existed a certain body of highly-developed men — men not of any one nation, but of all the advanced nations—who have held it in its fulness; and there have always been pupils of these men, who were specially studying it, while its broad principles have always been known in the outer world. This body of highly-developed men exists now, as in past ages, and Theosophical teaching is published to the Western world at their instigation, and through a few of their pupils.

Those who are ignorant have sometimes clamorously insisted that, if this be so, these truths ought to have been published long ago; and most unjustly they accuse the possessors of such knowledge of undue reticence in withholding them from the world at large. They forget that all who have really sought these truths have always been able to find them, and that it is only now that we in the Western world are truly beginning to seek. For many centuries Europe was content to live, for the most part, in the grossest superstition; and when a reaction at last set in from the absurdity and bigotry of those beliefs, it brought a period of atheism, which was just as conceited and bigoted in another direction. So that it is really only now that some of the humbler and more reasonable of our people are beginning to admit that they know nothing, and to enquire whether there is not real information available somewhere.

Though these reasonable enquirers are as yet but a small minority, the Theosophical Society has been founded in order to draw them together, and its books are put before the public so that those who will may read, mark, learn, and inwardly digest these great truths. Its mission is not to force its teaching upon reluctant minds, but simply to offer it, so that those may take it who feel the need for it. We are not in the least under the delusion of the poor arrogant missionary, who dares to condemn to an unpleasant eternity every one who will not pronounce his little provincial shibboleth; we are perfectly aware that all will at last be well for those who cannot as yet see their way to accept the truth, as well as for those who receive it with avidity. But the knowledge of this truth has, for us and for thousands of others, made life easier to bear and death easier to face; and it is simply the wish to share these benefits with our fellow-men that urges us to devote ourselves to writing and lecturing on these subjects.

The broad outlines of the great truths have been widely known in the world for thousands of years, and are so known at the present day. It is only we in the West who, in our incredible self-sufficiency, have remained ignorant of them, and scoffed at any fragment of them which may have come in our way. As in the case of any other science, so in this science of the soul, full details are known only to those who devote their lives to its pursuit. The men who fully know— those who are called Adepts— have patiently developed within themselves the powers necessary for perfect observation. For in this respect there is a difference between the methods of occult investigation and those of the more modern form of science; this latter devotes all its energy to the improvement of its instruments, while the former aims rather at the development of the observer.

THE METHOD OF OBSERVATION.

The detail of this development would take up more space than can be devoted to it in a preliminary manual such as this. The whole scheme will be found fully explained in other Theosophical works; for the moment let it suffice to say that it is entirely a question of vibration. All information which reaches a man from the world without reaches him by means of vibration of some sort, whether it be through senses of sight, hearing, or touch. Consequently, if a man is able to make himself sensitive to additional vibrations he will acquire additional information; he will become what is commonly called "clairvoyant.'

This word, as commonly used, means nothing more than a slight extension of normal vision; but it is possible for a man to become more and more sensitive to the subtler vibrations, until his consciousness, acting through many developed faculties, functions freely in new. and higher ways. He will then find new worlds of subtler matter opening up before him, though in reality they are only new portions of the world he already knows. He learns in this way that a vast unseen universe exists round him during his whole life, and that it is constantly affecting him in many ways, even though he remains blindly unconscious of it. But when he develops faculties whereby he can sense these other worlds it becomes possible for him to observe them scientifically, to repeat his observations many times, to compare them with those of others, to tabulate them, and draw deductions from them.

All this has been done—not once, but thousands of times. The Adepts of whom I spoke have done this to the fullest possible extent, but many efforts along the same line have been made by our own Theosophical students. The result of our investigations has been not only to verify much of the information given to us at the outset by those Adepts, but also to explain and amplify it very considerably.

The sight of this usually unseen portion of our world at once brings to our knowledge a vast body of entirely-new facts which are of the very deepest interest. It gradually solves for us many of the most difficult problems of life; it clears up for us many mysteries, so that we now see them to have been mysteries to us for so long, only because heretofore we saw so small a part of the facts, because we were looking at the various matters from below, and as isolated and unconnected fragments, instead of rising above them to a standpoint whence they are comprehensible as parts of a mighty whole. It settles in a moment many questions which have been much disputed—such, for example, as that of the continued existence of man after death. It affords us the true explanation of all the wildly impossible statements made by the churches about heaven, hell, and purgatory; it dispels our ignorance and removes our fear of the unknown by supplying us with a rational and orderly scheme. What this scheme is I will now endeavour to explain.

CHAPTER II. GENERAL PRINCIPLES.

It is my desire to make this statement of Theosophy as clear and readily comprehensible as possible, and for this reason I shall at every point give broad principles only, referring those who wish for detailed information to larger books, or to monographs upon particular subjects. I hope at the end of each chapter of this little treatise to give a list of such books as should be consulted by those who desire to go more deeply into this most fascinating system.

I shall begin, then, by a statement of the most striking of the broad general principles which emerge as a result of Theosophical study. There may be those who will find here matter which is incredible to them, or matter which runs entirely contrary to their preconceived ideas. If that be so, then I would ask such men to remember that I am not putting this forward as a theory—as a metaphysical speculation or a pious opinion of my own—-but as a definite scientific fact proved and examined over and over again, not only by myself, but by many others also.

Furthermore, I claim that it is a fact which may be verified at first hand by any person who is willing to devote the time and trouble necessary to fit himself for the investigation. I am not offering to the reader a creed to be swallowed like a pill; I am trying to set before him a system of study, and, above all, a life to live, I ask no blind faith from him; I simply suggest to him the consideration of the Theosophical teaching as a hypothesis, though to me it is no hypothesis, but a living fact.

If he finds it more satisfactory than others which have been presented to him, if it seems to him to solve more of the problems of life, to answer a greater number of the questions which inevitably arise for the thinking man, then he will pursue its study further, and will find in it, I hope and believe, the same ever-increasing satisfaction and joy that I have myself found. If, on the other hand, he thinks some other system preferable, no harm is done; he has simply learnt something of the tenets of a body of men with whom he is as yet unable to agree. I have sufficient faith in it myself to believe that, sooner or later, a time will come when he will agree with them—when he also will know what we know.

THE THREE GREAT TRUTHS.

In one of our earliest Theosophical books it was written that there are three truths which are absolute and cannot be lost, but yet may remain silent for lack of speech. They are as great as life itself, and yet as simple as the simplest mind of man. I can hardly do better than paraphrase these for the greatest of my general principles.

I will then give some corollaries which "follow naturally from them, and then, thirdly, some of the more prominent of the advantageous results which necessarily attend this definite knowledge. Having thus outlined the scheme in tabular form, I will take it up point by point, and endeavour to offer such elementary explanations as come within the scope of this little introductory book.

I. God exists, and He is good. He is the great life-giver who dwells within us and without us, is undying and eternally beneficent. He is not heard, nor seen, nor touched, yet is perceived by the man who desires perception. 2. Man is immortal, and his future is one whose glory and splendour have no limit.

3. A Divine law of absolute justice rules the world, so that each man is in truth his own judge, the dispenser of glory or gloom to himself, the decreer of his life, his reward, his punishment.

COROLLARIES.

To each of these great truths are attached certain others, subsidiary and explanatory.

From the first of them it follows:

1. That, in spite of appearances, all things are definitely and intelligently moving together for good; that all circumstances, however untoward they may seem, are in reality exactly what are needed; that everything around us tends, not to hinder us, but to help us, if it is only understood.

2. That, since the whole scheme thus tends to man's benefit, clearly it is his duty to learn to understand it.

3. That when he thus understands it, it is also his duty intelligently to co-operate in this scheme.

From the second great truth it follows:

1. That the true man is a soul, and that this body is only an appanage.

2. That he must, therefore, regard everything from the standpoint of the soul, and that in every case when an internal struggle takes place he must realize his identity with the higher and not with the lower.

3. That what we commonly call his life is only one day in his true and larger life.

4. That death is a matter of far less importance than is usually supposed, since it is by no means the end of life, but merely the passage from one stage of it to another.

5. That man has an immense evolution behind him, the study of which is most fascinating, interesting, and instructive.

6. That he has also a splendid evolution before him, the study of which will be even more fascinating and instructive.

7. That there is an absolute certainty of final attainment for every human soul, no matter how far he may seem to have strayed from the path of evolution.

From the third great truth it follows :

1. That every thought, word, or action is definitively not —not a reward or a punishment imposed from without, but a result inherent in the action itself, definitely connected with it in the relation of cause and effect, these being really but two inseparable parts of one whole.

2. That it is both the duty and interest of man to study this divine law closely, so that he may be able to adapt himself to it and to use it, as we use other great laws of nature.

3. That it is necessary for man to attain perfect control over himself, so that he may guide his life intelligently in accordance with this law.

ADVANTAGES GAINED FROM THIS KNOWLEDGE.

When this knowledge is fully assimilated, it changes the aspect of life so completely that it would be impossible for me to tabulate all the advantages which flow from it. I can only mention a few of the principal lines along which this change is produced, and the reader's own thought will, no doubt, supply some of the endless ramifications which are their necessary consequence.

But it must be understood that no vague knowledge will be sufficient. Such belief as most men accord to the assertions of their religions will be quite useless, since it produces no practical effect in their lives. But if we believe in these truths as we do in the other laws of nature—as we believe that fire bums and that water drowns —then the effect that they produce in our lives is enormous. For our belief in the laws of nature is sufficiently real to induce us to order our lives in accordance with it. Believing that fire bums, we take every precaution to avoid fire; believing that water drowns, we avoid going into water too deep for us unless we can swim.

Now these beliefs are so definite and real to us because they are founded on knowledge and illustrated by daily experience; and the beliefs of the Theosophical student are equally real and definite to him for exactly the same reason. And that is why we find following from them the results now to be described:

1. We gain a rational comprehension of life—we know how we should live and why, and we learn that life is worth living when properly understood.

2. We learn how to govern ourselves, and therefore how to develop ourselves.

3. We learn how best to help those whom we love, how to make ourselves useful to all with whom we come into contact, and ultimately to the whole human race.

4. We learn to view everything from the wider philosophical standpoint—never from the petty and purely personal side.

Consequently:

5. The troubles of life are no longer so large for us.

6. We have no sense of injustice in connection with our surroundings or our destiny.

7. We are altogether freed from the fear of death.

8. Our grief in connection with the death of those whom we love is very greatly mitigated.

9. We gain a totally different view . of the life after death, and we understand its place in our evolution.

10. We are altogether free from religious fears or worry, either for ourselves or for our friends—fears as to the salvation of the soul, for example.

11. We are no longer troubled by uncertainty as to our future fate, but live in perfect serenity and perfect fearlessness.

Now let us take these points in detail and endeavour briefly to explain them.

CHAPTER III THE DEITY.

When we lay down the existence of God as the first and greatest of our principles, it becomes necessary for us to define the sense in which we employ that much-abused, yet mighty word. We try to redeem it from the narrow limits imposed on it by the ignorance of undeveloped men, and to restore to it the splendid conception—splendid, though so infinitely below the reality— given to it by the founders of religions. And we distinguish between God as the Infinite Existence, and the manifestation of this Supreme Existence as a revealed God, evolving and guiding a universe. Only to this limited manifestation should the term "a personal God" be applied. God in Himself is beyond the bounds of personality, is "in all and through all" and indeed is all; and of the Infinite, the Absolute, the All, we can only say "He is."

For all practical purposes we need not go further than that marvellous and glorious manifestation of Him (a little less entirely beyond our comprehension) the great Guiding Force or Deity of our own solar system, whom philosophers have called the Logos. Of him is true all that we have ever heard predicated of God—all that is good, that is—not the blasphemous conceptions sometimes put forward, ascribing to Him human vices. But all that has ever been said of the love, the wisdom, the power, the patience and compassion, the omniscience, the omnipresence, the omnipotence—all of this, and much more, is true of the Logos of our system. Verily "in Him we live and move and have our being," not as a poetical expression, but (strange as it may seem) as a definite scientific fact; and so when we speak of the Deity our first thought is naturally of the Logos.

We do not vaguely hope that He may be; we do not even believe as a matter of faith that He is; we simply know it as we know that the sun shines, for to the trained and developed clairvoyant investigator this Mighty Existence is a definite certainty. Not that any merely human development can enable us directly to see Him, but that unmistakable evidence of His action and His purpose surrounds us on every side as we study the life of the unseen world, which is in reality only the higher part of this.

Here we meet the explanation of a dogma which is common to all religions —that of the Trinity. Incomprehensible as many of the statements made on this subject in our creeds may seem to the ordinary reader, they become significant and luminous when the truth is understood. As He shows Himself to us in His work, the Logos is undoubtedly triple—three and yet one, as religion has long ago told us; and as much of the explanation of this apparent mystery as the intellect of man at its present stage can grasp will be found in the books presently to be mentioned.

That He is within us as well as without us, or, in other words, that man himself is in essence divine, is another great truth which, though those who are blind to all but the outer and lower world may still argue about it, is an absolute certainty to the student of the higher side of life. Of the constitution of man's soul and its various vehicles we shall speak under the heading of the second of truths; suffice it for the moment to note that the inherent divinity is a fact, and that in it resides the assurance of the ultimate return of every human being to the divine level.

THE DIVINE SCHEME.

Perhaps none of our postulates will present greater difficulty to the average mind than the first corollary to this first great truth. Looking round us in daily life we see so much of the storm and stress, the sorrow and the suffering, so much that looks like the triumph of evil over good, that it seems almost impossible to suppose that all this apparent confusion is in reality part of an ordered progress. Yet this is the truth, and can be seen to be the truth so soon as we escape from the dust-cloud raised by the struggle in this outer world, and look upon it all from the vantage ground of the fuller knowledge and the inner peace.

Then the real motion of the complex machinery becomes apparent. Then it is seen that what have seemed to be counter-currents of evil prevailing against the stream of progress are merely trifling eddies into which for the moment a little water may turn aside, or tiny whirlpools on the surface, in which part of the water appears for the moment to be running backwards. But all the time the mighty river is sweeping steadily on its appointed course, bearing the superficial whirlpools along with it. Just so the great stream of evolution is moving evenly on its way, and what seems to us so terrible a tempest is the merest ruffling of its surface. Another analogy, very beautifully worked out, is given in Mr. C. H. Hinton's Scientific Romances, vol i., pp. i8 to 24.

Truly, as our third great truth tells us, absolute justice is meted out to all, and so, in whatever circumstances a man finds himself, he knows that he himself and none other has provided them; but he may also know much more than this. He may rest assured that under the action of evolutionary law matters are so arranged as to give him the best possible opportunity for developing within himself those qualities which he most needs. His circumstances are by no means necessarily those that he would have chosen for himself, but they are exactly what he has deserved; and, subject only to that consideration of his deserts (which frequently impose serious limitations), they are those best adapted for his progress. They may provide him with all sorts of difficulties, but these are offered only in order that he may learn to surmount them, and thereby develope within himself courage, determination, patience, perseverance, or whatever other quality he may lack. Men often speak as though the forces of Nature were conspiring against them, whereas as a matter of fact everything about them is carefully calculated to assist them on their upward way.

That, since there is a Divine scheme, it is man's part to try to understand it, is a proposition which surely needs no argument. Even were it only from motives of self-interest, those who have to live under a certain set of conditions would do well to familiarize themselves with them; and when a man's objects in life become altruistic it is still more necessary for him to comprehend, in order that he may help the more effectually.

It is undoubtedly part of this plan for man's evolution that he himself should intelligently co-operate in It as soon as he has developed sufficient intelligence to grasp it and sufficient good feeling to wish to aid. But indeed this Divine scheme is so wonderful and so beautiful that, when once a man sees it, nothing else is possible for him than to throw all his energies into the effort to become a worker in it, no matter how humble may be the part which he has to sustain.

For fuller information on the subjects of this chapter the reader is referred to Mrs. Besant's Esoteric Christianity and Ancient Wisdom, and to my own little book on The Christian Creed. Much light is also thrown on these conceptions from the Greek standpoint in Mr. G. R. S. Mead's Orpheus, and from the Gnostic-Christian in his Fragments of a Faith Forgotten.

I know, as my life grows older And mine eyes have clearer sight, That under each rank wrong somewhere There lies the root of right; That each sorrow has its purpose.

By the sorrowing oft unguessed; That, as sure as the sun brings morning.

Whatever is, is best.

I know that each sinful action.

As sure as the night brings shade, Is somewhere, some time punished,

Though the hour be long delayed I know that the soul is aided Sometimes by the heart's unrest. And to grow means oft to suffer;

But whatever is, is best.

I know that there are no errors In the great eternal plan, And that all things work together For the final good of man. And I know when my soul speeds onward In its grand eternal quest I shall say, as I look back earthward.

Whatever is, is best.

[The above appeared anonymously in an American newspaper.]

CHAPTER IV

THE CONSTITUTION OF MAN.

The astounding practical materialism to which we have been reduced in this country can hardly be more clearly shown than it is by the expressions that we employ in common life. We speak quite ordinarily of man as having a soul, of "saving" our souls, and so on, evidently regarding the physical body as the real man and the soul as a mere appanage, a vague something to be considered as the property of the body. With an idea so little defined as this, it can hardly be a matter of surprise that many people go a little further along the same lines, and doubt whether this vague something exists at all. So it would seem that the ordinary man is very often quite uncertain whether he possesses a soul or not; still less does he know that that soul is immortal. That he should remain in this pitiable condition of ignorance seems strange, for there is a very great deal of evidence available, even in the outer world, to show that man has an existence quite apart from his body, capable of being carried on at a distance from it while it is living, and entirely without it when it is dead.

Until we have entirely rid ourselves of this extraordinary delusion that the body is the man, it is quite impossible that we should at all appreciate the real facts of the case. A little investigation immediately shows us that the body is only a vehicle by mean s of which the man manifests himself in connection with this particular type of gross matter out of which our visible world is built.

Furthermore, it shows that other and subtler types of matter exist—not only the ether admitted by modern science as interpenetrating all known substances, but other types of matter which interpenetrate ether in turn, and are as much finer than ether as it is than solid matter.

The question will naturally occur to the reader as to how it will be possible for man to become conscious of the existence of types of matter so wonderfully fine, so minutely subdivided. The answer is that he can become conscious of them in the same way as he becomes conscious of the lower matter—by receiving vibrations from them.

And he is enabled to receive vibrations from them by reason of the fact that he possesses matter of these finer types as part of himself – that just as his body of dense matter is his vehicle for perceiving and communicating with the world of dense matter, so does the finer matter within him constitute for him a vehicle by means of which he can perceive and communicate with .the world of filler matter, which is imperceptible to the grosser physical senses. "'This is by no means a new idea. It will be remembered that St. Paul remarks that "there is a natural body, and there is a spiritual body," and that he furthermore refers to both the soul and the spirit in man, by no means employing the two words synonymously, as is so often ignorantly done at the present day. It speedily becomes evident that man is a far more complex being than is ordinarily supposed; that not only is he a spirit within a soul, but that this soul has various vehicles of different degrees of density, the physical body being only one, and the lowest of them. These various vehicles may all be described as bodies in relation to their respective levels of matter. It might be said that there exist around us a series of worlds one within the other (by interpenetration), and that •man possesses a body for each of these worlds by means of which he may observe it and Live in it.

He learns by degrees how to use these various bodies, and in that way gains a much more complete idea of the great complex world in which he lives; for all these other inner worlds are in reality still part of it. In this way he comes to understand very many things which before seemed mysterious to him; he ceases to identify himself with his bodies, and learns that they are only vestures which he may put off and resume or change without being himself in the least affected thereby. Once more we must repeat that all this is by no means metaphysical speculation or pious opinion, but definite scientific fact, thoroughly well-known experimentally to those who have studied Theosophy. Strange as it may seem to many to find precise statements taking the place of hypotheses upon questions such as these, I am speaking here of nothing that is not known by direct and constantly-repeated observation to a large number of students. Assuredly "we know whereof we speak," not by faith but by experiment, and therefore . we speak with confidence. .

To these inner worlds or different levels of nature we usually give the name of planes. We speak of the visible world as "the physical plane", though under that name we include also the gases and various grades of ether. To the next stage of materiality the name of "the astral plane" was given by the medieval alchemists (who were well aware of its existence), and we have adopted their title. Within this exists another world of still finer matter, of which we speak as "the mental plane", because of its matter is composed what is commonly called the mind in man. There are other still higher planes, but I need not trouble the reader with designations for them, since we are at present dealing only with man's manifestation in the lower worlds.

It must always be born in mind that all these worlds are in no way removed from us in space. In fact, they all occupy exactly the same space, and are all equally about us always. At the moment our consciousness is focused in and working through our physical brain, and thus we are conscious only of the physical world, and not even of the whole of that. But we have only to learn to focus that consciousness in one of these higher vehicles, and at once the physical fades from our view, and we see instead the world of matter which corresponds to the vehicle used. Recollect that all matter is in essence the same.

Astral matter does not differ in its nature from physical matter any more than ice differs in its nature from steam. It is simply the same thing in a different condition. Physical matter may become astral, or astral may become mental, if only it be sufficiently subdivided, and caused to vibrate with the proper degree of rapidity.

THE TRUE MAN.

What, then, is the true man? He is in truth an emanation from the Logos, a spark of the Divine fire. The spirit within him is of the very essence of the Deity, and that spirit wears his soul as a vesture—a vesture which encloses and individualizes it, and seems to our limited vision to separate it for a time from the rest of the Divine Life. The story of the original formation of the soul of man, and of the enfolding of the spirit within it, is a beautiful and interesting one, but too long for inclusion in a merely elementary work like this. It may be found in full detail in those of our books which deal with this part of the doctrine. Suffice it here to say that all three aspects of the Divine Life have their part in its inception, and that its formation is the culmination of that mighty sacrifice of the Logos in descending into matter, which has been called the Incarnation.

Thus the baby soul is born; and just as it is " made in the image of God"— threefold in aspect, as He is, and threefold in manifestation, as He is also—so is its method of evolution also a reflection of His descent into matter. The Divine Spark contains within it all potentiality, but it is only through long ages of evolution that all its possibilities can be realized. The appointed method for the evolution of the man's latent qualities seems to be by learning to vibrate in response to impacts from without. But at the level where he finds himself (that of the higher mental plane) the vibrations are far too fine to awaken this response at present; he must begin with those that are coarser and stronger, and having awakened his dormant sensibilities by their means he will gradually grow more and more sensitive until he is capable of perfect response at all levels to all possible rates of vibration. That is the material aspect of his progress; but regarded subjectively, to be able to respond to all vibrations means to be perfect in sympathy and compassion. And that is exactly the condition of the developed man—the adept, the spiritual teacher, the Christ. It needs the development within him of all the qualities which go to make up the perfect man; and this is the real work of his long life in matter. .

In this chapter we have brushed the surface of many subjects of extreme importance. Those who wish to study them further will find many Theosophical books to help them. On the constitution of man we would refer readers to Mrs. Besant's works, Man and his Bodies, The Self and its Sheaths, and The Seven Principles of Man, and also to my own book, Man Visible and Invisible, in which will be found many coloured illustrations of the different vehicles of man as they appear to clairvoyant sight.

On the use of the inner faculties refer to Clairvoyance.

On the formation and evolution of the soul to Mrs. Besant's Birth and Evolution of the Soul, Mr. Sinnett's Growth of the Soul, and my own Christian Creed and Man, Visible and Invisible.

On the spiritual evolution of man, Mrs. Besant's In the Outer Court and The Path of Discipleship, and the concluding chapters of my own little book, Invisible Helpers.

CHAPTER V. REINCARNATION.

Since the finer movements cannot at first affect the soul, he has to draw round him vestures of grosser matter through which the heavier vibrations can play; and so he takes upon himself successively the mental body, the astral body, and the physical body. This is a birth or incarnation –the commencement of a physical life. During that life all kinds of experiences come to him through his physical body, and from them he should learn some lessons and develop some qualities in himself.

After a time he begins to withdraw into himself, and puts off by degrees the vestures which he has assumed. The first of these to drop is the physical body, and his withdrawal from that is what we call death. It is not the end of his activities, as we so ignorantly suppose; nothing could be further from the fact. He is simply withdrawing from one effort, bearing back with him its results; and after a certain period of comparative repose he will make another effort of the same kind.

Thus, as has been said, what we ordinarily call his life is only one day in the real and wider life – a day at school, during which he learns certain lessons. But inasmuch as one short life of seventy or eighty years at most is not enough to give him an opportunity of learning all the lessons which this wonderful and beautiful world has to teach, and inasmuch as God means him to learn them all in His own good time, it is necessary that he should come back again many times, and live through many of these schooldays that we call lives, in different classes and under different circumstances, until all the lessons are learned; and then this lower schoolwork will be over, and he will pass to something higher and more glorious – the true divine lifework for which all this earthly school-life is fitting him.

That is what is called the doctrine of reincarnation or rebirth – a doctrine which was widely known in the ancient civilisations, and is even today held by the majority of the human race.

Of it Hume has written:- "What is incorruptible must also be ungenerable. The soul, therefore, if immortal, existed before our birth.....The metempsychosis is, therefore, the only system of this kind that Philosophy can hearken to." * (* Hume. "Essay on Immortality," London, 1875). Writing of the theories of metempsychosis in India and Greece, Max Muller says:- "There is something underlying them all which, if expressed in less mythological language, may stand the severest test of philosophical examination." # (# Max Muller, 'Theosophy or Psychological Religion,' p. 22, 1895 ed.) In his last and posthumous work this great Orientalist again refers to this doctrine, and expresses his personal belief in it.

And Huxley writes. "Like the doctrine of evolution itself, that of transmigration has its roots in the world of reality; and it may claim such support as the great argument from analogy is capable of supplying." Huxley, "Evolution and Ethics," p. 61, 1895 edition.

So it will be seen that modern as well as ancient writers recognize this hypothesis as one deserving of the most serious consideration.

It must not for a moment be confounded with a theory held by the ignorant, that it was possible for a soul which had reached humanity in its evolution to rebecome that of an animal.

No such retrogression is within the limits of possibility; when once man comes into existence— a human soul, inhabiting what we call in our books a causal body—he can never again fall back into what is in truth a lower kingdom of nature, whatever mistakes he may make or however he may fail to take advantage of his opportunities. If he is idle in the school of life, he may need to take the same lesson over and over again before he has really learnt it, but still on the whole progress is steady, even though it may often be slow. A few years ago the essence of this doctrine was prettily put thus in one of the magazines:

"A boy went to school. He was very little. All that he knew he had drawn in with his mother's milk. His teacher (who was God) placed him in the lowest class, and gave him, these lessons to learn: Thou shalt not kill. Thou shalt do no hurt to any living thing. Thou shalt not steal. So the man did not kill; but he was cruel, and he stole. At the end of the day (when his beard was gray—when the night was come) his teacher (who was God) said: Thou hast learned not to kill. But the other lessons thou hast not learned. Come back to-morrow.

"On the morrow he came back, a little boy. And his teacher (who was God) put him in a class a little higher and gave him these lessons to learn: Thou shalt do no hurt to any living thing. Thou shalt not steal. Thou shalt not cheat. So the man did no hurt to any living thing; but he stole and he cheated. And at the end of the day (when his beard was gray —when the night was come) his teacher (who was God) said: Thou hast learned to be merciful. But the other lessons thou hast not learned. Come back to-morrow.

"Again, on the morrow, he came back, a little boy. And his teacher (who was God) put him in a class yet a little higher, and gave him these lessons to learn: Thou shalt not steal. Thou shalt not cheat. Thou shalt not covet. So the man did not steal; but he cheated, and he coveted. And at the end of the day (when his beard was gray—when the night was come) his teacher (who was God) said: Thou hast learned not to steal. But the other lessons thou hast not learned. Come back, my child, to-morrow.

"This is what I have read in the faces of men and women, in the book of the world, and in the scroll of the heavens, which is writ in the stars." (Berry Benson, in The Century Magazine, May 1894).

I must not fill my pages with the many unanswerable arguments in favour of this doctrine of reincarnation; they are set forth very fully in our literature by a far abler pen than mine. Here I will say only this. Life presents us with many problems which, on any other hypothesis than this of reincarnation, seem utterly insoluble; this great truth does explain them, and therefore holds the field until another and more satisfactory hypothesis can be found. Like the rest of the teaching, this is not a hypothesis, but a matter of direct knowledge for many of us; but naturally our knowledge is not proof to others.

Yet good men and true have been sorrowfully forced to admit that they were unable to reconcile the state of affairs which exists in the world around us with the theory that God was both almighty and all-loving. They felt, when they looked upon all the heartbreaking sorrow and suffering, that either He was not almighty, and could not prevent it, or He was not all-loving, and did not care. In Theosophy we hold with determined conviction that He is both almighty and all-loving, and we reconcile with that certainty the existing facts of life by means of this basic doctrine of reincarnation. Surely the only hypothesis which allows us reasonably to recognize the perfection of power and love in the Deity is one which is worthy of careful examination.

For we understand that our present life is not our first, but that we each have behind us a long line of lives, by means of the experiences of which we have evolved from the condition of primitive man to our present position. Assuredly in these past lives we must have done both good and evil, and from every one of our actions a definite proportion of result must have followed under the inexorable law of justice. From the good follows always happiness and further opportunity; from the evil follows always sorrow and limitation.

So if we find ourselves limited in any way, the limitation is of our own making, or is merely due to the youth of the soul; if we have sorrow and suffering to endure, we ourselves alone are responsible. The manifold and complex destinies of men answer with rigid exactitude to the balance between the good and evil of their previous actions; and all is moving onward under the divine order towards the final consummation of glory.

There is, perhaps, no Theosophical teaching to which more violent objection is made than this great truth of reincarnation; yet it is in reality a most comforting doctrine. For it gives us time for the progress which lies before— time and opportunity to become "perfect, even as our Father in Heaven is perfect." Objectors chiefly found their protest on the fact that they have had so much trouble and sorrow in this life that they will not listen to any suggestion that it may be necessary to go through it all again. But this is obviously not argument; we are in search of truth, and when it is found we must not shrink from it, whether it be pleasant or unpleasant, though, as a matter of fact, as said above, reincarnation rightly understood is profoundly comforting.

Again, people often inquire why, if we have had so many previous lives, we do not remember any of them. Put very briefly, the answer to this is that some people do remember them; and the reason why the majority do not is because their consciousness is still focussed in one or the other of the lower sheaths. That sheath cannot be expected to recollect previous incarnations, because it has not had any; and the soul, which has, is not yet fully conscious on its own plane. But the memory of all the past is stored within that soul, and expresses itself here in the innate qualities with which the child is born; and when the man has evolved sufficiently to be able to focus his consciousness there instead of only in lower vehicles the entire history of that real and wider life will be open before him like a book.

The whole of this question is fully and beautifully worked out in Mrs. Besant's manual on Reincarnation, Dr. Jerome Anderson's Reincarnation, and in the chapters on that subject in The 'Ancient Wisdom, to which the attention of the reader is specially directed.

CHAPTER VI. THE WIDER OUTLOOK.

A little thought will soon show us what a radical change is introduced into the life of the man who realizes that his physical life is nothing but a day at school, and that his physical body is merely a temporary vesture assumed for the purpose of learning through it. He sees at once that this purpose of "learning the lesson" is the only one of any importance, and that the man who allows himself to be diverted from that purpose by any consideration is acting with inconceivable stupidity.

To him who knows the truth, the life of the ordinary person devoted exclusively to physical objects, to the pursuit of wealth or fame, appears the merest child's play—a senseless sacrifice of all that is really worth having for a few moments' gratification of the lower part of man's nature. The student "sets his affection on things above, and not on things of the earth," not only because he sees this to be the right course of action, but because he realizes very clearly the valuelessness of these things of earth. He always tries to take the higher point of view, for he sees that the lower is utterly unreliable—that the lower desires and feelings gather round him like a dense fog, and make it impossible for him to see anything clearly from that level.

Yet even when he is thoroughly convinced that the higher course is always the right one, and when he is fully determined to follow it, he will nevertheless sometimes encounter very strong temptations to take the lower course, and will be sensible of a great struggle within him. He will discover that there is "a law in the members warring against the law of the mind," as St. Paul says, so that "the good that I would, I do not, and the evil which I would not, that I do."

Now good religious people often make the most serious mistakes about this interior struggle which we have all felt to a greater or less extent. They usually accept one of two theories on the subject. Either they suppose that the lower promptings come from exterior tempting demons, or else they mourn over the terrible wickedness and blackness of their hearts, in that such fathomless evil still exists within them. Indeed, many of the best of men and women go through a vast amount of totally unnecessary suffering on this account.

The first point to have clearly in mind if one wishes to understand this matter is that the lower desire is not in truth our desire at all. Nor is it the work of some demon trying to destroy our souls. It is true that there sometimes are evil entities which are attracted by the base thought in man, and intensify it by their action; but such entities are man-made, every one of them, and impermanent. They are merely the artificial forms called into existence by the thought of other evil men, and they have a period of what seems almost like life, proportioned to the strength of the thought that created them.

But the undesirable prompting within us usually comes from quite another source. It has been mentioned how man draws round him vestures of matter at different levels, in order that he may descend into incarnation. But this matter is not dead matter (indeed, occult science teaches us that there is no such thing as dead matter anywhere), but is instinct with life; though it is life at a stage of evolution much earlier than our own—so much earlier that it is still moving on a downward course into lower matter, instead of rising again out of lower matter into higher. Consequently its tendency is always to press downwards toward the grosser material and the coarser vibrations which mean progress for it, but retrogression for us; and so it happens that the interest of the true man sometimes comes into collision with that of the living matter in some of his vehicles.

That is a very rough outline of the explanation of the curious internal strife that we sometimes feel—a strife which has suggested to poetic minds the idea of good and evil angels in conflict over the soul of man. A more detailed account will be found in The Astral Plane, p. 40, and also in The Other Side of Death. But in the meantime it is important that the man should realize that he is the higher force, always moving towards and battling for good, while this lower force is not he at all, but only an uncontrolled fragment of one of his lower vehicles. He must leaim to control it, to dominate it absolutely, and to keep it in order; but he should not, therefore, think of it. as evil, but as an outpouring of the Divine power moving on its orderly course, though that course in this instance happens to be downwards into matter, instead of upwards and away from it, as ours is. •

CHAPTER VII. DEATH.

One of the most important practical results of a thorough comprehension of Theosophical truth is the entire change which it necessarily brings about in our attitude towards death. It is impossible for us to calculate the vast amount of utterly unnecessary sorrow and terror and misery which mankind in the aggregate has suffered simply from its ignorance and superstition with regard to this one matter of death. There is among us a mass of false and foolish belief along this line which has worked untold evil in the past and is causing indescribable suffering in the present, and its eradication would be one of the greatest benefits that could be conferred upon the human race.

This benefit the Theosophical teaching at once confers on those who, from their study of philosophy in past lives, now find themselves able to accept it.

It robs death forthwith of all its terror and much of its sorrow, and enables us to see it in its true proportions and to understand its place in the scheme of our evolution.

While death is considered as the end of life, as a gateway into a dim but fearful unknown country, it is not unnaturally regarded with much misgiving, if not with positive terror. Since, in spite of all religious teaching to the contrary, this has been the view universally taken in the western world, many grisly horrors have sprung up around it, and have become matters of custom, thoughtlessly obeyed by many who should know better. All the ghastly paraphernalia of woe—the mutes, the plumes, the black velvet, the crape, the mourning garments, the odious black-edged notepaper—all these are nothing more than advertisements of ignorance on the part of those who employ them. The man who begins to understand what death is at once puts aside all this masquerade as childish folly, seeing that to mourn over the good fortune of his friend merely because it involves for himself the pain of an apparent separation from that friend, becomes, as soon as it is recognized, a display of selfishness. He cannot avoid feeling the wrench of the temporary separation, but he can avoid allowing his own pain to become a hindrance to the friend who has passed on.

He knows- that there can be no need to fear or to mourn over death, whether it comes to himself or to those whom he loves. It has come to them all often before, so that there is nothing unfamiliar about it. Instead of representing it as a ghastly king of terrors, it would be more accurate and more sensible to symbolize it as an angel bearing a golden key to admit us to the glorious realms of the higher life.

He realizes very definitely that life is continuous, and that the loss of the physical body is nothing more than the casting aside of a garment, which in no way changes the real man who is the wearer of the garment. He sees that death is simply a promotion from a life which is more than half-physical to one which is wholly astral, and therefore very much superior. So for himself he unfeignedly welcomes it, and when it comes to those whom he loves he recognizes at once the great advantage for them, even though he cannot but feel a certain amount of selfish regret that he should be temporarily separated from them. But he knows also that this separation is in fact only apparent, and not real. He knows that the so-called dead are near him still, and that he has only to cast off temporarily his physical body in sleep, in order to stand side by-side with them and commune with them as before.

He sees clearly that the world is one, and that the same Divine laws rule the whole of it, whether it be visible or invisible to physical sight. Consequently he has no feeling of nervousness or strangeness in passing from one part of it to the other, and no sort of uncertainty as to what he will find on the other side of the veil. The whole of the unseen world is so clearly and fully mapped out for him through the work of the Theosophical investigators that it is as well known to him as the physical life, and thus he is prepared to enter upon it without hesitation whenever it may be best for his evolution.

For full details of the various stages of this higher life we must refer the reader to the books specially devoted to this subject. It is sufficient here to say that the conditions into which the man passes are precisely those which he has made for himself. The thoughts and desires which he has encouraged within himself during earth-life take form as definite living entities hovering round him and reacting upon him until the energy which he poured into them is exhausted. When such thoughts and desires have been powerful and persistently evil, the companions so created may indeed be terrible; but happily such cases form a very small minority among the dwellers in the astral world. The worst that the ordinary man of the world usually provides for himself after death is a useless and unutterably wearisome existence, void of all rational interests—the natural sequence of a life wasted in self-indulgence, triviality, and gossip here on earth.

To this weariness active suffering may under certain conditions be added. If a man during earth-life has allowed strong physical desire to obtain a mastery over him—if, for example, he has become a slave to such a vice as avarice, sensuality, or drunkenness—he has laid up for himself much purgatorial suffering after death. For in losing the physical body he in no way loses these desires and passions; they remain as vivid as ever—nay, they are even more active when they have no longer the heavy particles of dense matter to set in motion. What he does lose is the power to gratify these passions; so that they remain as torturing, gnawing desires, unsatisfied and unsatisfiable. It will be seen that this makes a very real hell for the unfortunate man, though of course only a temporary one, since in process of time such desires must burn themselves out, expending their energy in the very suffering which they produce.

A terrible fate, truly; yet there are two points which we should bear in mind with regard to it. First, that the man has not only brought it on himself, but has determined its intensity and its duration for himself. He has allowed this desire to reach a certain strength during earth-life, and now he has to meet it and control it. If during physical life he has made efforts to repress or check it, he will have just so much the less difficulty in conquering it now: He has created for himself the monster with which now he has to struggle; whatever strength his antagonist possesses is just what he has given it. Therefore, his fate is not imposed upon him from without, but is simply of his own making.

Secondly, the suffering which he thus brings upon himself is the only way of escape for him. If it were possible for him to avoid it, and to pass through the astral life without this gradual wearing away of the lower desires, what would be the result? Obviously that he would enter upon his next physical life entirely under the domination of these passions. He would be a born drunkard, a sensualist, a miser; and long before it would be possible to teach him that he ought to try to control such passions they would have gown far too strong for control— they would have enslaved him, body and soul, and so another life would be thrown away, another opportunity would be lost. He would enter thus upon a vicious circle from which there appears no escape, and his evolution would be indefinitely delayed.

The Divine scheme is not thus defective. The passion exhausts itself during the astral life, and the man returns to physical existence without it.

True, the weakness of mind which allowed passion to dominate him is still there; true, also, he has made for himself for this new life an astral body-capable of expressing exactly the same passions as before, so that it would not be difficult for him to resume his old evil life. But the ego, the real man, has had a terrible lesson, and assuredly he will make every effort to prevent his lower manifestation from repeating that mistake, from falling again under the sway of that passion. He has still the germs of it within him, but if he has deserved good and wise parents they will help to develop the good in him and check the evil, the germs will remain unfructified and will atrophy, and so in the next life after that they will not appear at all. So by slow degrees man conquers his evil qualities, and evolves virtues to replace them.

On the other hand, the man who is intelligent and helpful, who understands the conditions of this non-physical existence and takes the trouble to adapt himself to them and make the most of them, finds opening before him a splendid vista of opportunities both for acquiring fresh knowledge and for doing useful work. He discovers that life away from this dense body has a vividness and brilliancy to which all earthly enjoyment is as moonlight unto sunlight, and that through his clear knowledge and calm confidence the power of the endless life shines out upon all those around him. He may become a centre of peace and joy unspeakable to hundreds of his fellow-men, and may do more good in a few years of that astral existence than ever he could have done in the longest physical life.

He is well aware, too, that there lies before him another and still grander stage of this wonderful post-mortem life. Just as by his desires and his lower thoughts he has made for himself the surroundings of his astral life, so has he by his higher thought and his nobler aspirations made for himself a life in the heaven-world. For heaven is not a dream, but a living and glorious reality. Not a city far away beyond the stars, with gates of pearl and streets of gold, reserved for the habitation of a favoured few, but a state of consciousness into which every man will pass during the interval between his lives on earth. Not an eternal abiding-place truly, but a condition of bliss indescribable lasting through many centuries. Not even that alone, for although it contains the reality which underlies all the best and most spiritual ideas of Heaven which have been propounded in various religions, yet it must by no means be considered from that point of view only.

It is a realm of nature which is of exceeding importance to us—a vast and splendid world of vivid life in which we are living now, as well as in the periods intervening between physical incarnations. It is only our lack of development, only the limitation imposed upon us by this robe of flesh, that prevents us from fully realizing that all the glory of the highest heaven is about us here and now, and that influences flowing from that world are ever playing upon us, if we will only understand and receive them. Impossible as this may seem to the man of the world, it is the plainest of realities to the occultist; and to those who have not yet grasped this fundamental truth we can but repeat the advice given by the Buddhist teacher:—"Do not complain and cry and pray, but open your eyes and see. The light is all about you, if you would only cast the bandage from your eyes and look. It is so wonderful, so beautiful, so far beyond what any man has dreamt of or prayed for, and it is for ever and for ever." {The Soul of a People, p. 163.)

When the astral body, which is the vehicle of the lower thought and desire, has gradually been worn away and left behind, the man finds himself inhabiting that higher vehicle of finer matter which we have called the mental body.

In this vehicle he is able to respond to the vibrations which reach him from the corresponding matter in the external world—the matter of the mental plane. His time of purgatory is over, the lower part of his nature has burnt itself away, and now there remain only the higher thoughts and aspirations which he has poured forth during earth-life. These cluster round him, and make a sort of shell about him, through the medium of which he is able to respond to certain types of vibration in this refined matter. These thoughts which surround him are the powers by which he draws upon the wealth of the heaven-world. This mental plane is a reflection of the Divine Mind—a storehouse of infinite extent from which the person enjoying heaven is able to draw just according to the power of his own thoughts and aspirations generated during the physical and astral life.

All religions have spoken of the bliss of Heaven, yet few of them have put before us with sufficient clearness this leading idea which alone explains rationally how for all alike such bliss is possible—which is, indeed, the keynote of the conception—the fact that each man makes his own heaven by selection from the ineffable splendours of the Thought of God Himself. A man decides for himself both the length and the character of his heaven-life by the causes which he himself generates during his earth-life; therefore, he cannot but have exactly the amount which he has deserved and exactly the quality of joy which is best suited to his idiosyncrasies. This is a world in which every being must, from the very fact of his consciousness there, be enjoying the highest spiritual bliss of which he is capable— a world whose power of response to his- aspirations is limited only by his capacity to aspire.

Further details as to the astral life will be found in The Astral Plane; the heaven-life is described in The Deva chanic Plane, and information about both is also given in Death and After, and in The Other Side of Death.

CHAPTER VIII. MAN'S PAST AND FUTURE.

When we have once grasped the fact that man has reached his present position through a long and varied series of lives, a question naturally arises in our minds as to how far we can obtain any information about this earlier evolution, which would obviously be of absorbing interest to us. Fortunately such information is available, not only by tradition, but also in another and much more certain way. I have no space here to dilate upon the marvels of psychometry, but must simply say that there is abundant evidence to show that nothing can happen without indelibly recording itself—that there exists a kind of memory of Nature from which can be recovered with absolute accuracy a true, full, and perfect picture of any scene or event since the world began. Those to whom this subject is entirely new, and who consequently seek for evidence, should consult Dr. Buchanan's Psychometry or Professor Denton's Soul of Things; but all occult students are familiar with the possibility, and most of them with the method, of reading these records of the past.

In essence this memory of Nature must be the Divine Memory, far away beyond human reach; but it is assuredly reflected into lower planes so that, as far as events on these lower planes are concerned, it is recoverable by the trained intelligence of man. All that passes before a mirror, for instance, is reflected on its surface, and to our dim eyes it seems that the images make no impression upon that surface, but that each passes away and leaves no trace. Yet that may not be so; it is not difficult to imagine that an impression may be left, somewhat as the impression of every sound is left upon the sensitive cylinder of a phonograph; and it may be possible to recover the impression from the mirror just as it is recoverable from the phonograph.

The higher psychometry shows us that this not only may be so, but is so; and that not a mirror only, but any physical object, retains the impression of all that has happened within its sight, as it were. We have thus at our disposal a faultlessly accurate method of arriving at the earlier history of our world and of mankind, and in this way much that is of the most entrancing interest can be observed in every detail, as though the scenes were being specially rehearsed for our benefit. (See Clairvoyance, p. 88.)

Investigations into the past conducted by these methods show a long process of gradual evolution, slow but never-ceasing. They show the Divine Life rising from kingdom to kingdom, through the mineral, the vegetable, the animal, until it reaches the human, and thus binding them all together into one common brotherhood. They show the development of man under the action of two great laws—first the law of evolution, which steadily presses him onward and upward, and secondly the law of divine justice, or cause and effect, which brings him inevitably the result of his every action, and thus gradually teaches him to live intelligently in harmony with the first law.

This long process of evolution has been carried out not only on this earth, but on other globes connected with it; but the subject is much too vast to be fully treated in an elementary book such as this. It forms the principal theme of Madame Blavatsky's monumental work, The Secret Doctrine; but before commencing that students are advised to read the chapters on this subject in Mrs. Besant's Ancient Wisdom and Mr. Sinnett's Growth of the Soul.

The books just mentioned' will afford the fullest available information not only as to man's past, but as to his future; and though the glory that awaits him is such as no tongue can tell, something at least may be understood of the earlier stages which lead towards it. That man is divine even now, and that he will presently unfold within himself the potentialities of divinity, is an idea which appears to shock some good people, and to be considered by them to savour of blasphemy. Why it should be so is not easy to see, for Jesus himself reminds the Jews around him of the saying in their Scriptures, "I said, ye are Gods," and the doctrine of the deification of man was quite commonly held by the Fathers of the Church. But in these later days much of the earlier and purer doctrine has been forgotten and misunderstood; and the truth now seems to be held in its fulness only by the student of occultism.

Sometimes men ask why, if man was at the first a spark of the Divine, it should be necessary for him to go through all these aeons of evolution, involving so much sorrow and suffering, only in order to be still Divine at the end of it all. But those who make this objection have not yet comprehended the scheme. That which came forth from the Divine was not yet man—not yet even a spark, for there was no developed individualization in it. It was simply a great cloud of Divine essence, though capable of condensing eventually into many sparks.

The difference between its condition when issuing forth and when returning is exactly like that between a great mass of shining nebulous matter, and the solar system which is eventually formed out of it. The nebula is beautiful, no doubt, but vague and useless; the suns formed from it by slow evolution pour life and heat and light upon many worlds and their inhabitants.

Or we may take another analogy. The human body is composed of countless millions of tiny particles, and some of them are constantly being thrown off from it. Suppose that it were possible for each of these particles to go through some kind of evolution by means of which it would in time become a human being, we should not say that because it had been in a certain sense human at the beginning of that evolution it had, therefore, not gained anything when it reached the end. The essence comes forth as a mere outpouring of force, even though it be Divine force; it returns in the form of thousands of millions of mighty adepts, each capable of himself developing into a Logos.

Thus it will be seen that we are abundantly justified in the statement that the future of man is a future to whose glory and splendour there is no limit. And a most important point to remember is that this magnificent future is for all without exception. He whom we call the good man—that is, the man whose will moves with the Divine Will, whose actions are such as to help the march of evolution—makes rapid progress on the upward path; while the man who unintelligently opposes himself to the great current by striving to pursue selfish aims instead of working for the good of the whole, will be able to progress only very slowly and erratically. But the Divine Will is infinitely stronger than any human will, and the working of the great scheme is perfect. The man who does not learn his lesson the first time has simply to try over and over again until he does learn it; the Divine patience is infinite, and sooner or later every human being attains the goal appointed for him. There is no fear and no uncertainty, but only perfect peace for those who know the Law and the Will.

CHAPTER IX. CAUSE AND EFFECT.

In previous chapters we have constantly had to take into consideration this mighty law of action and reaction under which every man necessarily receives his just desert; for without this law the rest of the Divine scheme would be incomprehensible to us. It is well worth our while to try to obtain a true appreciation of this law, and the first step towards doing that is to disabuse our minds entirely of the ecclesiastical idea of reward and punishment as following upon human action. It is inevitable that we should connect with that idea the thought of a judge administering such reward or punishment, and then at once follows the further possibility that the judge may be more lenient in one case than in another, that he may be swayed by circumstances, that an appeal may be made to him, and that in that way the incidence of the law may be modified or even escaped altogether.

Every one of these suggestions is in the highest degree misleading, and the whole body of thought to which they belong must be exorcised and utterly cast out before we can arrive at any real understanding of the facts. If a man put his hand upon a bar of red-hot iron, under ordinary circumstances he would be badly burnt; yet it would not occur to him to say that God had punished him for putting his hand on the bar. He would realize that what had happened was precisely what might have been expected under the action of the laws of Nature, and that one who understood what heat is and how it acts could explain exactly the production of the bum.

It IS to be observed that the man's intention in no way affects the physical result; whether he seized that bar in order to do some harm with it or in order to save someone else from injury, he would be burnt just the same. Of course, in other and higher ways the results would be quite different; in the one case he would have done a noble deed, and would have the approval of his conscience, while in the other he could feel only remorse. But the physical burn would be there in one case just as much as in the other.

To obtain a true conception of the working of this law of cause and effect we must think of it as acting automatically, in exactly the same way. If we have a heavy weight hanging from the ceiling by a rope, and I exert a certain amount of force in pushing against that weight, we know by the laws of mechanics that that weight will press back against my hand with exactly the same amount of force; and this reaction will operate without the slightest reference to my reason for disturbing its equilibrium. Similarly the man who commits an evil action disturbs the equilibrium of the great current of evolution; and that mighty current invariably adjusts that equilibrium at his expense.

It must not be therefore supposed for a moment that the intention of the action makes no difference; on the contrary it is the most important factor connected with it, even though it does not affect the result upon the physical plane. We are apt to forget that the intention is itself a force, and a force acting upon the mental plane, where the matter is so much finer and vibrates so much more rapidly than on our lower level, that the same amount of energy will produce enormously greater effect. The physical action will produce its result on the physical plane, but the mental energy of the intention will work out its own result simultaneously in the matter of the mental plane, totally irrespective of the other; and its effect is certain to be very much the more important of the two. In this way it will be seen that an absolutely perfect adjustment is always achieved; for however mixed the motives may be, and however good and evil may be mingled in the physical results, the equilibrium will always be perfectly readjusted, and along every line perfect justice must be done.

We must not forget that it is the man himself and no other who builds his future character as well as produces his future circumstances. Speaking very generally, it may be said that, while his actions in one life produce his environment in the next, his thoughts in the one life are the chief factors in the evolution of his character for the next. The method by which all this works is an exceedingly interesting study, but it would take us far too long to detail it here; it may be found very fully elaborated in Mrs. Besant's manual on Karma, and also in the chapter referring to this subject in her Ancient Wisdom, and in Mr. Sinnett's Esoteric Buddhism, to which the reader may be referred.

It is obvious that all these facts furnish us with exceedingly good reasons for many of our ethical precepts. If thought be a mighty power capable of producing upon its own plane results far more important than any that can be achieved in physical life, then the necessity that man should control that force immediately becomes apparent. Not only is the man building his own future character by means of his thought, but he is also constantly and inevitably affecting those around him by its means.

Hence there lies upon him a very serious responsibility as to the use which he makes of this power. If the feeling of annoyance or hatred arises in the heart of the ordinary man, his natural impulse is to express it in some way either in word or in action. The ordinary rules of civilized society, however, forbid him to do that, and dictate that he should as far as possible repress all outward sign of his feelings. If he succeeds in doing this he is apt to congratulate himself, and to consider that he has done the whole of his duty. The occult student, however, knows that it is necessary for him to carry his self-control a great deal further than that, and that he must absolutely repress the thought of irritation as well as its outward expression. For he knows that his feelings set in motion tremendous forces upon the astral plane, that these will act against the object of his irritation just as surely as a blow struck upon the physical plane, and that in many cases the results produced will be far more serious and lasting.

It is true in a very real sense that thoughts are things. To clairvoyant sight thoughts take definite form and colour, the latter, of course, depending upon the rate of vibration connected with them. The study of these forms and colours is of great interest. A description of them illustrated with coloured drawings will be found in an article in Lucifer for September, 1896.

These considerations open up to us possibilities in various directions. Since it is easily possible to do harm by thought, it is also possible to do good by it. Currents may be set in motion which will carry mental help and comfort to many a suffering friend, and in this way a whole new world of usefulness opens before us. Many a grateful soul has been oppressed by a feeling that for want of physical wealth he was unable to do anything in return for the kindness lavished upon him by another; but here is a method by which he can be of the greatest service to him in a realm where physical wealth or its absence makes no difference.

All who can think can help others; and all who can help others ought to help. In this case, as in every other, knowledge is power, and those who understand the law can use the law. Knowing what effects upon themselves and upon others will be produced by certain thoughts, they can deliberately arrange to produce these results. In this way a man can not only steadily mould his character in his present life, but can decide exactly what it shall be in the next. For a thought is a vibration in the matter of the mental body, and the same thought persistently repeated evokes corresponding vibrations (an octave higher, as it were) in the matter of the causal body. In this way qualities are gradually built into the soul itself, and they will certainly reappear as part of the stock-in-trade with which he commences his next incarnation. It is in this way, by working from below upwards, that the faculties and qualities of the soul are gradually evolved, and thus man takes his evolution largely into his own hands and begins to co-operate intelligently in the great scheme of the Deity.

For further information on this subject the best book to study is Mrs. Besant's upon Thought Power, its Control and Culture.